American
GRUNT

Ridiculous Stories of a Life Lived at $8.00 an Hour

Kevin Cramer

Ballast Books, LLC
www.ballastbooks.com

Copyright © 2023 by Kevin Cramer

ISBN: 978-1-955026-74-1

Printed in the USA

Published by Ballast Books
www.ballastbooks.com

For more information, bulk orders, appearances, or speaking requests, please email: info@ballastbooks.com

For Henry and Miranda—the reason
I work so damn hard.

Table of Contents

Introduction

"Work hard, kid, and you will be rewarded with a piece of the American Dream."

– Every suburban dad born between 1939 and 1963

It came from a good place. They wanted you to follow the path that had worked for them—the path that got them the home and the mid-size sedan and the patch of lawn they'd constantly bitch about having to maintain. Then on Saturday night during the three-and-a-half glorious hours they got to relax during the week, they'd crack open a can of the same cheap beer they'd been drinking since high school and think, *If I teach my kids to work hard, this will go on for eternity. There will always be solid jobs here in the land of milk and honey for anyone who's willing to roll up their sleeves.*

It made sense. Their fathers had come back from the war and gotten factory jobs that paid for the house they grew up in and the annual summer trip to visit Aunt Ruth and Uncle Kenny in some boring midwestern town with a boring midwestern lake. Because of their mothers' and fathers' hard work, Baby Boomers were able to go to college, thus becoming something easy to reply upon being asked by a new acquaintance, "What do you do for a living?"

"Why, I'm the assistant regional manager for one of the Tri-State Area's leading office supply companies," they could say proudly.

And the new acquaintance would nod and think to themselves, *Now that's someone who rolled up their sleeves.*

My father worked in a blast furnace in Braddock, Pennsylvania, during the summers to pay for his college education. He'd graduate in the spring of 1969 and by the fall was teaching high school chemistry. At twenty-two years old, he was already in the job he'd retire from. My mother was an elementary school teacher until I showed up and ruined that gig. After a fifteen-year absence from the job market raising her kids, she'd end up working as an education professor at Penn State until she retired in 2012. In my father's life, he had two jobs. I believe my mother had four.

I lost count somewhere around fifty.

This is the story of a guy in his mid-forties who somehow ended up with more degrees than salaried jobs over the years—and the path he's taken toward accepting life as an occupational nomad. Every single anecdote you'll read in the following pages is biased in my favor because that's the benefit you get when you're the one controlling the narrative. (Pro tip, don't be a dick to writers!) Many names have been changed to protect the guilty.

Anyway, I hope the upcoming chapters resonate with the growing number of us who are working harder and harder for less and less while being forced to redefine what constitutes success. Maybe it's simply about the act of surviving a life spent working for dopes and interacting with morons. Perhaps the shared strife is truly what bonds us with others and pushes us forward on an eternal quest for something better.

Yeah, I'm the one who wrote that last sentence, and I'm not buying it, either. I just hope you laugh at the stories.

CHAPTER 1

Hellhound

I n the 1980s, it was an FCC requirement that every film or television show taking place in the American suburbs opened with a paperboy in a striped shirt and backward ballcap happily riding down the street on a bike, chucking the *Tweed County Gazette* into random yards while waving at friendly neighbors who for some odd reason were out on the porch sipping coffee in robes. To an eleven-year-old, becoming one of those scrappy young entrepreneurs seemed like the opportunity of a lifetime.

"Wait, they'll pay me to ride my bike around and chuck stuff at people's houses? Sign me the hell up!"

The Pittsburgh Press was established in 1884 and for over a century was the second largest newspaper in Pennsylvania. It was an information engine full of everything the people of the region wanted, including Steelers insight, Steelers opinions, Steelers breakdowns, local obituaries, and Steeler game recaps. In short, it was a solid company to help usher any sixth grader into the great American workforce.

After a brief phone interview, a bunch of newspapers started showing up outside my garage. I got a crudely drawn map, a bunch of tiny receipt stubs, and a giant canvas bag with a strap that was tailored less for a middle schooler and more for an NBA power forward. So one Monday

3

in the spring of 1989, I proudly filled my canoe-size sack with newspapers, hopped on my Huffy, and entered the glorious world of employment. I rode up Shady Drive, turned right onto Maple, and coasted down the hill. As I turned left onto Beech, the oversize sack slipped off my lap and got wedged between the pedal and the wheel—locking the brakes and causing me to fly headfirst to the asphalt. Before I'd delivered my first paper, I was bleeding. Fortunately, I was too young to understand the concept of harbingers.

There are tropes we take for granted without even remotely thinking about their practicality. The happy, bike-riding, newspaper-hurling kid pedaling down Main Street is one of them. As it turns out, there are things in the world like rain, snow, and squirrels that can severely impact the integrity of the flimsy lump of information the customers paid $2.50 a week to obtain. Consequently, leaving it in the yard exposed to the elements isn't an optimum delivery method. As I'd quickly find out, unlike the television kids, you didn't get to smile and bomb the paper at the house going thirty miles per hour. No, you had to walk up and place the paper between the screen door and the actual door, a detail that made the job infinitely less fun and typically led to unwanted conversations with old people about how much they dislike the restrictive diet that damned Asian doctor put them on.

My eleven-year-old self didn't realize it at the time, but being a paperboy was incredible preparation for life in the modern American workforce. You quickly realize that the amount of shit you have to put up with doesn't remotely justify the compensation you're receiving for putting up with it. During the week, I made a nickel per paper, which I think would've been pretty good money in 1920 when kids bit on quarters just to make sure they were real, then ran off and bought forty acres of land with the windfall. With the number of houses on my route, I was supposed to make almost two bucks a day during the week. But the real bonanza came on Sunday when I made fifteen cents per paper and the route volume doubled because everyone wanted to laugh at the funnies and get 20 percent off of everything at Kmart. I theoretically made like *five or six* bucks on Sunday.

Back then, the Sunday paper was special. So special in fact that it came in about nine parts that you had to assemble like an Ikea coffee table at five a.m. When you finally put it together, each one had the volume, dimensions, and weight of the tree stump that pulled the bumper off your uncle's truck. The canvas sack they'd provided for the job was woefully inadequate. While it could easily hold forty or fifty weekday papers, at most it could hold eight of those beasts.

"So what brings you in for surgery today, Mr. Cramer?"

"Well, thirty-five years ago, I stuffed ten Sunday papers in my sack at once and..."

"Ah, that explains the X-ray. Consider yourself lucky. Eleven and you'd have never seen another sunrise."

After my first Sunday took around three-and-a-half hours and people at the end of the route complained that their breakfast got cold while they breathlessly waited for their Steelers news, my parents came to the dismaying realization that they too now worked for *The Pittsburgh Press*. Every Sunday at 7:00 a.m. for three years, we'd load the remnants of a small forest into our Chevy Lumina and drive around the neighborhood—which my dad absolutely loved considering his alarm rang at 5:15 a.m. Monday through Friday.

I can envision him grunting into his pillow, "Can't we just give him twelve bucks a week to spend on baseball cards ourselves?"

"Well, he *is* learning financial responsibility," my mom would reply. "And that's a big lesson."

"Thirty years from now, this kid better be a hedge fund manager who can buy us a new house and not some struggling middle-aged nonfiction writer."

"Oh, Paul, I'm sure we won't have to worry about that nightmare."

Anyway, because of my paper route, Paul and Cathie Cramer often got roped into ridiculous scenarios that I can only now understand as a parent myself—like when a random F1 tornado hit at 4:00 a.m. on the Sunday morning before Christmas in 1990. Because of it, we had to retrieve drenched papers from all around the front yard as the awning from our side porch tumbled away and the transformer across the street exploded in a crazy burst of electric purple that set our neighbor's pine tree on fire. Having survived all that mayhem, my parents, my little sister, and I spread each of the forty-eight papers out on our garage floor and used a battery-powered hairdryer to bring them back from the dead.

I distinctly remember my parents going from agitated to amused and back fifteen times before sunrise. After almost four hours of blowing hot air around the garage, the papers were crinkly but dry-ish. It was almost nine o'clock before we got going—which meant that certain folks were already awake and ready to pounce.

"This is damp! And the Lifestyle section is missing!"

At thirteen years old, I responded how you'd expect a skinny kid with braces, glasses, and acne to respond. "The storm was really bad. Rain, uh, makes things wet and..."

"Where are the *coupons*?"

"Uh, fire trucks...had to come to my neighbor's house..."

"The only reason I pay for the paper is because I make up for it in *savings!*"

At this point, my dad would roll down the window as he idled the car out in the street and with the voice of an inner-city schoolteacher who'd been up since 4:00 a.m. and didn't know where his awning was growled, "What's the problem?"

The customer would look up hesitantly. "The Shop 'n Save circular is missing! And this one panel of Doonesbury is all smeared!"

"Most of the papers are in Baltimore by now," my dad snapped. "Be thankful you got anything. Kev, get in the car."

I'd smile sheepishly. "We dried them in the garage with a—"

"Kev, get in the damn car!"

And those would be the people who'd owe me $2.50 the next Saturday, pay with three ones and insist on getting their fifty cents back.

Saturday was collection day. Which meant I had to go around the neighborhood with a little green zip sack and knock on doors like a super timid mobster.

"Hey, Mister Dybzinski. You actually owe fifteen dollars because you haven't paid since February 8."

"Fifteen dollars! I remember when a paper only cost a penny!"

"Well, it, uh…costs more now."

To which he'd shuffle through a wallet that clearly held at least thirty bucks and say, "Well, I only have five." Later I assume he'd wonder who the hell was throwing all the rocks into his yard.

Now don't get me wrong. Ninety percent of the people were super nice. In fact, what I most remember from my days as a paper carrier are the warm conversations over iced tea that I'd have with some of the lonely old folks on my route. At first it annoyed me that my Saturday afternoons ended up shot because I couldn't get off Mrs. Burkovic's porch without a twenty-minute story about VE Day, but eventually I realized that the old folks were always home to pay me, so I accepted the trade-off. Everyone else had kids to shuttle to dance recitals or hauled their camper up to Lake Erie fifteen weekends in a row—so after I rang the doorbell there was a lot of kicking at the welcome mat, listening for any hints of shuffling around inside the house, ringing the doorbell again, and then slowly grumbling my way across the yard. Consequently, I'd only collect sixty-five of the seventy-eight dollars the *Press* expected from me that week, thus *paying* thirteen bucks for the privilege of delivering papers. Then just before my bike got repossessed, a miracle blizzard would hit. The weather guy would say stuff like…

"Make sure to bring your pets inside today, folks. This storm is going to pack a wallop that no living thing should be forced to endure—unless you're a paper carrier who really needs that $22.50 from the Campanettis, because trust me, they aren't going anywhere today."

Finally getting paid to do my job for the first time in a month would warm my toes just enough to stave off the nastier effects of frostbite. But in the end when I purchased the Toronto Blue Jays team set that now sits in a random shoebox I've been shoving in basement closets for the last thirty years, it was all worth it.

I also distinctly remember the first time my bullheadedness got me in trouble with my employer. It was a significant moment in my life because, as you'll see, unchecked stubbornness would become a bit of a theme over the years. Sometimes it takes a while to truly understand where you took the first steps on the path that would lead to your adult self. Why do I see work as a necessary evil rather than a means to gain power or prestige? Why do I value money infinitely less than my own pride? Why won't I just put my head down and listen? Dear god, why can't I just take the easy road for once? For me, those questions began at a quaint red brick home on Penn Drive.

In that house lived a retired couple whose last name was Lamp. Their home was behind a large row of pine trees with a driveway to the right and a set of long concrete stairs that gently ascended from the driveway up to the front door. I trembled before that house the way kids in other towns quiver before the old Magruder Mansion where the Great Hicksville Bloodbath of 1915 occurred. Not because the house itself was particularly creepy or haunted. No, it was because they had a huge Dalmatian.

And that dog was an asshole.

Here's the thing I've learned about suburban dog owners: there's so much love interfering with their judgment that not a single one of them realizes how shitty their dog is.

"I know he's big and intimidating and barks all night and ripped off four of the census guy's fingers, but when he's asleep at my feet while I'm watching my programs, he's just a <u>sweetheart</u>."

Because of the layout of the house, I could never tell if the dog was in the backyard or not. Consequently, I had to creep up the stairs like a ninja, slowly ease open the door, and then haul ass back to the street where I'd catch my breath, thankful to have survived another day.

Then came the fateful Thursday that would shape my attitude about workplace compliance. Like every other day, I'd tiptoed the whole way up the stairs. I'd slowly pulled open the thin, white storm door, gently placing the paper inside. I'd done everything as quiet as foam padding. Then just as I was about to ease the door shut, a gust of wind blew it out of my hand, and it slammed into the frame with a BANG. It was like realizing there was a gas leak just after you'd struck a match. My throat filled with concrete.

The Dalmatian came tearing around the side of the house like a goddamn velociraptor, growling with a fury not often heard by survivors. I couldn't outrun it. I was trapped. I did the only thing I could do: I threw the storm door back open, blocked my groin with my canvas sack, and made myself as skinny as possible in the narrow space between the two doors. Inches away, the dog growled and snapped at my legs through the tiny opening.

I started violently knocking with the free hand that wasn't attempting to fend off canine teeth. "Open the door! Your dog is trying to fucking kill me! Open the door!"[1*]

After what seemed like two hours but was probably only twenty seconds, I heard the knob turn. The door behind me swung inward, causing me to stumble back into the living room. Mr. Lamp grabbed his Dalmatian by the collar and started talking to it in the same voice he'd use when telling it there were treats in the kitchen.

"Hey, Barney, that's the paper boy. You know that. He delivers the paper every *day*. What are you doing? What are you doing, boy?"

As I tried to get my pulse down under a thousand beats per minute, that jerk dog got an ear rub.

I can still hear Mr. Lamp's hearty laugh as he busted out the excuse everyone uses when their dog's behavior sucks. "Oh, don't worry, he's just playing."

[1*] As far as I remember, this is the very first time I used the F word.

I checked myself to find that I was indeed bleeding, but it was most likely from smacking my ankle off the bricks trying to wedge myself in the door. The dog had snapped through my canvas sack a couple times (which I was now very, very glad I had in front of my junk), but otherwise I was okay.

"Well, that'll get the ol' blood pumping, huh?" Mr. Lamp said.

"I got more papers to…get to…people," I said, stumbling out the door and running down the stairs to the safety of the road.

Cut to the next day. I once again stood trembling at the end of the driveway, now thoroughly terrified. The images I had of the demon dog roaring around the house to kill me were no longer fuzzy daydreams of a nightmare future. They were now legitimate PTSD-inducing memories. I took a deep breath. Protocol said in no uncertain terms that papers needed to be delivered onto covered porches or left between the two doors. Here was my moment of truth. I was about to learn that sometimes you have to put everything on the line to earn that nickel because that's what your employer expects. That's what the paying customer expects. That's what society…

The paper hit the ground at the end of the driveway. And I walked away.

And so it went the next day. And the day after that. There was only one house I ever chucked the paper at like those kids in the movies. It was a quaint, red brick house on Penn Drive.

Then one day a note showed up with my papers in the handwriting of the route manager who'd dropped them off. The note read:

Kevin,

Mr. and Mrs. Lamp have called three times to complain that their paper is being left at the end of their driveway or thrown into the yard. Please remember that it's your job to place it in their front door.

Thank you,
Linda

It was a nice note. A nice note that I completely ignored.

As the Lamps continued to get more and more irritated at having to walk the twenty yards to the end of their driveway to get their paper each day, the less and less guilty I felt about it. For over a year, I shook as I thought of approaching that house. I'd start thinking about it in seventh period at school. It would distract me at basketball practice. Simply not worrying about it was incredibly freeing. I could actually concentrate on social studies and occasionally hit a jump shot. Then after about three weeks, I got a call.

"Hey, Kevin, it's Linda from the *Press*. How are you?"

"Uh, good."

"So what's going on with the Lamps? This is odd. You've been with us almost two years and we've never had a single complaint. Now these people call us almost every day."

"Did they tell you their giant dog attacked me?"

There was a long pause. "No, they didn't mention that."

"Well, that's why."

"Okay, I know that was probably very scary, but these people aren't happy, and I really need you to resume putting the paper in their door."

Damn it, I was going to have to go back to being terrified every afternoon. Unless…

"No, I'm not doing that."

There was an audible sigh on the other end of the line. "Okay. I will…let them know."

When Linda called back the next day, she asked if I'd be amenable to leaving the paper in a box next to the garage door if they promised to have their dog tied up or inside during my typical delivery window. I told her I'd be amenable. For another year and a half, I put the paper in the box outside their garage. They left an envelope containing the $2.50 they owed every Saturday, and I never interacted with them again.

I'd won my first workplace negotiation. I no longer had to face the hell hound.

I spent just over three years marching around the neighborhood delivering the residents of Trafford, Pennsylvania, news of the outside world. When other paper carriers quit, the *Press* began giving me parts of the routes that bordered mine. As I got older, I could do it all in less time, so all it really meant was more money. I planned on doing it until I got drafted into the minor leagues—which at fourteen I figured was inevitable considering I was at least the third best pitcher in my small town.

As it turned out, life was a pretty damn good pitcher as well. And the curve ball it threw at me was completely unhittable.

At the end of 1991, the management of the *Press* announced a plan to streamline their distribution system, which would've eliminated a bunch of good truck driver and circulation jobs. This quite obviously chapped the Teamsters Union in a city that was still mourning the rapid and unexpected collapse of the steel industry. As I write this in the 2020s, Pittsburgh has reinvented itself as a hub of robotics and bio-medical research. In the early 1990s, however, it was an economically depressed area searching for a way forward after its identity swiftly disappeared. Fighting for these six hundred truck driver jobs galvanized a city built on organized labor exactly one hundred years after Andrew Carnegie brought in the Pinkertons to crush the Homestead Strike. Public sentiment was quite clearly on the side of the workers—which led to something that probably could've only happened in that particular city at that particular time.

After months of failed negotiations, the drivers walked off the job on May 17, 1992. Suddenly I had no papers to deliver. I figured it might last a couple days. Or a week. Or two. But it just kept going. At fourteen, you're not really prepared to end up caught in the middle of a major labor dispute that paralyzes the city you live in. It dragged on and on and on.

It was unprecedented. A major American city just didn't have a newspaper anymore. Nobody knew what to do. The Penguins swept the Blackhawks to win their second consecutive Stanley Cup championship. Almost no printed record of it exists. Then on September 21, a student at Woodland Hills High School in Churchill, PA, fired a pistol six times in a crowded second-floor hallway in what was most likely a failed gang hit. Incredibly only one student was struck—in the shoulder off a ricochet. It was a massively lucky break.

I only know so much about it because the shooting happened directly outside of my father's classroom. He was an accidental hero by keeping his students inside for an extra thirty seconds with, "The bell doesn't dismiss you. I dismiss you." As he was finishing up relaying their assignment, he heard a pop and turned to see the overhead light in the hallway explode—at which point he was unintentionally valiant by walking out into the hall and shuffling kids out of the way of what he thought was simply falling glass from a defective fluorescent bulb.

While the shooter was still firing.

To this day he jokes, "I told them, 'Don't worry about the kid with the gun. The real danger is all this glass on the floor.'"

The gunman turned and ran down the stairwell, out of the school, and was eventually apprehended by police in the woods a few hours later. Whether my dad actually saved anyone in the hallway that day is debatable. But even if he had no idea what was happening, because of him, there were definitely fewer kids in the line of fire.

Perhaps the weirdest thing is that the incident is almost completely forgotten—even here in Pittsburgh. This was seven years before school shootings truly became an unfortunate and dreadful part of American life. It should've been big news. But there was no major newspaper in the region to cover it. In doing research for this chapter, the only thing I could find was a tiny UPI story and a link to some guy's blog that said, "Hey, anyone remember that shooting on the second-floor sophomore year?"

As for the *Press*, they tried to print two papers in late July using scabs brought in from out of town, but all that resulted in was a bunch of broken windshields. In the end, what finally settled the strike was the complete and total collapse of the newspaper that had been a Pittsburgh institution for 108 years. Eventually it was sold to a company that produced a much smaller paper, and by mid-January of 1993, Pittsburgh was once again circulating the daily news. It had been eight months and a day. The new *Pittsburgh Post-Gazette* saved money by phasing out delivery kids in favor of adult drivers. As would happen many times in the future, I didn't leave my first job. It left me.

CHAPTER 2

Muffin Men

Modern life is chocked full of things you don't give a minute's thought to. Take the supermarket. You show up, park the car, grab a cart, go in through the big wooshy doors, and it's just full of bananas and sliced meats and Pop Tarts waiting for you to pick them off the shelf. Until the summer before I went to college, I never contemplated how all that stuff got there.

My best friend of thirty years is a comic genius named Chris who would've been the most famous man alive in the pratfall era of silent films. He's also a semi-deranged metalhead drummer who looks like he spends his nights harvesting the organs of the unholy. Imagine the world's goofiest Satanic priest and you're probably pretty close. Back in the summer of 1995, we were just two wayward eighteen-year-olds with unkempt facial hair and thrashpunk haircuts. By late July, my baseball season was over, and I was essentially just waiting around for college to start. Chris had been spending his summer volunteering at youth soccer camps, all of which had concluded by that point as well. This left us without much to do except drive around Pittsburgh's shitty eastern suburbs causing chaos. We desperately needed something to occupy our time before we obliterated the miniscule chance either of us had of making anything of ourselves. Fortunately, just such an opportunity arose.

Chris's uncle Joe drove a box truck for Entenmann's, a company specializing in quality morning foods like English muffins, breads, bagels, and donuts. Uncle Joe was having some sort of surgery that was going to put him out of commission for a few weeks. Without him, the residents of eastern Allegheny and western Westmoreland Counties would be muffinless for an indeterminate period that would no doubt end in riots and bloodshed. The world needed heroes. And we were about to step up—mainly because Chris's dad said to Uncle Joe…

"Have Chris do it. I'm pretty sure he and his friend Kevin have figured out how to make bombs, and I'd like to keep them out of jail as long as possible."

And then Uncle Joe said to Chris, "Hey, how about helping me out by driving my truck for the next couple weeks?"

And then Chris said to me, "I gotta do my uncle Joe's Entenmann's route for a while. I'll pay you fifty bucks if you help me out."

And I said, "Can we have muffin battles in inappropriate places at inappropriate times?"

And Chris said, "Fuck yeah, we can have muffin battles in inappropriate places at inappropriate times. Why do you think I asked you to come along?"

And I said, "I'm in."

So on my eighteenth birthday, I got up at 4:00 a.m. to go meet Chris next to his Uncle Joe's box truck in the black silence of the early morning. The Conrail train yards across the street hadn't even woken yet. We'd spent most of the previous weeks lifting weights and setting off improvised explosives underneath abandoned machinery. Pretending to be responsible citizens was going to be a clear departure from our everyday routine.

As Chris started up the truck, he began laughing and bonked his head off the horn. "Holy shit, we're *muffin men*! What the hell are we doing?"

"Actual work so our dads aren't ashamed of us for a while?"

"Oh, we'll figure out a way to fuck this up. Don't worry, they'll be ashamed before this is over," he said, shifting into drive and jerking the truck into the road.

The first stop was always the Entenmann's warehouse neatly tucked behind a Sheetz gas station off Route 286. Sunrise produced a whirlwind of activity as drivers from all over the region backed their trucks into loading docks, warehouse guys checked manifests, and everyone loaded crates onto dollies while saying stuff like, "Another day, another dollar."

The warehouse guy assigned to our route was a supremely pudgy, baby-faced guy who constantly nudged you with his elbows in a desperate attempt to be your friend for a few minutes. Chris and I still argue about whether he had a mustache. I say he did. Chris is adamant that he didn't. Either way, the minute we stepped into the warehouse, he was there to greet us with hearty handshakes.

"You Joe's nephews?" he asked with the optimism of a golden retriever presenting a tennis ball.

"That's us."

"Welcome to the warehouse! I'm Fat Andy," he said, walking over to a tower of plastic crates filled with various products. "Any questions before we start?"

"Yes," Chris said. "You *seriously* want us to call you Fat Andy?"

He nodded excitedly. "Let's get you fellas loaded up!"

As we dollied all of the crates into the back of the truck, we'd quickly come to learn that Fat Andy was terrible at small talk. Instead of commenting on football or the weather, he'd just go straight to his odd warehouse guy fantasies.

"Reports are that the checkout girls at Giant Eagle are easy," Fat Andy said, his eyebrows hopping up his forehead. "Two strappin' young guys come strolling in with ten crates of delicious—I'm not saying you're gonna get lucky, but," elbow bump, "you're gonna have a good time."

I hauled a crate up the ramp. "Fat Andy, are you suggesting that the checkout girls at Giant Eagle are so easy that they'll see us stocking muffins and immediately clock out to have sex with us somewhere in the store?"

Fat Andy chuckled. "I doubt they'd even clock out. Ha ha…"

"I'm not certain I'd want to be with a girl that's that willing, Andy."

Chris's voice rang out from the back of the truck. "Speak for yourself!"

"Yes, sir," Andy said, holding his hand up for a high five. "You guys are getting some checkout-girl action. Don't spare Fat Andy the details tomorrow!"

Chris hopped to the concrete floor and slammed the ramp back underneath the truck. "I'm gonna find a girl named Brenda and we're gonna do it in the meat section! The *meats*! But only if her name is Brenda!" he shouted, pumping his crotch fifteen different ways.

Chris is a weird dude.

I hopped up on the bumper and pulled down the overhead door, locking it with a metal-on-metal clink as Chris acknowledged Fat Andy's high-five request with a smack heard around the warehouse.

Our job was to deliver the products Andy had given us to ten different supermarkets along Route 30 between East McKeesport and Greensburg. At each stop we had to pull the truck around back, read the printout to see what the store had ordered for the day, pull the corresponding items, load them onto a dolly, then wheel them in through the back of the store. At the doors would always be some sort of delivery manager to either meticulously check our goods or send us through with a disinterested wave.

From there it seemed like a straightforward process—put the crap on the shelves and move on. But like most undertakings in your average American job, it was at least one standard deviation tougher than it needed to be. Each day brought with it a different-colored bread tag to help us immediately recognize what was "fresh" and what was "not particularly fresh."

Now pay attention to this next part because after I reveal it, I'm probably going to have to look over my shoulder the rest of my life due to threats from the multibillion-dollar muffin industry (or Big Breakfast, as they're often called). A large part of the job was removing the really old packages from the shelves completely, then stuffing the fresh ones way in the back where the gremlins lived. At that point, we'd move the "closer to expired" packages to the front where customers were more likely to grab them. So if you want fresh muffins, you gotta reach toward the...

"Hey, hey, get out of here. Hey..."

Sorry about that, I had to fight off an assassin.

Anyway, Monday we'd pull the green tags and shove the blue ones into the void. Tuesday it was white and yellow. Wednesday it was orange and pink. By Saturday we'd be pulling the blue ones we'd delivered on Monday. They'd go back to the warehouse to be redistributed to discount supermarkets and food pantries—or if we drivers felt a mighty hankering, we could feast on all the almost-but-not-quite-stale bagels we could handle. It was one of the few perks of the job.

As we exited our very first store, Chris tore open the plastic covering on one of our returns and ripped into an English muffin like a pit bull. "Instead of taking these back to the warehouse, we should drive down the road chucking them into people's yards like breakfast paperboys!"

"Actually, as a paperboy you're not supposed to..."

Chris took the rest of the muffins and joyously tossed them in the air like he'd just slid down a rainbow. "Muffins for everyone!" he yelled as they rained from the sky. One of them landed on the roof of the store. His smile was contagious. "What a great job!"

This enthusiasm would not last.

Having to arrange the product by colored tags added loads of mostly unnecessary time as we ended up in an atoll of muffin packages trying to make sure each one was placed correctly. After twenty some years, Uncle Joe had it down to a science. We...did not. Because of this, on that first day, we progressively got further and further behind. Uncle Joe was typically done and back home by noon every day. By then, we were only on our fifth store. It led to some...complications. By the time we got to the Shop 'n Save in Jeanette at one thirty, the back door was closed and nobody was around. We pulled the truck up to the door and rang the buzzer. No answer. Rang the buzzer again. No answer. Rang the buzzer again...

"Yeah, what?" crackled an agitated voice.

"We have your Entenmann's delivery."

"No deliveries after noon. Come back tomorrow."

"Sorry. It's our first day, and we're running a little behind."

No answer. Ring the buzzer. No answer.

Chris seemed to briefly consider ripping the metal door off the hinges. Instead he just grunted and hopped back in the truck. "Fine, you don't get your shit. What do I care?"

Having one less store that first day was actually a huge benefit because we immediately went from comically behind to just behind. Even so, we got to our last stop at the Davis Supermarket in Greensburg at around four thirty, which might as well have been midnight in supermarket time. It was also a full twelve hours since we left for the warehouse. Both of us were now stressed, exhausted, and incredibly sick of muffins.

When we got there, the back door was locked, so we decided to park in the lot and haul our stuff in through the front—which seemed like a reasonable adaptation.

It was not.

The store manager, one of those guys who wore a crinkled short-sleeve shirt with a red tie, came hustling out of his throne room as quickly as his loafers could carry him. "What the hell is this?" he shouted.

"We have your Entenmann's—"

"You don't come through the front door! Who told you to come through the front?"

"No one. The back door was locked so—"

"The front door is where the *customers* enter!"

Chris looked at the guy's name plate. The name BRUCE was stamped on it in big, bold letters. Underneath his name in slightly smaller letters was the word MANAGER. "It's been a long day, Bruce Manager. Wow, your last name is Manager? That's convenient."

"Destiny is real," I said.

"That's not my last name. It's my job title!" he sneered. "You think being three hours late is funny?"

Chris took a deep breath to avoid strangling the guy with his own tie. "Well, the sign says the muffins are in aisle two so..."

I was about to get one of my first experiences in the dangers of giving people more power than their minds can handle. Bruce Manager was angry that life hadn't provided him the opportunity to be a cop or an assistant principal. Either that or he was going through a divorce and didn't have anyone to take it out on but the two dudes unlucky enough to be late with his muffins.

"Count 'em," he commanded.

"What?" Chris said, turning back around.

"I don't trust that you dropouts can count. Count 'em. Right here," he said, ripping the paper manifest off the top of the tray I was holding.

Now what I haven't mentioned thus far is that there was a small computer in the back of the truck. It was there to make drivers double-check the product count. If the printout you got at the warehouse said that the Norwin Foodland needed five packages of blueberry muffins, you had to enter a five in an electronic spreadsheet before you went into the store. In the end when the computer did the math, the count had to match the desired total for each location. Doubling the work apparently made it tougher for drivers to forget certain items as they rushed through their deliveries.

For 1995, the little computer bolted to the wall was incredibly advanced. You used a small digital pen to write on the screen, and the internal processors recognized your scribble and turned it into a clear, readable number in a tiny box next to the item in question. The problem was the technology was nowhere near perfected. Damn near every time you wrote a one, the computer turned it into a seven. And if you didn't notice right away, you'd do all the work to make sure the orders matched only to have the thing say you were six off when you actually weren't. It led to a ton of confusion and a lot of kicking things in the back of the truck.

The computer was glitching like crazy as we loaded the products for Davis Market. No matter what we did, we couldn't get the count to match.

"I don't know," Chris growled. "This thing is turning nines into eights and twos into fives and threes into dicks…"

"We've counted it four times," I said. "It's right. Don't worry about the computer."

Chris let the pen swing from the wire. "Screw it."

All this wouldn't have been a huge deal if not for Bruce Manager's need to flex his nuts. Right there in the front of the store, he pulled up a stool and sat down to watch us count muffin packages. So we did. Chris took half the crates, and I took the other half. Under Bruce's watchful eye, we walked our fingers across the plastic, running a silent tally in our heads.

"I got seventy," I said.

"I got seventy-nine," Chris answered back.

"I'm supposed to have one fifty. You're one off," Bruce Manager scowled, now with customers and cashiers uncomfortably watching from the checkouts. "Count 'em again. Out loud."

We counted again. Out loud. Once again, seventy and seventy-nine.

He smacked the printout and angrily shook his head. "I wouldn't let either of you work here. I wouldn't let you sweep the damn floors."

Chris about chewed through his tongue. "We're just doing this for my uncle Joe because…"

"I don't care what your excuse is. Count 'em again." He pointed at Chris. "Just you. All of 'em."

I could tell the rage inside Chris was nearly at a boil. It was starting to get seriously uncomfortable. This dude was absolutely set on belittling us in front of his customers over one solitary muffin package. Obviously, I wasn't pleased with being called a dropout but also recognized that we were in fact really damn late and currently not doing much to counteract Bruce Manager's assessment of our cognitive abilities. Also, it was my birthday, for fuck's sake. I just wanted to get home.

Chris, on the other hand…

"One-forty-seven, one-forty-eight," Chris said, dropping his head, veins bursting from his forearms as he nearly turned the last package into paste. "…one-forty-nine."

Bruce Manager was about to say something smarmy that was going to get him put through the plate-glass window at the front of the store. If I didn't do something fast, the next time Chris and I hung out would be sometime in the mid-2030s.

As Chris and Bruce Manager had one of the dumber stare downs in modern history, I deftly slipped a package of bagels out from the trays and slowly kicked it around behind me.

"Oh shit," I said, feigning surprise. "Have we been counting this one that fell out?" I said, reaching for it on the floor. "Well, that makes one fifty right there."

"There ya go," Chris said with beads of sweat balling on his forehead. "One fifty."

Bruce Manager began a sarcastic slow clap. "Wow, they *can* count."[2*]

At the insult, Chris exhaled in a manner normally reserved for rodeo bulls. And this is where Bruce Manager should've been a professional, realized he'd proved his point, and let us walk away to do our job. But he was on a roll and wanted to see how far he could push it.

He pointed his stubby finger at us. "First thing I'm doing when I get back to the office is calling the Entenmann's warehouse to let them know how much time I had to waste shitting around with their dropout muffin vendors."

And…volcano.

Chris took two menacing strides toward the guy and leaned so far into him that he nearly fell off his stool. "I. DON'T. GIVE. A. FUCK!"

[2*] Technically, we still couldn't, but that's beside the point.

The front of the store went silent. The beeps, clanks, and quiet conversations all ceased. Bruce Manager, now realizing he'd pushed himself right into complete powerlessness, huffed, "Well...that's not appropriate." For some reason, he turned and glanced at me for support.

"Don't look at me," I said. "I don't give a fuck, either."

Knowing the situation was escaping him, Bruce Manager clenched his jaw and waved toward aisle two. "Go."

We silently hauled our wares through the store as the beeps, clanks, and quiet conversations resumed. We finished up and drove the forty-five minutes home. It was probably the longest Chris and I had ever spent together in silence. We thought for sure we'd cost Uncle Joe his job. We'd found a way to disappoint our fathers damn near immediately.

That night, Chris solemnly called Uncle Joe to let him know how we'd let him down—only to have Joe laugh and explain that as long as we got the products to their destination, there was no one at the warehouse that would remotely care about the complaints of some random store manager in Greensburg. It was an interesting glimpse into the world outside of high school that we weren't prepared for. When you're a kid, standing up to authority typically comes with an automatic punishment. But in a country enraptured with capitalism, we weren't important enough to be given a detention slip. It was freeing—depressingly, bafflingly freeing.

We were barely in the warehouse doors the next morning when Fat Andy greeted us, wringing his hands with anticipation. "There's my boys. How much checkout (kitty) did you get yesterday?"

"None, Andy," I said as I picked up a few trays and walked them into the back of the truck. "Buddy, I promise if we get laid on the job, we'll call the warehouse immediately."

"Holding you to it," Andy replied. "I'm telling you the Giant Eagle girls are *eassssssy!*"

I guess we could've easily taken his interest as creepy, but he seemed more like a dude who'd never had younger brothers to mentor, and since there wasn't really much he could teach us about the job itself, informing us about the promiscuousness of the Giant Eagle girls was his offbeat attempt to pass something down. It was oddly endearing.

Each day we'd get slightly timelier. Tuesday we got to the Jeanette Shop 'n Save at one instead of one thirty, but when we rang the buzzer, there was still no answer. Wednesday we got there at twelve thirty. No answer. Thursday we actually saw them shut the door as we were pulling up.

"Hey," we yelled through the door. "We have your Entenmann's delivery!"

The guy was obviously still in earshot. "We told you already. No deliveries after noon!"

"It's 12:03!"

"Well, that's after noon, ain't it?"

By this time, Chris was almost as pissed as he'd been when he nearly killed Bruce Manager. "That's it," he said, kicking the truck tire. "Tomorrow all we give them is whole wheat bread. No blueberry muffins, just a whole aisle of the one thing nobody fuckin' wants."

I chuckled at the thought of the world's most disappointing supermarket aisle. We couldn't actually pull that off. Could we? More on this later.

By Friday, Fat Andy's disappointment that we hadn't somehow gotten lucky in a Giant Eagle was starting to wear on us. Dude was a sad puppy every time we'd relay that we didn't have time to squeeze in a quickie with a girl we'd just met. We started to assume that Andy was still living with his mother.

He'd give us an elbow bump. "Hey, I heard you guys were running late yesterday. Does that mean you were, ya know…getting a little…"

"No, Andy. It means we're not good at our job yet."

"Ah, you guys are killing me!"

We wondered privately why Fat Andy was so adamant about the effortlessness of seducing the Giant Eagle girls, but asking meant we might find out, so we didn't. We also never inquired as to why the Shop 'n Save and Foodland girls were apparently devout Catholics.

As luck would have it, my ex-girlfriend Colleen worked as a cashier at the Giant Eagle in East McKeesport. She was a quiet, puffy-cheeked redhead with dark brown eyes that always looked like they were plotting a robbery. Unfortunately for Colleen, she was the first girl I ever seriously dated, which meant I was woefully inept at basic things like… paying attention to her. We made it about five months, which was four more than she realistically should've afforded me. Seeing her across the store each morning was somewhat awkward—right up until I decided to make it *really* awkward.

The East McKeesport Giant Eagle was typically our first stop. Early in the morning, there was almost no one in the store, so when we arrived on Thursday, Colleen was leaning against the register fiddling with the name tag on her vest.

"Hey, no leaning on the registers," I said, sneaking up behind her, causing her to immediately pretend like she was working.

She reached over and slugged me. "Uh, you prick. I thought you were my boss."

"Hey, I don't have a lot of time, but I need a favor," I said.

Intrigued, she squinted at me. "Okay."

"I need you to have sex with me somewhere in the store. But just for pretend."[3*]

She blinked about fifty times. "What?"

Chris butted in. "There's a guy at the warehouse who desperately needs to hear that one of us did a little," honk noises and finger miming, "with a Giant Eagle checkout girl."

"We're pretty sure if he doesn't, he turns back into a package of donuts at midnight," I added. "All we need is the story."

Colleen puffed her lips. "So you're asking my permission to tell some random guy at your warehouse that you had sex with me at work?"

"Uh, yes," I said, slightly ashamed after hearing it out loud. "Unless there's a girl who works here named Brenda. Then Chris can take care of it."

[3*] This was the first time we'd spoken in months.

Colleen wrinkled her eyebrows. "Brenda doesn't work the morning shift. Also, she's like forty-five and smells like cigars."

Chris smiled. "I *don't* care."

Colleen looked at me with a skeptical glimmer. "What do I get in return?"

"I don't know. We have lots of…muffins."

"Backrub. My house. Tomorrow night. My parents are going out of town."

This was getting dicey. In order to have pretend sex to placate Fat Andy, I was now being put in a situation that could lead to real sex with an ex-girlfriend I had no desire to get back together with. The most troubling thing of all was that I knew her birthday was the next weekend, and if I followed through, I'd be perilously close to obligated to buy her something. Still, though, at eighteen all thoughts began downstairs instead of upstairs.

"Uh, sure," I answered.

An old woman plopped a basket of groceries down on the conveyor belt, and Colleen turned back to the register. "Call me," she said, turning to toss a flirt over her shoulder.

Chris smacked me on the back. "Well, that went well!"

I nodded. "Fat Andy might be on to something. That was much easier than it should've been."

Without getting into the mostly boring details, the next Monday when Fat Andy approached with that hopeful gleam, I cut him off before he could speak. "Talked to this Giant Eagle girl Thursday morning," I told him. "I'm not gonna say much, but Friday night I got home from her place at three a.m."

Fat Andy stopped like he'd walked into a screen door. I half expected him to float to the ceiling in a halo of light and proclaim, "You are the chosen one, my child."

He put his hand up for a stunned high five. "I told you!" he yelped. "Did Fat Andy tell you or what?"

"Fat Andy, you did indeed tell me," I said, smacking his hand.

He pumped his fist. "That's what I'm talking about!" There were collar grabs and rib pokes and some very serious nods of approval. He was so excited that his mustache may well have dropped clean off his face, thus inducing the possibility that Chris and I are both right.

What I left out of the story I told Fat Andy was how little actually happened that night and how most of the money Chris promised me for helping him deliver muffins was now invested in some crappy piece of jewelry that I'd give to Colleen about a half hour before we broke up for the second time that year—at her birthday party.

Some may ask me, was it worth it just to see the smile on Fat Andy's face in that moment? Just to know he walked a little taller that day? To give a man hope that all things are possible? The answer of course is fuck no. I'd much rather have had the fifty bucks. But though I'd essentially break even on the experience monetarily, there was, in fact, one memory that made my time as a substitute muffin truck driver's assistant more than worthwhile.

On Friday we hustled through our usual stops, skipping a few along the way just so we could finally get to the Jeanette Shop 'n Save before noon. Their aisle hadn't been stocked since Saturday. Looking only at the Entenmann's shelves, you could've reasonably assumed a hurricane was coming. Because of it, we were expecting some sort of Bruce Manager situation. But to our surprise, no one said a thing as we walked in the back doors at 11:00 a.m. and started stacking muffins. Everything looked totally normal.

Except for one special "eff you" package.

The day before when I'd heard Chris suggest that we should "give them a million of what nobody wants," it dawned on me that we had an abundance of something that almost nobody can stand. Our truck was filled with the junk mail of the food industry.

Heels.

The crappy end pieces of a normal loaf of bread drive most of the world insane. Many a roommate has gone to fix a sandwich only to yell, "Ah, maaaaaan," when they find nothing but two flat pieces of disappointment. There's never been a restaurant that advertised *"a lip-smacking delight piled high with garlic peppercorn turkey breast, two slices of delicious Colby Jack, our special homestyle honey mustard, and a fresh dill pickle—served between two heels."*

Which made them perfect for our special delivery.

Thursday afternoon we got back to Chris's house, parked the truck in the alley, and spent a half hour meticulously taking the heels out of each of our returns and putting them all into one single package, cracking up as we did it—heel after heel after heel until we'd made an entire loaf.

A whole loaf of heels.

Look, I know what we did was probably illegal and due to the fact that we assuredly didn't wear gloves as we did it more than a little gross. And lord knows we weren't punishing the people actually responsible for our inconvenience. We were penalizing some random customer who'd now be out $2.49 and stuck with bread they couldn't use. It was a dumb and kind of mean thing to do. But I'm asking you to put all that aside and focus on the humor here. Hey, I risked my life to give you insider muffin secrets; the least you can do is not judge me for my teenage ethics.

That Friday we giggled like a third-grade sleepover as we put the heel loaf on the shelf with all the others. We walked out the door having executed one of the more ridiculous worker revolts in history. And the best thing was that by the time we came back on Monday, it was gone. Which either meant the managers did quality control on each individual package—or someone bought it. And that's the thing I can't quit laughing about all these years later—the thought of some poor soul from Jeanette opening the bread for their morning toast, pulling out the first heel, setting it aside, and then immediately finding another heel. And then another. And another.

"What the hell?" they yell in my dreams. "This is a physical impossibility! Surely it can't be *all* heels! And yet the more I uncover, the deeper the mystery becomes!"

What I learned from the experience is that as fun as delivering muffins was, I probably couldn't do it every day of my life. Dealing with small-minded people trying to wield power over their tiny fiefdoms would eventually drive me to madness.

After two weeks, Uncle Joe came back to work. A week after that, I took off for Florida and my freshman year of college. As for Chris, he decided he loved supermarkets so much, he'd become a butcher and work in them for the next three decades and counting.

Recently, Uncle Joe relayed that Fat Andy is no longer with us. Here's hoping he found his way to the easiest Giant Eagle in the sky.

CHAPTER 3

Forklift

U pon returning home from my freshman year, sitting around my
parents' house doing nothing began to gnaw at my insides. Down
in Florida, I was always busy with class and baseball practice. Now that I
was back in Pennsylvania without anything to do, however, I was slowly
going insane from boredom—until my mom circled a square in the
want ads and left it on the kitchen table.

CAROL HARRIS STAFFING
Seeking college students for summer positions!
Clerical, light industrial, warehouse
Call now!

Two days later, I ended up at an office building in Monroeville,
where a very nice woman named Lisa took me through an interview
that was essentially the following...
"How are your typing skills?"
"Mediocre."
"Do you have dress shoes?"
"I think so."
"Are you familiar with Windows 95?"

"I'd say we're acquaintances at best."

The last answer was met with a sigh and a lot of sifting through manila folders. "Can you lift heavy things?"

"I can lift heavy things."

There was more paper shuffling before she gave me a smile. "Okay, when we have something, we'll call you."

It would be another week at home doing odd jobs in the yard before I got a frantic call from Lisa one Friday just before dinner. Duquesne University apparently realized moments before a weekend conference that they'd forgotten to put in a request to the physical plant and thus hadn't set up any of the vendor displays yet—which even to a college kid prone to leaving full glasses of milk on the counter all afternoon still seemed like a massive oversight.

"Yeah, I guess I can do that," I said. "When do you need me?"

"Can you be there in half an hour?"

Truth was, the only way I was getting downtown in a half hour was if I'd left fifteen minutes before she called, but at that point, I wasn't passing on anything. I said yes, hung up, and rushed down the stairs.

It was not a particularly complicated job. At around six, I entered a big empty conference room where a guy in a Duquesne University polo gave me instructions on how to put together banner stands and a laminated Xerox document showing where everything needed to go. Only about twelve of the forty booths needed the bigger trusses assembled. The rest only required small stands bookending those white plastic folding tables that even the most remote tribes of the Amazon have forty of stacked against the wall of a rarely used storage hut. I followed the directions, put everything together, and moved the tables around. Two hours later as I was setting up the last booth, the guy in charge returned to the conference room to check on my progress.

I unlocked the table legs and stood up. "So, uh, what else needs done?"

"You set up the tables, too?"

"Was I not supposed to?"

The guy looked at me like I'd pulled a dove out of my previously empty hands. "Well, um, yes. But um...we were expecting you to be here until at least ten o'clock. It's not even eight yet." He looked at his watch, put his hands on his hips, and glanced around the room. "I guess I'll sign off on your hours and you can get out of here. Thanks for coming down on such short notice. And for getting it all done so quickly. Wow."

The dude signed his name on my timesheet, and I headed home feeling pretty good about myself. I'd put in a solid two hours of hard work, going above and beyond what the folks at Duquesne had expect... *Wait a minute.* In my head, I heard the supervisor's pleased confusion at the fact that I'd gotten it all done so quickly. *"Wow, we were expecting you to be here until at least ten o'clock..."*

As I zipped down the Parkway, I was hit with the depressing realization of how my work ethic had screwed me. At six bucks an hour, I had a choice. That choice was to work really hard for twelve bucks or nowhere near as hard for twenty-four. And I'd chosen the former. I wasn't aware yet that when you're paid by the hour in a corporate setting, there's absolutely no reward for doing a great job. Nope, in hourly America, excellent is overkill. It would be a long time before I realized that the only real goal of the hourly employee is to not be lousy enough for management to justify the hassle it would take to hire someone else.

My first paycheck came about a week later. I opened it to find a blue slip of paper with my name on it and $9.86 that was *all mine.* For the next few weeks, I was Carol Harris's go-to guy for three-hour jobs setting up conference rooms—which meant that I got up early, unfolded tables, and was back home by lunchtime. I'd learned my lesson, though. When one of my jobs only took me forty-five minutes, I tore the whole thing down and did it again. After that, I sat there for a good hour fiddling with a single wingnut until someone came in to check on me.

"How are we coming along in here?"

I slithered out from beneath the table. "Perfect timing. One last wingnut to tighten."

"Really? You're done already? We thought this would be a four-hour job."

One of the things I learned that summer is that people who never set up conference rooms severely overestimate the amount of time it takes to set up conference rooms. Either that or I was the Baryshnikov of unfolding tables—a possibility I'm not ruling out.

For a while, the work was spotty. I'd get two or three jobs a week until one Friday when Lisa called. "Hey, Kevin, you live in Trafford, right?"

"Yup."

"We might have something for you starting Monday if you want steadier work."

In 1869, at the age of twenty-two, a now-overlooked industrialist named George Westinghouse invented a braking system for trains that relied on compressed air instead of a person running from car to car in order to pull the brakes manually. It was a much better method than the old one seeing as stopping a rolling multi-ton bullet was no longer exclusively reliant on Wally's endurance. Though a New Yorker, Westinghouse chose the town of Wilmerding, Pennsylvania, to manufacture his new brakes both for its proximity to the steel mills of Pittsburgh and because it was bisected by the Pennsylvania Railroad. Over the next decade, the Wilmerding Air Brake Company (WABCO) became such a success that other company towns began to spring up in the hills around it. One of those towns was Trafford, named for the borough in Manchester, England, where Westinghouse ran his overseas operations. In late 1903, when the Westinghouse foundry opened in Trafford, Pennsylvania, it immediately became the world's largest.

For decades, the giant brick buildings along the creek below town churned out raw American power, molding steel for railroad parts, electrical substations, and transformer coils. But though Trafford wasn't a mill town itself, it was irrevocably tied to the steel industry and thus couldn't avoid the hard times of the 1970s. The Westinghouse

Corporation struggled to keep up with cheaper, foreign-made alternatives, finally culminating with the loss of over three hundred jobs on September 19, 1985, when the plant shut down for good. When our family moved to town the very next year, the Westinghouse buildings were an abandoned, rusty hulk of distress. The complex sat vacant for years. It was the rust belt personified.

Gradually, however, life returned to the facility. By 1996, one of the buildings housed the distribution warehouse for Chelsea Building Products. Such is where I found myself at 6:55 a.m. one Monday morning sitting in a cinderblock break room with thirty other people who were all silently sipping on gas station coffee and staring at the same wall clock waiting for someone with authority to say, "All right, let's get to it."

I was put on a four-man team with a forklift driver in his early thirties named Greg who had long hair and played guitar in a local metal band; Alex, a tiny Italian dude who was our supervisor and thus always called away whenever the hard work began; and an old guy named Paul with fading Navy tattoos who loved to make dick jokes but was too Catholic to actually use the word penis. And thus we were treated to daily tales of his legendary "hangdown."

My presence on the team was necessary because when Chelsea transferred the inventory from their older, smaller warehouse earlier in the year, their mantra was not, "Let's develop a clear plan as to where we put everything so as not to cause chaos when the new facility opens," it was, "Hell, just drop it anywhere."

Unsurprisingly, this wasn't the best plan for avoiding shipping delays. The workers who buzzed around us all day knew what they needed but didn't know where any of the shit in the 150,000 square foot warehouse actually was. Bundles of gutters were sitting on top of bales of door tracks, which were sitting on top of crates of siding. Consequently, orders were not what most businesses would describe as "filled in a timely manner."

For nine hours a day, Alex would use a portable scanner to figure out what products were in a specific group of open-ended steel containers, then give a printout to Paul as to what we needed to pull. Paul and I would then remove those bundles, stack them in a different crate, and leave it for Greg, who would load the whole monstrosity on the forklift and drive it off to a section along the back wall that was now god forbid actually organized by product, size, and color.

It was brutal work. Each bundle was roughly eight feet long and weighed between eighty and a hundred fifty pounds depending on the product inside. We'd remove and stack hundreds of these things a day. In fact, the work was so tough that when I came back from lunch on Wednesday, Alex gave me a pat on the back.

"Congrats, buddy. You made it longer than any of the other guys they sent us. I can learn your name now."

"It's only my third day," I said, astonished. "And it's Kevin."

Truthfully, one of the big reasons I stuck around was that if I quit, I knew my dad would invent something much more arduous at home. Every day when my alarm went off at 6:30 a.m. and I pictured a utopia where I wasn't deadlifting gutters all day, I'd hear my father's voice saying something like, "Kev, since you're not working today, I'm gonna need you to walk the old refrigerator to Ohio."

Each day the work got exponentially more difficult. Early on they realized I was a monkey who could easily climb the twelve-foot-tall stacks of crates, so instead of haggling with everyone else in the warehouse who needed the lift, Alex would say, "Kevin, could you go up there and check that label at the top for me real quick? And if it says GB-1021, why don't you just push it down to Paul and Greg?"

So by the end of the day, not only had I lifted about five tons, I'd also scaled the equivalent of Pike's Peak in twelve-foot chunks. But by far the worst development of the summer was that someone who clearly worked elsewhere decided that they needed to test the heat to be ready for winter. For some reason, this meant the goddamned system had to run the entirety of July. I imagine the June department meeting at Chelsea headquarters went something like this…

"Okay, any last items?"

"Sir, we're going to need to test the heating system in the new warehouse in Trafford. It hasn't been used in eleven years."

"Is there any way we can test it over a weekend when nobody's working?"

"I'm sure we could, but how would we tell it was operational unless there were employees in there to pass out from heatstroke?"

"Ah, yes. Good thinking, Simmons."

My dad used to have to clean the carbon deposits off the sides of the open hearth at the Homestead Works. "You could only stand it for twenty seconds or so before you had to go back down the ramp and another guy came up to replace you," he once told me. "There were five guys in a line, and we just rotated for the entire shift." He had to wear one of those reflective silver suits that volcanologists wear next to bubbling calderas just so his skin didn't literally catch on fire.

Okay, so *that* was probably worse. But there were days in the Chelsea warehouse where it was over a hundred twenty degrees in there—and if I know anything about saunas, it's that you're supposed to relax on a bench and not march around carrying building supplies. And yet I wasn't the one melting the quickest. It wasn't even Paul whose single-pocket T-shirts were always three shades darker by the afternoon. No, it was most definitely Greg.

What you don't realize unless you've driven a forklift is that the only place for the engine compartment is literally right underneath the driver's seat—which functions as a nice butt warmer in January. In a needlessly heated warehouse in July, however…

I remember Greg being slumped over the steering wheel one ninety-four-degree day as Paul and I rearranged bundles on the warehouse floor. Sweat was dripping from his forehead at a rate that could show up on radar. Another few minutes and he'd bear a striking resemblance to the ghoulish skeletons on his Cannibal Corpse T-shirt. Finally, he turned off the forklift and melted out of the seat.

"Kevin, I'm going to teach you how to drive the forklift. I need a break from the swamp ass. Half hour. I'll pull bundles."

"Wouldn't I need to take some kind of training course? And get certified?"

"As long as you don't fuck up too bad, nobody will know." He tried to peel away the hair stuck to his forehead and looked deep into my eyes. "Alligators could live in my ass right now. I'm begging you."

I looked at the forklift. I looked back at him. "I don't know if I want alligators to be able to survive in my ass, Greg."

Paul wiped his forehead and chuckled. "I had alligators in my pants, I'd smack 'em away with my hangdown," he said, shaking his hips back and forth, engulfed in a world of heat-induced madness where he was fending off reptiles with his cock. "Get out of here, gator!"

My whole goal in life is to be Paul when I'm seventy.

Greg put his hands on my shoulders. "I'll buy you an iced tea. I just need a break."

Truth was I super wanted to drive the forklift but figured if I showed initial reluctance, I might be able to get a cold drink out of the deal. Mission accomplished. I grinned and excitedly jumped into the seat. It was warm and squishy. Uncomfortably warm and squishy. I barely cared because again…I was about to drive the freaking forklift.

"Okay," Greg said. "It's not that different than a car. Gas. Brake. Wheel. This lever here only has three settings. It's got to be in neutral to turn it on. Pull it back to go in reverse. Throw it forward to go forward. These levers over here are how you control the forks."

I grabbed the lever and thrust the forks forward, then pulled them back. I raised and lowered them. This was going to be awesome. I was about to illegally drive heavy, unsafe stuff around the back of the warehouse. The plan was perfect. Right up until…

"What is Kevin doing on the forklift?"

We turned to see Alex rounding the corner sipping on an ice-cold Pepsi and looking like a man who'd spent the last few hours doing paperwork in an air-conditioned office.

Greg was devastated. "Uh…he wanted to see how it worked."

I nodded. "I, uh…wanted to see how it worked."

Alex sipped his drink and pointed. "He can't be on there. OSHA'd have a conniption." He scanned us up and down. "You guys on break? Need me to clock you out? Don't see a lot of work going on back here."

Greg sighed and slithered back up into the swamp. Though his plans were thwarted, he knew exactly how to get Alex to leave us alone. Greg pointed to the bundles spread across the floor. "Actually, Alex, you're just in time to help us with this load."

Alex wiped the back of his neck with the handkerchief he kept in his pocket. "Oh, well, I just came back to check your progress. I have a meeting soon," he said, squinting at his watch. "I'll be back as soon as it's done to help you guys out." He gave a thumbs-up and smiled as he walked off to a meeting that would inevitably "take much longer than anticipated," even though he "had every intention" of assisting us for the last two hours.

Long story short, I never got my iced tea.

As it turned out, this was most likely a fortunate break. Because get this...forklifts are fuckin' dangerous. It was a lesson I'd learn later that summer.

There are three things you need to know to properly set up this story.

Number one: the warehouse was so large that simply walking from the front to the back took three or four minutes. Thus, we had these little battery-operated carts that you could trolley around in at twelve miles per hour. They were essentially a bumper car–sized vehicle that was a combination of a scooter and a bright yellow tank. To use them, you stood in the center between two metal casings that housed the battery assembly and the motor and made it go by gripping a rubber-coated handlebar. Every time I got on one and needed to back up, I'd initially hiccup forward before I remembered that my knuckles had to roll back toward my wrists to make it do what I wanted. I screwed it up every single time.

Number two: the entire place was a labyrinth of crates. It was row after row after row of product-filled containers stacked four high—which essentially made long, twelve-foot-tall steel barriers that you couldn't see over or through.

Number three: there was a greasy-haired guy in the warehouse who was impossible to ignore. His name was Mike, and due to his Tourette's Syndrome, you knew where he was at every moment. All day, every day, "FUCK, FUCK, FUCK, FUCKERS, FUCKING FUCKCAKES, MOTHERFUCKIN' FUCKFUCK!" In the end, we all knew he couldn't help it, so as annoying as it was, it somehow turned into background static. It was as much a part of the warehouse audioscape as the clangs, bangs, and honks.

Anyway, one Friday afternoon, Alex forgot his hammer up front and sent me in a cart to go fetch it. I was excited. Driving around at jogging speed wasn't much, but it created more of a breeze than the otherwise dead July air, so you took what you could get. I found the hammer by the loading docks and turned to head back, giving myself a well-deserved palm smack to the forehead when I accidentally threw the cart forward into the wall before I backed it up.

As I rolled down one of the alleys to the left of all the crates, a forklift carrying a couple ten-foot-long strips of siding made a left turn out of the stacks and slowly started to drive in my direction. It wasn't a big deal. I could just turn and duck down any of the other rows to get around it. So I did. I couldn't see what was around the corner, but if nothing else, I was pretty confident that at least Swearing Mike wasn't pulling a crate on the other side because I'd have heard the cussing from two miles away. And then…

"Oh, FUCK, FUCK, FUCK ME!"

It's hard to describe how suddenly it happened. I turned the corner just in time to see Mike catch the tail of a crate against one of the other enclosures in the row. There's a reason you never turn the forklift while carrying a load with the forks elevated. It's so you don't accidentally nick something and send a thousand pounds of product crashing to the ground. Even the dope nineteen-year-old temp who OSHA wouldn't let drive one knew that.

The blue, eight-foot-long steel crate alone weighed over two hundred pounds. With the bundles that were now sliding off the forks with it, the whole load was somewhere north of eight hundred. To this day I can still see it in crystal-clear HD as it all slid sideways off the forks and began to drop toward my head.

BOOM!

Hundreds of pounds of steel and aluminum crashed to the concrete floor, the blue crate landing on the front of my cart—a cart that I'd somehow for the very first time instinctively thrown into reverse. If I'd have done what I always did and initially jerked forward instead—you wouldn't be reading this sentence. Actively thinking about it still gives me the jibblies. In the nanosecond I had to react, I have no idea how my brain succeeded in a task where it had previously failed 100 percent of the time. It just did.

From the forklift, Mike shot a terrified look in my direction. "Oh fuck. Oh fuck, dude! Are you fucking okay? Fuck, fuck, I'm sorry, man. Fuck! Fuck!"

I didn't have a lot of words in response. "That was close," was all I managed to utter. I took a deep breath, backed up, and slowly cruised past all the debris.

A minute later, Alex had his hammer back. "What was that crash?" he asked.

"Swearing Mike dropped a crate," I answered.

Alex suddenly looked very concerned. "Nobody got hurt, did they? Did you see it?"

I pointed to the severely dented front of the cart. "Uh, yup."

It was in that moment, looking at the damaged cart, that I realized I almost left home for work and never came back. I wasn't a cop. I wasn't a firefighter. I wasn't a soldier. I hadn't signed up to put my life on the line for the greater good. I was just trying to pay for my Intro to Mass Communication textbook. Luckily, I was still too young to properly internalize the haphazard fragility of existence and quickly brushed the whole thing off.

It seemed that Alex completely understood how close I'd come to being hauled out of there under a tarp—and how close he'd come to a lot of unwanted paperwork. "Do you need a break? Maybe clock out early? I don't know. You tell me."

I didn't really understand the question. I was still alive and breathing. Nothing had been crushed or broken other than my perception of Swearing Mike's attention to detail.

"Why would I want to clock out early?"

Greg, Paul, and Alex all shook their heads in pity and admiration as if I'd reminded them exactly how dumb and carefree it was to be nineteen. Paul laughed and patted me on the back. "How are you tucking that giant hangdown into your pants every day, son?"

"One leg at a time, Paul. One leg at a time."

Alex took us all to lunch on the last day of the project after we'd seemingly done the impossible and got the warehouse in order. The three temps Carol Harris had sent Chelsea Building Products before me had lasted a total of four-and-a-half days. I lasted the final nine weeks. Enjoying the pizza that Alex bought for us on that final afternoon, I grinned. I'd made it through the summer...barely.

CHAPTER 4

Assembly

N ot wishing to flounder around again looking for work when I got home after my sophomore year, I called Carol Harris the day after I got back to let them know I was available. I knew the work wouldn't exactly be a dream come true, but wherever they sent me would allow me to play ultimate frisbee and drive around town pulling stupid pranks with Chris, which was really all I cared about anyway.

I got a call almost right away.

Otis Spunkmeyer is a brand name that can only be taken seriously if your principal products are delicious baked goods or party supplies. It is a terrible name for your high-end hotel chain. Luckily, Spunkmeyer stayed in their lane and mass-produced gooey desserts that seemed as if they'd come straight from Grandma's oven.[4*]

If you could produce a job that was exactly the opposite of the Chelsea Building Products warehouse, this was it. Whereas Chelsea was dirty and disorganized, the Spunkmeyer factory was spotless and orderly. Where Chelsea redefined the word sweltering, Spunkmeyer kept the place just warm enough for you to wonder why you were shivering. Where Chelsea felt like tetanus was around every

---

[4*] He wrote, deftly angling for a crate of free stuff.

corner, Spunkmeyer was an assault of light and stainless steel—a site where a cough was cause for reprimand and a sneeze grounds for execution.

The amount of preparation necessary to enter the workplace was staggering. You may be surprised to learn that the average person doesn't like hairs from strangers in their cookies. (Keebler, Oreo, Ahoy, et. al, 1979) Consequently, there was a room just off the factory floor where everyone was transmogrified into a lunch lady.

I cannot emphasize enough how dopey you feel in a hair net and booties. You could roll into the parking lot on a Harley wearing a jacket with spikes, and by the time you clock in, you will be a docile, droopy-shouldered geek. As I adjusted the elastic band across my forehead, it suddenly occurred to me how much of our everyday self-assurance depends on not looking like a dickhead. I held a small wake for my confidence as I pulled some weird little slippers over my boots. The only saving grace of the whole experience was that at least I didn't look any stupider than anyone el...

Suddenly, a supervisor appeared in front of me with what can only be described as the piece of cloth they put over your *(redacted)* when filming nude scenes. "For your beard," he said. He flipped it in the air for me to catch and immediately walked away to avoid protest.

"Fantastic." I sighed, reluctantly strapping on my very own chin diaper.

As everyone else packed the cookies into boxes, I was stationed at the end of the line to take said boxes off the conveyor belt and stack them onto pallets to be taken away to shipping—a process made 25 percent tougher because the booties on my feet weren't exactly what anyone would call "grippy." The whole thing was surreal and comical. I mean at Chelsea, the work was five times as brutal, but it definitely made your voice deeper. At this place, with everyone shuffling around wearing goofy little transparent hats in a room that was mental-ward white, my brain started to do odd things.

As the hours went by, I began to look around. The supervisor was a happy-go-lucky guy in a shirt, tie, and little blue vest. He was five-foot-five tops. The floor manager was an older woman with short gray hair who might have been four-foot-eleven. And *their* boss was pudgy guy with a well-trimmed white beard who was somehow shorter than the guy in the vest. As a collective, they were great—laughing and keeping our spirits up the whole time. They were uncommonly, some might say disturbingly, happy people. In fact, the bearded guy would sometimes randomly break into song over by the giant cylinders of dough and…

Wait, am I the tallest one in here? Noooo…way.

Now outside of a few days at one factory near Pittsburgh, I don't have a ton of cookie-manufacturing experience. Walk into a cookie factory in Kalamazoo or Texarkana and everyone might be grouchy and six-foot-six. Truthfully, if we were packing almonds, I could've had the exact same supervisors and not noticed squat. Really, the only other thing that would've triggered the connection is if we were making little wooden toys, so it's doubtful that *all* people who dedicate their lives to cookie production resemble elves. That can't really be a thing.

Can it?

One thing I can tell you for sure is that most everyone who sews flags for a living are old women who are "done with the bullshit." I found this out on my next assignment at a company called Perspectives that produced the nylon banners people would fly outside their homes to support the local high school or college team.

Was it the worst job I've ever had? No. Was it my worst job's annoying stepsister? Most definitely. I showed up to a noisy warehouse full of various contraptions feeding giant spools of fabric into other contraptions—which didn't seem mind-numbingly horrendous until I was led to a small, windowless room off the factory floor where sixteen cantankerous women sat hunched over sewing machines.

My supervisor gestured to the women, none of whom waved back when I put up my hand to say hello. "When they're done with their product, they will drop it into the cardboard box beside them. At that point, you go pick up the flags, bring them back to this table, fold them, and stack them for shipping."

"So I'm folding flags all day?" I said.

"Oh no," the supervisor said. "Again, you have to walk around and pick them out of the boxes, too. There's much more to it than just folding."

"I better be on my game, then."

At 8:00 a.m., the sewing machines began to hum as I stood there in the front of the room like a substitute teacher awkwardly trying to supervise a state-administered test. I had no chair to relax in, so when I didn't have flags to fold, I could only stand there doing calf raises with my hands in my pockets wishing I was anywhere else on the planet. All I could do to pass the time was pretend I was a sociologist brought in to observe the primeval hierarchies that develop in a room full of white women from the sticks of Westmoreland County. Honestly, it was like *Mean Girls*, but with menopausal smokers named Debbie and Carol.

Without knowing a thing about any of them, it was quite obvious where everyone's place in the pecking order was. The hardworking women with no time for gossip sat up front while the quiet younger women retreated to the back hoping not to be noticed. But the stars around which everything revolved were stationed across the aisle from each other in the third row—women whose overdyed hair suggested they were thirty-five and whose leather faces suggested they'd died a month ago. They were the type of women who'd ask, "Anyone care if I light up a quick cigarette?" in a way that implied hell would come to those who did. Even when they weren't puffing away, they made the air in the room much tougher to breathe. All day, it was conversations like…

"You know what I heard? I heard Shelly's not coming back," Debbie would say. "She's going to stay home with the baby."

"Well, it must be nice to have a husband that works for the highway department," Carol would answer. "How *she* scored a man like that…"

"Oh, I think we *know* how she scored a man like that."

"Tammy said the baby looks like it hatched from an egg."

"Is anyone really surprised? You ask me, I think she was drinking through most of it." Suddenly there'd be a loud snap in my direction. "Honey, there are three in my box. That's the last time there will be more than one. Is that understood?"

"Oh hush," Carol would say as I hustled over. "He's trying as hard as he can. Don't let her scare you, baby. You haven't said a word all morning."

"I'm just...quiet," I'd answer, trying to reveal nothing so if I missed a flag pull, they didn't know where I slept.

"Strong, silent type? Mmm-mmm-mmm-mmm, what I wouldn't give..."

It wasn't really harassment by 1990s standards. I mean, they mostly just treated me as if I was an extra sewing machine in the corner. I can't imagine how dreadful and distressing it would've been had things been reversed and I was a young woman in a room full of comparably shiver-inducing older men. I'm certain that I can't properly comprehend that kind of nightmare. Ladies, you have my unyielding sympathy.

I'm not certain how my brain survived the onslaught, but I made it to four o'clock and mercifully walked out the door into a world I wasn't certain was still there. About a half hour after I got home, Lisa called to inquire whether I aimed to go back the next day.

"How was it?" she asked.

"Uh," I stammered. "You know how every once in a while scientists might need test subjects for ethically questionable experiments?" I asked. "I'd rather do that."

She chuckled on the other end. "Gotcha. I'll see what else I can find. Don't worry about it. So far you're only the second person to return from lunch."

Quitting a job before I'd seen it through to the end was a foreign concept, and truthfully, I felt unreasonably guilty all night and into the next morning—right up until 8:00 a.m. when I wasn't listening to Debbie and Carol give detailed biological accounts of their hot flashes. That afternoon I happily cut the grass for my dad.

Anyway, the next Monday I got the assignment that I'd reluctantly drive to for the next two and a half months. IDL, Incorporated was housed in a big steel warehouse just off of Route 22 in Export, PA. I spent the summer on various assembly lines building and packaging stuff you see in department stores all the time but your brain doesn't consciously register. If at any point during the late 1990s you ever thought, *Boy, our kitchen would be perfect if not for the ugly handles on all the cabinets,* then headed out to Wal-Mart to remedy the situation, you might be familiar with my work. If so, you may be inclined to say, "Honey, come quick, the guy who wrote this book made the delightful 1 ¼ inch Williamsburg knobs that have delighted our guests for over two decades! What are the chances?"

Well, the chances are terrible. Sorry for toying with your emotions. They are, however, damn near 100 percent that I helped make the bin you rummaged through to find them.

I was one of sixteen people working the assembly line that cranked out those bins seven hours a day for three straight weeks. To my left, a very irritable, plump woman sat on an uncomfortable metal stool, stapling slotted plastic tracks to the precut wooden pieces that would eventually constitute the top and bottom of the bin. The pieces were then handed to two AC/DC fans named Jeff who were definitely kings of the Vo-Tech bus in the mid-eighties. The Jeffs worked as a team to nail the bins together, then put the open-faced box on the conveyor belt—which meant for me it was go time.

Behind me there was a giant pallet stacked with triangular pieces of brown fiberboard. It was my job to slide them into the plastic slots as the damn thing slowly traveled to the right. Each bin got eleven.

In life there are tasks that seem incredibly simple right up to the moment you try to accomplish them. Putting pants on a baby comes to mind. Ramming these dividers into the marked slots as the box traveled by required a level of concentration I was unprepared to carry out at 8:00 a.m. on a Monday. The first morning was an absolute disaster. There was a little red button that you could press to shut down the belt if something was going wrong. I probably hit it fifteen times before noon to avoid drifting into the next station as I chased an unfinished bin down the line.

The guy who designed the whole process was a bearded hick named Harry who was one of those shitheads who grinds your knuckles when you shake his hand—a quirk I discovered in the break room almost as soon as I arrived.

"I'm Harry, the floor manager," he said, sticking out his hand for a shake.

"Kevin," I said, extending my palm in response.

"Welcome to IDL." And he looked right into my eyes like a sociopath and made my metacarpals do the wave for a good ten seconds. Not going to lie, it hurt like hell. I definitely winced.

"What's the matter? Can't take a man's handshake?" Harry chuckled.

Knowing I couldn't outcrush him, I went to a place I knew he didn't want to venture. "I've never held hands with a *girl* this long, buddy."

The pressure released immediately. "Man's handshake. That's what...I wasn't holding your hand. I ain't some queer."

"If you say so."

I believe the above interaction is why he didn't immediately blow his top when I kept stopping the belt.

Harry walked around the pallets and put his hands on his hips. "What seems to be the problem?"

"I'm gonna get a good system here soon," I answered. "I think if I grab six and put those in, then turn around and grab the other five instead of trying to fumble with all eleven at once..."

"Whoa! What's with this six and five bullshit? Each bin needs eleven."

"Six plus five is eleven."

"Look, don't be doing your own dance. You pick up eleven dividers and put them in. I designed it so we wouldn't have down time. When the belt's down, that's what we call *down time*. Understand?"

He clearly hadn't processed a word I'd said. "You're the boss," I replied.

"Oh, I ain't the boss. Donald's the boss. I'm just the floor manager," he said, leaning on the stack of dividers. "Perfect day for bow hunting. Probably go out after work," he mentioned randomly—obviously trying to show me he wasn't one of those East End softies who'd never squelched through the mud of state game lands 153. I just gave him a thumbs-up and hit the button to restart the belt. He drummed on the pallet and awkwardly headed off.

The crazy thing about the experience was how quickly my brain adapted to the task. Monday morning, I was stopping the belt every few minutes. But by Tuesday afternoon I was able to put those things in with my eyes closed. By the third week I was slamming them in behind my back just to give myself a challenge.[5*]

The most critical thing I learned is that when performing the same menial task over and over, you must develop a completely different relationship with time than you have in the normal world. On an assembly line, the clock is a zombie grunting in your ear, and it will eat your brain the minute you turn to look at it. The more you imagine a happy-go-lucky future where you're walking out the door into the sunshine, the less material that future becomes. Being aware the parking lot exists ensures you will never get there. As anyone who's ever had a similar job can attest, it's why some eight-hour days take two hours and others take seventeen. I believe physicists call it the shitty job paradox.

Anyway, like most businesses, IDL was obsessed with getting maximum value out of their workers while putting minimum thought into how to best accomplish that goal. Periodically one of the machines would break. One time the bander let loose and started shooting strips of white plastic all over the warehouse floor like a ski-ball machine

---

[5 *] Doing some quick math, if we churned out one bin every ninety seconds, it meant that I was slotting in somewhere around 3,300 dividers a day. My hands are cramping just thinking about it.

spewing out a million tickets in some second grader's dream. This would cause Harry a giant headache as he raced over with his tools to try and diagnose the problem. Unfortunately, this also meant that the assembly line would be down for an unspecified amount of time, leaving us with nothing to reliably accomplish. Rather than giving everyone a well-deserved fifteen-minute break, however, the bosses would immediately mobilize and begin haranguing everyone into doing useless things during the down time.

"We don't pay you to stand around and gab! You got time to lean, you got time to clean!"

Five minutes later the warehouse would be overrun with people slowly and aimlessly walking around behind push brooms. Wall Street was caught completely off guard when IDL immediately shot into the Fortune 500.

One day when the belt fried, I was outside behind the building breaking down boxes and throwing them into the CARDBOARD ONLY dumpster with a baby-faced kid named Mikey and a trendy pot-head we all called Tappy. As we tossed the corrugated strips over the edge, I was struck with a thought. I climbed up the side and peered in. Unlike the other dumpster, which was full of old yogurt cups and jagged pieces of metal, this one was simply full of comfortable, some might say bed-like, pieces of cardboard.

"Ballpark figure, Tappy," I asked, "how long does it take Harry to fix the belt?"

He shrugged. "Half hour. Forty-five minutes?"

"You guys ever looked in here?"

They didn't have to ask why I brought it up. "So what's the plan?" Mikey asked.

"One guy's the sentinel. Other two nap. Rotate every fifteen minutes. Three bangs on the side of the dumpster when the belt's back up," I said.

Mikey won the rock, paper, scissors battle to see who joined me on first nap. As he climbed in, he suddenly stopped. "There's a warning sticker that says pretty clearly that we're not allowed to play in, on, or around the dumpster," he joked.

"It doesn't say anything about *relaxing* in a dumpster, Mikey. Our plans break no protocols."

Each of us got a glorious thirty minutes of sleep. From that day forward any time anything broke, the three of us immediately rushed to take out the cardboard.

Other than the aforementioned relationship with time, another big lesson I took from the IDL experience is that intelligence is not necessarily a requirement for leadership. In fact, as I'd discover in job after job—quite often the two are inversely proportional. At nineteen, however, I was still naïve enough to think that hard work and smarts were the main reasons people got promoted into positions of authority.

Such were my beliefs until I met Donald.

Donald was a guy in his forties who looked as if he came straight from the set of a low-budget porn film. He had greasy, curly hair, a big black mustache, wore polo shirts with lots of unnecessary flair, and had a perpetual look on his face that suggested he wasn't certain if the fart he let out came with a drink. And holy shit, it was astonishing the crap this guy got away with only to stroll back in the next day still in charge of things.

About two weeks in, something went wrong at the end of the line. I was gathering dividers when I heard Donald yell, "You stupid son of a bitch!" And then a random screwdriver hit the concrete floor a few feet away from me and went skidding off. As Donald stomped and ranted, I turned to the Jeffs.

"Did you guys just see a screwdriver go skipping by us?"

Wide eyed, Jeff answered, "Yeah. Donald just threw it at Marty."

Further background here: Marty was a dude in his fifties who mentally approached things much more slowly and more deliberately than those he worked around. And he wasn't the only one. Because of the repetitive nature of the work, IDL was a perfect job for people who most likely fell somewhere on the Autism spectrum. As I'd find out,

Donald's anger was almost always directed at these people—the ones he knew wouldn't fight back.

I started contemplating what would've happened if the screwdriver had accidentally hit me or, god forbid, he'd thrown it at me directly. I inherently knew what my reaction *should* be—immediately walk off the job, call Carol Harris, and then own IDL. But I'm pretty certain at nineteen, I'd have given the screwdriver back to Donald at the speed of one of my fastballs, which at that point were sitting in the low nineties. And we'd have all gotten to see an ambulance.

How Donald retained his job, I have no idea. The only thing I can fathom is that he had pictures of the owner desecrating gravesites. One time he got so mad at Harry for not driving the forklift fast enough that he pushed Harry out, hopped in, stomped on the gas, and zipped from one end of the warehouse to the other. Unfortunately, in his haste and foolishness, he left the forks up and blasted into every single hanging florescent light in the back of the warehouse, one after the other. They went swinging on their chains back and forth, crashing into each other like one of those perpetual-motion tchotchkes with the silver balls. The whole warehouse flinched as glass and plastic rained down from the ceiling. Of course, Donald obliviously drove off, only to come back five minutes later, see the debris all over the floor and yell…

"Who the *fuck* broke all the lights?"

The higher-ups who were too cowardly to fire Donald occasionally showed up to inspect the assembly lines. We called them the "Men in Slacks." And while they didn't have Donald's reckless temper, they weren't exactly the brightest rocks in the barrel, either. Our biggest assembly line of the summer was reserved for a few thousand Formica Flooring displays that I believe were going to all the Home Depots in the country. Up at the front, Tappy and one of the Jeffs glued two pieces of Formica together, then sent them down a sixty-foot belt through some heaters and people doing quality control. At the end of the line, my job was to scrape off the excess dried glue and then stack them in boxes to send to shipping.

From the start, it didn't go well. The boards weren't bonding fast enough and subsequently were falling apart on the line. I spent the better part of three days standing around waiting to scrape boards that never reached me. This necessitated an investigation by the Men in Slacks. After a full morning of pointing and rubbing their chins, they huddled in the corner to talk strategy. While they conversed, Tappy came down and grabbed me.

"Hey, man, can you help me find some wood? I gotta make a... thing."

We spent the next fifteen minutes scouring the warehouse for scrap, which we found by busting up some broken old pallets out back. Each of us hauled an armload of wood back to the line.

I dumped it all at his station. "So what do we have to make here?"

"They said the big problem is that I need both hands to press the pieces together, so I need to build a contraption to hold the bottle of glue. I don't know."

"Is this contraption going to be automatic somehow?" I asked.

"No."

"Then wouldn't you still need one hand to squeeze the glue?"

"Yeah."

"Can't you just set the bottle down while you and Jeff are pressing the pieces togeth—"

"Yeah."

"So what's the point of—"

"Dude, we get paid the same no matter what we're doing. Don't stress about it."

The fatty he'd smoked at breakfast couldn't have fried my mind as much as the stoner logic he'd just unleashed. There was something liberating about the sheer futility of the work we were about to embark upon. And it didn't matter.

It took Tappy and me forty-five minutes to nail this bullshit thing together. All the while, the Men in Slacks nodded. After almost two hours of the belt producing nothing, they were ready to try their new gadget—only to find that it actually added a bunch of time to the process because like a toddler trying to help cook dinner, it was really just in the way. After it failed, Tappy turned to the Men in Slacks and said, "So far the ones that made it to the end without breaking were in the vice longer. I was timing it. Sixty seconds and they're good to go."

"We need to be churning these out every forty-five seconds to fulfill the order."

I nodded. "Even quicker now that we just spent all this time with the belt down to build the glue holder."

"Exactly," said one of the Slacksmen. "We're open to ideas here."

Realizing that simple solutions weren't what they desired, I pointed at the ceiling. "What if we rented a crane, cut a hole in the roof, and dangled the glue bottle from a bungee cord?"

I'm not kidding, these dudes stared up at the ceiling for a good twenty seconds as if giving serious contemplation to the idea. "Cutting a hole in the roof is impractical, but dangling the glue bottle *from* the roof could work."

Long story short, in the end the Men in Slacks declared, "I know it's been a long and frustrating process, but we've figured out that the pieces need to be left in the vice for at least sixty seconds in order for the glue to dry properly."

I looked over at Tappy when they made their declaration. A couple of blinks were his only reaction.

Anyway, after eleven weeks of that nonsense, I headed back to Florida in late August—where I now had experience to draw on in my film classes based on an opportunity I'd also gotten that summer.

CHAPTER 5

Snacks

For Christmas in 1992, my family got an RCA camcorder. It was about six pounds, had a giant battery, and a compartment for a VHS tape. My parents thought it would be a nice gift for all of us so we could record the last remaining vestiges of a childhood my sister and I were quickly escaping from. What my father didn't anticipate, however, was that it would be used much less by him to record precious family moments and much more by his son to film oddball comedy skits with his weirdo buddy Chris.

Until that point, I'd never shown much of an interest in anything other than baseball. But once we got that camera, I found I really liked making stupid little movies. Being a lower-middle-class kid with absolutely no link to the film industry, however, it didn't seem like a particularly realistic life goal. My only connection was through a woman I'd met at my aunt Diane's wedding in South Carolina whose ex-boyfriend ran a production company in Pittsburgh. Luckily, my aunt is an electrical engineer who I'm pretty sure was almost solely responsible for getting Horry County's power grid back online after five different hurricanes. In other words, she gets shit done. She pounced on that nominal connection, and I got home from IDL one afternoon to find a note on the counter.

John Boyce Productions
(412) 123-1234
*Your aunt said they're expecting you to call

So I called—nervously. At that point, I knew I could stack boxes and lift bundles of aluminum siding, but working for a legitimate production company seemed like it might be a large jump in responsibility I wasn't prepared for. Outside of pressing power on our camcorder and occasionally adjusting the zoom, I didn't really know much about film. I was going to be in way over my head. And I was—just not for the reasons I imagined.

The voice on the other end of the phone was chipper but stressed. "John Boyce Productions, this is Billy."

"Hey, I, uh…was told to call. My aunt, uh…said you might need, uh…"

"So you're the guy?"

"Uh, maybe. I'm *a* guy. Not sure I'm *the* guy."

"Nope, you're the guy. We got a shoot coming up next week. And we need a guy. And you're the guy."

Billy gave me the address of their office downtown and a time to meet. The following Tuesday, I found myself desperately trying to find a parking spot next to a ten-story building on the corner of First and Market. I walked into a spacious, first-floor office that was somehow both conspicuously empty and insanely busy. There were only three people in the room, but they buzzed around like casually dressed bees as they juggled fourteen phone calls, flipped through binders, and chugged coffee at three in the afternoon.

When I awkwardly opened the door and started looking around, Billy buried his phone in his neck and asked, "Are you the guy?"

"I'm the guy."

Words can't express the love I have for the two characters I was about to meet. Billy was a scattershot dude who was shaped like a pear and always looked like he'd just rolled out of bed. His assistant Damian was a suave dude who popped anxiety medication like candy and had a fantastic head full of silver hair—though he was maybe thirty-one.

"Okay," Damian said, rushing over to hand me a binder. "Here's your call sheet. Make sure your contact info on the back page is correct. Over there in the corner is all the stuff. Billy wrote up a list of the things you need to get tonight." He stopped abruptly. "Nice to meet you. I'm Damian. Should've led with that." Just then, a fashionable young woman in a scarf entered the office. Damian pointed to her. "That's Lisa. She does wardrobe. Lisa, say hi to…" He didn't know my name yet.

"Kevin," I answered.

"The K-man," Damian said. "He's our new craft service guy."

I had no idea what craft service was. But apparently I was the guy for it. As it turned out, craft service is pretty much the worst job on any production—unless you really love going to the supermarket and then having to justify what you bought to a bunch of people you barely know. Then it's ideal. Essentially, my purpose was to supply the entire crew with snacks to keep them happy through all the inevitable down-time—then deal with the resulting trash. I was blissfully unaware of the actual job parameters as I loaded coffee filters, paper towels, packets of old Sweet Tarts, a case of Sprite, and a giant cooler into the bed of my dad's truck. Then before I left, Billy walked over and handed me a hundred fifty bucks in cash.

"This should cover it. We'll reimburse you if you go over. But try not to go over."

To that point, it was the largest wad of cash I'd ever held. In my hand was an entire week of toiling away at IDL. And they'd just handed it over to a nineteen-year-old they met ten minutes ago. I mean, if I just drove off and never came back, I could've scored a hundred fifty bucks, a nice cooler, and a bunch of candy. I gave passing thought to the idea until I remembered my parents' address and phone number were in the call binder.

So that night I hit the Giant Eagle in Monroeville and filled up a cart with Diet Coke, M&M's, cookies, mini bags of chips, one of those vegetable wheels where everything gets devoured but the cauliflower, a hundred bottles of water, and a load of Entenmann's bagels that had no doubt been lovingly dollied onto a delivery truck that morning by a gentleman named Fat Andy. All was well...until I woke up at 4:30 a.m. and promptly started the day with a major problem.

John Boyce had supplied me with three half-full cans of Folgers Classic Roast and a huge Thermos to transport it in. I was expected to provide the morning jolt to an entire crew of electricians, producers, actors, and executives, which made it one of the most important jobs on set. And as I stood there in my parents' kitchen before sunrise, I suddenly realized I'd never made a cup of coffee in my life.

My dad was not what you'd call "pleased" when I woke him up to ask for help. He gave reluctant assistance, but it was obvious he didn't know what he was doing, either, and was only awake because that's the crap you do for your kids.

I got two reactions on my coffee later that morning.

"Whooooa! Now *that's* coffee! *That's* the punch in the face you need at 7:00 a.m. Well done, sir. *Well* done!"

And...

"Oh my god, is this varnish stripper? Humans can't drink this. Find someone to make a Starbucks run immediately."

On subsequent shoots, they just had me go to Dunkin Donuts.

My first shoot was for United Healthcare at a medical clinic in Pittsburgh's Hill District. Going in that morning, I thought I'd be spending the day studying the crew, silently nodding to myself, and taking mental notes on how to utilize dollies and best position the lights. Instead, I was mainly trapped in the break room listening to the grips complain that the M&M's were gone and how I really should've bought more. It was somehow less glamorous than napping in a dumpster. And while everyone else got to go home when the shoot wrapped at five, I still had to go back to the supermarket to prepare for the next day. It wasn't even close to what I'd envisioned.

Truthfully, I might not have continued with John Boyce if not for two things. First of all, when I took the cooler back to the office on Friday, Billy handed me a check for $300, which at the time seemed like Hamptons money. The second factor was a simple handshake.

John Boyce was Billy's older brother and literally his complete opposite. He was fit, perfectly tanned, wore silk shirts, and drove a sporty BMW convertible that matched the color of his jet-black mobster hair. Everything about him screamed fake—right up until you talked to him.

He looked me in the eyes, conveying the type of sincerity you don't expect from rich guys. "Billy and Damian said you did a bang-up job for us," he said, shaking firmly without so much as entertaining the thought of grinding my knuckles. "Really appreciate it and I hope we'll see you again soon."

Any thought I had of ditching them immediately vanished. "Yeah, sure. Thank you for the opportunity."

Unfortunately, they'd quickly learn that my main quality as an employee was being young, strong, and stupid. It was never, "Hey, Kevin, you're going to college for this stuff. What do you think of this shot?" Nope, it was, "Hey, don't try to lift that heavy, awkward thing. That's what we have Kevin for."

"I thought he was here to make terrible coffee and not buy enough M&M's."

"He's a jack of all trades."

The more shoots I was called to, the more I found myself unloading the lighting trucks, setting up equipment, and moving furniture around. The more I helped, the more I was asked to do. Once when filming at a big house in a wealthy neighborhood, the director wasn't smitten with the unnecessarily large barrel cactus the homeowners had sitting beside the sliding doors.

"Can we get that cactus out of here?" he asked. "It looks out of place with the rest of the decor."

Damian snapped his fingers. "Kevin, cactus…"

After I picked it up, I was told to take it downstairs to the basement to get it fully out of the way. Which I did. Upon ascending the stairs again, however…

"The left side of the shot is too empty now. Where's that cactus?"

"Kevin, where's the cactus?"

"In the basement where you told me to—"

Thirty seconds later, I found myself bringing this sixty-pound blob of death spikes back up the stairs and setting it exactly where it was originally—only to have the director look through the camera for a few moments and decide, "Nah, I still don't like it. What else can we put there?"

So the cactus and I made a return trip down the stairs. End of story, right?

Nope! Fifteen minutes later, I'm in the garage filling up the cooler with ice when Damian bursts in, sweating through his shirt. "Where'd you put the cactus? We need it immediately."

"In the basement where you—"

"I'll deal with the ice. Go."

And once again, I lugged that monster up the stairs—only this time as I was stepping through the archway into the living room, one of the lighting guys was in such a hurry that he tried to squeeze past *a guy with a fucking cactus.* As he did, he accidentally hip-checked the pot. Like young lovers on a moonlight night, the plant and I were no longer two beings, but one.

"Set it down right there," the director grumbled, pointing to the exact same spot where it had been sitting when I arrived that morning.

I carefully went to my knees, desperately trying to ensure that the five-inch needle currently puncturing my chest didn't break off inside of me. I grunted as it exited my skin, set the cactus down, and walked myself straight to the bathroom. An hour later, Damian was the first and only person to notice or care about the large red dot on my shirt.

"Cactus accident?" he asked nonchalantly.

"Pretty sure some of my blood is in the shot."

He slapped me on the shoulder. "We all get our fifteen minutes of fame somehow."

Not every director was that indecisive. Some were just clueless. Once we were at a studio filming a commercial for the Children's Hospital of Pittsburgh. The guy directing the spot looked like he'd just flown in from surfing Half Moon Bay and had a personality to match. He was generally pretty cool. The only problem for everyone on set was that this guy had a nemesis. And that nemesis was Pennsylvania's most adorable three-year-old boy.

He was a little Korean kid whose smile outshined the lights. Wardrobe had dressed him in overalls and a striped shirt in order to accelerate the melting of hearts. For the commercial, half of the kid's job was to play with trucks against a white background, and the other half was to act out the old nursery rhyme that starts with "one two, buckle my shoe."

All morning while we were setting up, the kid was zipping around like excited little boys do, running and screeching and giggling. Unfortunately, he was also in everyone's way. Somewhat by default, I got assigned to keep him occupied on the other side of the studio while they got all the lights and cameras in place. For an hour, we zoomed toys around. In my head, all I could think was, *Holy hell, I'm getting paid to play Tonka Trucks. This is the best day of my life.* We were actually having so much fun that I didn't realize they were calling for him until one of the producers blared my name across the studio.

"Kevin! Let's go! We need Trevor on set!"

"Oh. Hold on. We have to get back from Mars. We built a space fort..." Nobody cared. I turned to the kid. "Hey, buddy, let's race back to the cameras!"

"Okay, little guy," the director said, leading him to his mark. "Remember, it's 'one, two, buckle my shoe. Three, four, shut the door. Five, six, pick up sticks. Seven, eight, lay them straight. Nine, ten, a big fat hen!' And we're going to give a big smile and get super-*duper* excited when we say big fat hen! Okay?"

"Yes," the kid said with supreme confidence.

They cracked the slate for take one. "And action…"

The kid gave a big, toothy grin. "One, two, buckle my shoe. Eight, nine, lay them straight. Seven, eight, A BIG FAT HEN!" And he threw his arms in the air with a smile so big it knocked the camera out of focus. The entire crew had to stifle laughter so as not to screw with the sound. It was the very definition of precious—for the first twelve takes.

Fifteen minutes later, the director was forcing a smile to mask his frustration. "Take thirteen. Action."

"One, two, buckle my sticks. Three, four, pick up sticks. Shut the door. A BIG FAT HEN!"

I mean, the kid was absolutely crushing the big fat hen part, but by take twenty-four, no one was laughing. The whole crew was slowly inching away from the set, looking at their watches. The snack table got raided as everyone tried to disassociate themselves from a disaster that seemed to have no end in sight.

I was restocking the snack bags when Damian came over, eyelids twitching. "How are we doing on water?"

"Good," I answered. "Hey, quick question—the director knows about editing, right? He understands the kid doesn't have to go through the whole thing at once. He can break it into smaller chunks."

"You'd assume," Damian answered.

"It seems like we've wasted fifty minutes on something that should've taken five."

"It seems that way because that's exactly what's happening."

It was a good ten more takes before Damian finally pulled the guy aside and said, "Just a suggestion, but a month ago, this kid was still pooping himself. Perhaps it's a bit much to ask him to remember twenty-six consecutive words."

The only thing that outshined the little boy's smile all day was the light bulb that appeared over the director's head. Though it was rough going for a while, the end product turned out just as delightful as everyone had hoped. The only real problem was that immediately upon airing, hundreds of grandmothers in the Tri-State area overdosed on cuteness and passed away with their hands over their hearts.

For three years, I was the first one on set in the morning and the last one to leave. A typical shoot had me busting my ass for the first two-and-a-half hours, pissing around for nine, and then busting my ass for the last two and a half. I loved the job and the people, but in the end, I was mainly learning about what kind of donuts to buy and how to illegally sneak trash into Taco Bell dumpsters. Francis Ford Coppola was not hearing my footsteps.

The main thing I did learn about film from John Boyce Productions is that there's a huge difference between the plan and actually getting the desired shot. Storyboards contain a lot of wishful thinking. For instance, we were at an apartment complex filming a follow-up to a weirdly popular commercial for Shop 'n Save's line of Pizza D'Italia products. The basic story is that an Italian exchange student named Antonio finds American life too complicated and pines for the old country. Then he discovers "a little slice of home" with Pizza D'Italia. The saga ends with him riding away on the back of a hot girl's motorcycle, thus providing the audience with a needed dose of reality.

Cut to the sequel where Antonio and the motorcycle girl are no longer an item. His heart aches for her as he's moving into his new apartment. After twenty-two seconds of commercial time mourning his lost love and gorging on pizza, Antonio hauls in one last box. As he does, he spies the girl who lives across the hall as she opens her door. They share a look. She smiles. Perhaps he's found something new. Pizza D'Italia now has capicola or something.

The actress in the commercial was an Italian girl with newswoman hair, somewhere around twenty-three, and stunningly, spill things on your pants when she walked into the room gorgeous. In fact, she was so pretty that I wasn't even a little bit nervous to talk to her. I had no chance, and I knew it. Consequently, since every other dude on set was a blathering idiot in her presence, we ended up chatting in the break room. It was there that she admitted she was apprehensive because she was primarily a model and hadn't done much acting. It was also where I learned she was pretty cool, which led to perhaps my biggest contribution to any shoot—ya know, other than the M&M's.

The final shot was the scene where she was supposed to give Antonio a coy smile, then duck inside her apartment. But the girl was so nervous to be on camera that the physical act of smiling suddenly became impossible.

The director would cut and say, "Kelly, everything was good, but we need a bigger smile. Like you're surprised a cute guy is suddenly living across the hall where grouchy old Mr. Jagatelli used to live. We want happy surprise. Happy surprise. Okay?"

She'd politely nod and then on the next take give the type of smile you'd give in a hostage video. After four or five tries, it was apparent that something drastic needed to be done. Without her returning a natural smile, Antonio would just seem creepy, which we were all pretty certain the people at Shop 'n Save didn't want to associate with their pizza.

Pizza D'Italia – Sketchy dudes eat it alone!

Fortunately, this being a commercial for frozen pizza, there were a bunch of cardboard boxes laying around. Damian was sitting at the dining room table massaging his temples when I asked to borrow his Sharpie. I tore apart a pizza box, wrote on it, then slid it across to him. All he had to do was nod. Desperate times called for desperate measures.

On the next shot, just after the director yelled action, Antonio glanced back at the actress, who was unlocking her door. Just as she turned to look at him, I held up the pizza box behind the camera. With an arrow pointing to Antonio, it read…

HE SMELLS LIKE PEPPERONI

She didn't smile so much as try not to crack up, but it worked.

"Hey, great!" the director said with surprise. "Exactly what we're looking for. I think we got it, but let's do a couple more to make sure."

I furiously scribbled on the other boxes.

"And…action."

YOU CAN DO BETTER

The director slid his headphones around his neck. "Wow! Great job, Kelly. We got some momentum now. Let's keep rolling. Fumble with your keys. Now put the key in the door. You look up. Notice Antonio…"

HE IS A SELFISH LOVER

I'm not sure which take ended up in the commercial, but she nailed it.

The other thing I learned about filming commercials is that while directors seem to be in charge of everything, in reality they aren't. The people who actually have the final say are a cabal of random executives from the company paying for the commercial. As far as I can gather, their main purpose is to justify the money they're spending by making everyone stay well past when they should've gone home.

"Kevin, we have an urgent run for you to make," Damian said to me once during a Hoover vacuums shoot. "I need you to hurry to the Kmart down the hill and pick up as many bouquets of dried flowers as you can for," he took out his wallet and started to count bills, "sixty… three dollars. Go."

"What do we need them for? In case there's multiple types and I have to decide which ones to buy."

"According to the executives, the dirt we put on the carpet doesn't look enough like dirt."

"How does dirt not look like dirt?"

"Don't try to make sense of it," Damian replied. "If I teach you one thing that you take with you through life, it's 'don't try to make sense of anything.'"

"What about coffee grounds? We have a lot of them around and…"

"Already tried. They said it looked too much like coffee grounds."

"By default then, won't these look too much like dried flowers?"

Damian threw his hands in the air. "What'd I *just* tell you about trying to make sense of anything?"

"So…buy the flowers that look the most like dirt?"

Damian sighed and ran back in the house. "Remember to keep the receipt."

When the commercial went national a month or so later, people from California to Maine saw the crushed flowers I'd bought being swept up into the Power Suck 9000 or whatever deluxe new unit Hoover was pedaling at the time. I'm certain those people also thought to themselves, *Now that's some real dirt being extracted from that carpet. I hope I never read a book that tells me otherwise. That'd be like Santa Claus all over again.*

One final thing I learned at John Boyce is that filming food is a near-impossible task. We did spots with dogs and baby chickens and butterflies, all of which were somehow easier to capture visually than spaghetti. For one of our Shop 'n Save commercials, they brought in chefs whose entire job was to cook food that *looked* spectacular. And it did. Being near it turned you into a Pavlovian dog—though, as I can attest when I was later offered some of the gorgeous lasagna they'd made, flavor was not a priority. Anyway, the special effects team pumped in steam to make it look like a whole meal just came out of the oven as the camera circled around a big oak table showcasing all these (supposedly) appetizing delicacies from the Shop 'n Save Italian Market.

They started to film the food scene at around five p.m. Three hours later, the executives were still saying things like, "It needs to look fresher. I'm not seeing enough freshness."

Of course they didn't give anyone a single piece of advice on how to make the food look "fresher" other than to say it didn't look fresh enough. They seemed to be shocked that the noodles weren't physically sparkling. I was sitting on the stairs doing absolutely nothing as the tension in the room next to me began to drift out into the rest of the house. The producers were asking the executives questions in very pleasant tones, but it was obvious that if given total immunity, they'd have slapped them.

I was staring at my shoes, praying to hear something along the lines of, "Okay, we got it," when Damian walked into the hallway miming choking someone. Suddenly, he perked up. "Clean up craft service. Snacks, waters, everything." He stopped. "Leave the pretzels."

So I spent a half hour taking everything out to the truck except this big, half-full jug of Utz pretzels, which Damian had me set on an end table right next to the executives—who started eating them out of boredom. Upon returning to the stairs, I realized the brilliance of Damian's plan.

"Any way we could get three waters?" I heard them ask from the other room.

Damian's answer was just the right combination of compassionate and rude. "Oh, we packed those up."

"Coke, Gatorade? Anything to drink?"

"All gone. Yeah, sorry. Packed in with all our gear." He shouted to me. "Right, Kev?"

"Gonna be impossible to dig out at this point!" I yelled from the hallway.

"You heard the man," Damian said. "Impossible to dig out at this point."

Oddly the food in the next shot looked fresh as the morning dew.

If I'm being honest, working with John Boyce Productions didn't really enhance my love of film or teach me a ton about the industry other than what crap I didn't want to do. Really, all I learned was that film sets are pretty fun places to work right up until something goes haywire. And something *always* goes haywire.

CHAPTER 6

Not a Cop

When I first got to Flagler College in St. Augustine, Florida, for my freshman year, all the guys on my dorm floor squeezed into the hallway for a welcome meeting. Sitting in a folding chair underneath the fire extinguisher was a redneck with a buzz cut and an earring who spent an hour going over all the behaviors that'd get you a one-way ticket back to the shitty hometown you were trying to escape from. His name was Sumner, and he was our resident advisor—or, in more basic terms, an upperclassman who gets free room and board in exchange for making sure the freshmen don't die or burn down the building. I'm not sure why, but I thought to myself, *Two years from now, that'll be me.*

When I returned for my junior year, I fulfilled my prophecy. Though I'd spent most of my freshman year on probation for kicking in a door, the administration decided it might be a good idea to round out the staff with someone who fully understood trouble—so I became an outlier on a crew that mainly consisted of ultra-Christian kids with their sights set on becoming preachers or prosecutors. Anyway, a large majority of the job was sitting behind a desk with a walkie talkie every third day and letting kids who'd forgotten their keys back into the dorms. Occasionally you got called to tell someone to turn down their music. And every hour you had to do rounds, which consisted of walking up and down the hallway desperately hoping no one was doing anything stupid enough to force your intervention.

I actually liked being an RA. I was good at it. Nobody knew just how many problems I'd quashed behind the scenes before they became explosions. I knew from being a rowdy kid myself that in order to have a decent floor, you had to set up an environment where the guys weren't actively looking to break the rules just to prove they weren't prisoners. Let them get away with small stuff and they typically don't want to try the big stuff.

At the end of the year, one of the kids on my floor laughed as he was moving out. "Cramer, I gotta admit something."

"About the rabbit?"

His jaw dropped. Pets were explicitly not allowed. "You knew about Mr. Flops?"

I chuckled. "Dude, you guys were so worried about getting caught with the bunny, I knew I didn't have to worry about your whole suite doing anything else."

"So we hid him in the bathroom when you came around for no reason?"

"Buddy, it was one fuckin' rabbit. You guys were running a dog-fighting ring, I'd have said something."

To be honest, a job I originally applied for simply to cut my loans in half showed me I was surprisingly decent at things like counseling and leadership. And I'd have absolutely done it again my senior year—if my senior year hadn't been postponed.

I got home that summer and once again phoned up Carol Harris Temps to let them know I was back in town.

"How about IDL again? They always need summertime help," Lisa asked.

I paused. I did *not* want to go back to IDL. But I also knew that if I declined, one of the other options was folding flags in an estrogen dungeon. So I accepted.

Except for the inept management team, almost no one I knew from the previous summer was still there. I'd forgotten exactly how bad it sucked until the hour between two and three o'clock lasted an entire moon cycle. I drove home full of existential dread wondering how the hell I was going to survive three-and-a-half months of mind-numbing drudgery.

Turned out I wouldn't have to worry about it for long.

On my second day, I was put at the final station of an assembly line where my job was to fit a heavy-duty cardboard lid on these huge boxes of Frigidaire parts, then use an air-pressured staple gun to seal the box for shipping. A guy in his fifties with a long biker beard was stationed across from me. We'd simultaneously staple the corners of the box shut, then carefully pick the two-hundred-pound container off the belt and set it down on a skid. Once five or six were stacked on top of each other, Harry would drop an empty pallet, take the full one away, and the process would start all over again.

It was about 3:54—six minutes from the glorious whistle that would send me out into the bright, sunny world again. The last box of the day was halfway down the belt as we stapled the one in front of us like we'd done a hundred times already that afternoon. We lifted the box. We shuffled to the right. But this time as we went to set it on the skid, Biker Beard somehow got tangled in his air hose. The synchronicity we'd developed to that point was suddenly and violently thrown out of whack.

I was preparing to slide it on top of four other boxes when it slammed into the right side of my groin, pinning my hip against the containers already stacked on the skid. For the briefest of moments, the weight of the refrigerator parts had nowhere to go—causing my hip to bend in a direction that evolution hadn't planned for. The back of the box thudded to the floor as I somehow managed to keep the front of it off the ground. Biker Beard shuffled over to help me push it on top of the others.

"Damned air hose," he said. "Gets me once a day."

It was the type of thing that happens in blue-collar jobs ten times a day. The nature of the work dictates that you get banged around, so unless there's a ton of blood, you just shake it off and keep going. I grunted my way through the final box, set my air hose down, and limped out to my truck without letting anyone know. I didn't think it was a big deal. Sure, it hurt, but I was young and athletic—whatever the hell happened would go away by the time I woke up in the morning.

It did not go away by the time I woke up in the morning.

In fact, when I got up on Wednesday, I took one step out of bed, felt a molten sledgehammer smash me in the pelvis, and immediately collapsed to the floor. There was a burning pain all the way up the inside of my leg. In subsequent doctor's appointments over the next month, I'd learn that I partially tore my groin and inguinal ligament, popped a hernia, and severely bruised my right testicle. It was what experts in the medical field call "a quadruple suck." I still deal with the remnants of it all these years later.

I can hear someone yelling, "Why didn't you hire a lawyer? That's a big payout!"

But that just felt like a lot of crap I didn't want to deal with, especially since I didn't let anyone know what happened before I left. So at twenty years old, I hobbled around all summer with a cane as I waited for my surgery, which was scheduled for the beginning of August. This obviously meant that the one real skill I possessed—lifting heavy, awkward shit—was no longer a bankable asset. I had to find something where I could essentially just sit around.

Enter Weaver Security, another company my mom circled in the want ads. About a month after I left IDL, I landed myself a knock-off police uniform and an assignment—the 8:00 a.m. to four p.m. weekend shift at Ranbar Chemical in the tiny town of Manor. When I arrived on my first day, I was greeted by the overnight guy, a self-professed "patriot" named Ed who had stickers of eagles all over his truck and was almost certainly affiliated with some sort of dopey militia who ran around the Westmoreland County woods shooting their AR-15s at dot-matrix printouts of Bill Clinton and Janet Reno.

As we stood outside the guard shack next to picturesque Brush Creek, he spit to the ground and shook his head mournfully. "I'll tell ya what, Kevin, I'm fifty-nine years old, and I've spent my life watching this country lose its industrial base. They'll move this place to China in six months. You watch. You just watch."

It was the very first thing he said to me after I introduced myself.

Ed handed me a ring of keys and an object that looked like a metal canteen infused with a small analog clock. I'm certain that now they use some high-tech GPS system to make sure the guards are doing their rounds, but this was 1998, so we had to haul around a goofy contraption. A large part of my job was to walk around the complex, locate thirteen different keys hanging from the walls, and twist them into a keyhole in the top of the canteen. This process would then imprint a dot on a roll of special paper, thus letting the supervisors know I'd gone everywhere I was required to go at the correct times.

In general, rounds took me about fifteen minutes every two hours, so a majority of the day I was just sitting in the booth watching the World Cup on a tiny black-and-white television. It was a beautiful setting. Deer, foxes, and groundhogs all walked down the hill to drink from the creek while big flocks of turkeys gobbled through the woods. A tree right outside the guard shack attracted cardinals and blue jays and orioles and other birds that also double as baseball mascots. With no one else there on the weekends, it was actually a pleasant place to spend the day. For seven of the eight hours, I was a bit like Thoreau—if Thoreau had been babysitting noxious chemicals.

The other hour, however, was a shiver-inducing walk full of creepy shadows and constant dread. The inside of the plant itself was straight out of a low-budget horror movie. There were six buildings full of peeling paint, cracked windows, and rusty scaffoldings. All around were giant tanks connected to pressure gauges and covered in warning labels that featured skulls and fire—often both.

Not only was I surrounded by deadly chemicals everywhere I walked, every step felt like I was about to be accosted by a vampire.

And that was during the day. I had to cover Ed's night shift a few times, and holy shit, you want jump right out of your pants? Startle a raccoon next to the Sulphur Dioxide tank in the pitch black of 4:00 a.m. Since then, I've been to some supposedly terrifying haunted houses around Halloween and...meh.

"Sorry, zombie, I know you're doing your best, but...you ain't that raccoon."

If hidden critters weren't bad enough, I'd occasionally get a call from the plant manager as I was relaxing at the desk.

"Hey, Kevin, it's Roger. Look, it's probably no big deal, but the FBI just sent a memo to all small chemical plants about terrorists trying to get their hands on some ammonium chlorate. I guess it's more likely they're going to target smaller facilities that might only have one security guard on the weekends—I guess, ya know...like *you* there. But, uh, don't worry about it. Just keep your eyes peeled and don't let anyone in the gate. Anyway...have a good night."

I hung up the phone, picturing myself heroically defending America from the Libyans with nothing but a television antenna and a whole lot of guts—all while knowing that I was much more likely to be the dim-witted guard in every heist movie that goes to check the criminal's credentials and ends up slumped over a railing. For two months, I mentally freaked out every time I saw a car turning around in the parking lot.

One Saturday morning, Roger swung by in person. He opened the door to the guard booth and took a step inside. "Hey, Kev, weird question but you haven't seen any super-tiny black-and-orange spiders on your rounds, have you?"

"Not that I can think of. Why?"

He looked around. "Well, uh, we just got this shipment in from Guatemala, and long story short, there's some little guys around here now that sent one of the day-shift fellas to the hospital. If you see one, don't try to smash it. They can jump." He stared up at the sky for a moment. "Anyway, I'd call 911 if one nips ya. Have a good day. Oh, let Ed know."

And he shut the door and walked off.

So not only was I surrounded by deadly chemicals, apparently we also had tropical doom spiders hopping around. Of course I went on rounds just after his warning to find two of the little bastards chilling on the door to the laboratory. Suddenly I was in a standoff with these dime-sized monsters trying to calculate their leaping radius and debating just how much I wanted to reach for the knob. After a good five minutes of hoping they'd scuttle away toward other endeavors, I decided it was a good day to find out how closely the bosses checked the paper inside the black canteen.

The answer: not that closely.

And while the terrorists never showed up and the spiders never got me, there was one incident that for a moment at least was even worse than an unexpected raccoon. The very last key I had to insert was in a giant room that was dubbed Zone 5. I got to it by walking down a ramp from the Zone 4 building next to a huge map of Pennsylvania that I always stopped to analyze because I'm obsessed with geography and couldn't live with myself if I didn't know all the counties that Sinnemahoning Creek passed through. It was the first place on rounds that didn't feel like all of my movements were being closely scrutinized by demons who were upset I was in their house. But one time in early September, I didn't stop to look at the map.

Because that time was very, very different.

In December of 1984, a methyl isocyanate leak at the Union Carbide plant in Bhopal, India, exposed over five hundred thousand locals to a toxic cloud that some estimates claim killed over eight thousand people. It's one of the single deadliest industrial accidents in world history and is often cited as what can happen when large companies blatantly put profits ahead of safety. While on a much smaller scale, these were the types of chemicals stored at the facility I crisscrossed every weekend. And while an unscheduled release of said chemicals wouldn't have resulted in the catastrophic human toll seen in a much more populous region of the world, it would not have been particularly healthy for the 3,200 residents of Manor, PA, either.

Inside Zone 5 were two huge tanks of hydrogen sulfide or dimethylamine or something worse. I can't remember exactly what was in them, but I do know that if they escaped from the tanks, one of the ways to find out was to ask the Grim Reaper when he tapped on your shoulder. Whatever was stored in there was deadly enough that an entire system was set up to monitor the air in that part of the facility. Every fifteen minutes, it would spit out a little printout like a drug store receipt full of numbers whose meaning I wasn't privy to.

Toward the end of my rounds that September morning, I unlocked the door to Zone 4 and immediately knew something was off. Over the random creaks and thumps of the plant came a sound from over in Zone 5 that instinctively made me hold my breath.

WAAAAMP WAAAAMP WAAAMP (pause) WAAAAMP WAAAMP WAAAMP!

It was like a giant robotic crow being systematically tortured. I pulled my undershirt up over my nose and hobbled away as fast as my recently repaired groin could carry me. And thank god I thought to pull up my T-shirt because that thin layer of cotton doubled as a high-quality respirator. As many a historian has lamented about the Bhopal Disaster, "If only more people had been wearing shirts from random ultimate frisbee tournaments, countless lives could've been saved."

I hustled toward the guard shack about three hundred yards from the shrieking alarm inside Zone 5. With my arms shaking and certain the gas was already in the process of bubbling through my bloodstream, all I could think of was getting on the horn to Roger to let him know to alert the police. If it was my last act on earth before I collapsed right there at the desk, well then by God I had to make sure I kept the people of Manor from being forever linked to the unfortunate residents of Bhopal.

I was so jittery I could barely open the desk drawer to find the business card on which Ed had written Roger's phone number. I peered out across the parking lot as I dialed, expecting to see a fine yellow mist slowly rolling toward me like a closing fist. It was an eternity between rings. What if he was out fishing? What if his kid had a soccer game? The fate of thousands of people might just rest on…

"Hello?"

I tried to get the words out as quickly as I could. "Roger, it's Kevin down at Ranbar. We have an emergency. The Zone 5 alarm is going nuts. Who do we need to alert first, the police or the fire depart—"

"Eh, don't worry about it. The system is probably out of paper."

My mind was racing so fast I barely registered what he'd said. "What?"

"The little box that spits out the air-quality readout? Ninety-nine percent chance it's out of paper. There's a box in the corner with other rolls. Open it up, put a new one in, and feed it through the slot. Once you do that, the system will reset itself and turn the siren off."

While the fact that I wasn't about to be poisoned by the air around me was indeed welcome news, I couldn't help but want to chuck the phone through the window and into the creek. "So let me get this straight," I said. "If the alarm goes off, it's either because everyone in Manor is going to die or—the reader is out of paper?"

He paused. "Well, I never thought of it that way, but yes."

"You know there could just be a blinky light that says, 'change paper,' right?"

"Well, yeah. I guess that'd be…I mean, I didn't design the system."

I let out a long breath. "Oh-kay."

"I guess if you weren't awake before, you're awake now." He laughed. "Well, all right. Sorry you got a little scare there. Have a good day, buddy."

And he hung up. I promptly walked back across the complex and changed out the paper. Sure enough, the siren ceased. In the newfound silence, I was pretty certain I discovered what happened at Three Mile Island.

"Yeah, we just assumed the system was out of paper and we'd get to it after our smoke break. Then out of nowhere—BOOM! If only we'd had some sort of warning."

Anyway, Ranbar was my main job for Weaver Security, but sometimes they needed me to cover shifts at different places when other guards called off sick. I ended up spending five nights at a factory out in Hunker (real town name) where they made mobile home caps. They'd recently had a bad storm that caused part of a wall to collapse, so I guess I was there to make sure nobody came through the unguarded tarp to steal valuable camper hoods.

One of the other places Weaver sent me was the bar at the Sheraton Four Points out in Greensburg. My job was to stand outside the door and check IDs at a place where the clientele was mainly people in their late forties who were sweating through their dress clothes. It wasn't the type of spot that underage kids were risking their fakes to enter. Consequently, all I really did most of the night was delight groups of retired women by asking for identification.

Oddly, one underage kid did keep slipping into the bar. The first time I worked at the Sheraton was six weeks before my twenty-first birthday, which I always found funny considering that for a little while at least, every time I stepped inside, I was actually breaking the main law I'd been hired to enforce.

Luckily there were no real incidents, especially since I was still recovering from surgery. The only thing that came close was when I was asked to assist the bartender in helping a tubby drunk dude off his barstool. The dude hadn't convinced any females to follow him to his room that night and, because of it, was now as smashed as a cheap guitar. As we guided him into the lobby, he was amicable. Pleasant even. Right up until I inquired if he needed a taxi. Why that question set him off, only the alcohol knows.

"You're not a real cop," he said, accentuating his statement by poking me in the chest. And if there's one thing I know about super-drunk guys, it's that they don't just poke once. They're in it for a few. Anticipating another, I calmly took a step back.

Just behind me was a lounge area with a television and a couple armchairs. Most people got to it by going down two small wooden stairs—but not this dude. Nope, this guy whiffed on his second poke, toppled forward, missed the first step, and became what I can only describe as a catapulted walrus. It would've been a trophy-winning belly flop if he'd hit water instead of carpet. The air in his lungs escaped with the same sound you'd hear from a squeaky toilet seat. I thought for sure that's where he'd remain until we called the coroner, but instead, he crawled over to the coffee table, used it to hoist himself up, and staggered away like a boxer searching for his corner. He entered a stairwell, and that's the last we saw of him. Rumor has it, he haunts the hotel to this day.

My surgery was in mid-August, after which I was bedridden for a week, minus excruciating trips to the bathroom. Since my rehab was going to take well into October, my parents and I decided it would be best to delay my senior year until January—which meant I was stuck at home while everyone I knew was off at school. Two weeks later when I could finally hobble around again, I went back to Ranbar. But that was only on weekends. I needed something to fill that weekday void—preferably something that would pay me for essentially doing nothing until I fully healed from the operation.

Every year I crashed Chris's family reunion where we'd eat ravioli, act stupid, and eat more ravioli. That year, I struck up a conversation with his uncle Nick by the beer coolers. Nick was a gregarious man with a bushy black mustache who played in an up-tempo Serbian jam band. He also owned a small production company in the tiny shopping center just down the road from my house.

Nick pulled a beer out of the ice and patted me on the shoulder. "When are you headed back to Florida?"

"Eh, I just had surgery on my leg, so I'm not going back until January."

He cracked open his beer. "Wait, you're going to be around for the next few months? Aren't you studying film and video down there?"

"Yeah."

"I got a project for you starting Monday if you want it."

Well, that was easy.

Up to that point, Nick's main source of revenue had come from filming and editing high school sporting events. His wife Donna, however, worked for Federated Investors, a nationally known financial firm with their own twenty-seven-story building downtown. On very short notice, the CEO needed someone to film a roundtable discussion about investment strategies heading into the new millennium. Donna recommended Nick, and before he knew it, he was hauling all his equipment into the city to film the least riveting discussion in modern history.

What he recorded that day was four old white guys in stuffy suits sitting in a bland room speaking in subdued tones about potential investor pitfalls as the world hurtled toward Y2K. Nick made it as interesting as he could by interspersing wide shots and closeups, utilizing graphics and underlaying music, but it was still about as interesting as waiting for a bus. Most of it sounded like this...

"Well, Eugene, you have to ask yourself, is it wise to pull some of your assets out of the markets and into, let's say, precious metals due to all this looming computer trouble?"

"That's a good question, Walter. It really depends on whether society collapses or not. If it doesn't, your investments should be fine where they are. But if it does, money itself might become worthless. So in summary, we won't know until after January 1, 2000. By then, we should have a better handle on what we should be telling investors now."

"Sage advice, Eugene. Frederick, what are your thoughts?"

"Well, it is hard to say, fellows. But as I told my daughter this morning at breakfast, I now know that Y2K isn't a rock and roll band."

To the other three guys, that was comedy gold. One even slapped his own knee.

Frederick's joke was by far the high point of the video. But apparently fiduciaries aren't exactly looking for blockbuster-level excitement, so when Federated reviewed the finished product, they said, "Fantastic! We need twenty-five hundred by October." Consequently Nick, as a one-man operation used to putting together volleyball highlights for thirty families, now had an overwhelming order he was in no way equipped to fill.

And that's where I came in. Nick had twenty-four VCRs in a giant block on the wall in his edit suite. My job was to put the original copy of the Y2K discussion in the main VCR and twenty-four blank tapes in the huge bank of machines along the wall. After that, I'd press play on the main VCR and hit record on all the others. Just under ninety minutes later, I'd hit stop, rewind the original, pull out all the newly recorded tapes, do a quick quality control check, slap on some stickers, shove them in a box, then start the process all over again.

After Nick went home for the day, I'd work from around seven until one or two in the morning depending on how bored I was. I kept hoping that just once the guys on the tape would dance or start a fistfight or something. But alas, they just sat there speculating about the markets using insider business terms. By the time we finished the order, however, I could essentially lip sync the entire eighty-eight-minute discussion. Had anyone stopped me on the street and asked my opinion on mitigating investment risk in relation to Y2K, I would've sounded incredibly well informed.

"See, you gotta check the five-year Lipper Averages coming out of previous market disruptions to get a realistic picture of what we're facing here," I'd have told the imaginary person in this fictitious scenario—having zero idea what I was actually saying.

Somehow through many consecutive late nights, we got the order done on time. In early October, those boxes of Federated tapes were the first things over twenty pounds I'd lifted since Biker Beard stole my summer. Nick and I put them in the back of my truck for two trips downtown. Within a year, Federated was flying Nick all over the country to film their shareholder meetings. In other words, someone else was now freezing their ass off to record November soccer games. And Nick now drives a much nicer car.

As for me, I worked both jobs until December when I'd have been home from college anyway. Then in January, I gloriously headed south again.

CHAPTER 7

Touristy

At Flagler, I played ultimate frisbee with a big redhead named Opie who was tolerable as long as you only got him in about seven-minute doses. In the end he's completely irrelevant to this story except for the fact that he was heading home to New Jersey for the summer and needed someone to hold his job for him until he got back. Most summer jobs in St. Augustine were about the same anyway—you either worked for some restaurant or some store that was trying to pry money away from Yankees on vacation—so when Opie asked if I'd fill in for him, I gave it zero thought before saying yes. All I knew was that I'd need money for food and rent.

This was my first foray into the hell they call retail.

Before I launch into the bizarre stories I encountered at this place, there's no way to introduce the store itself without addressing the fact that it was cringe-inducingly racist toward Native Americans. It was called Teepee Town (see, you just cringed), and while it wasn't quite as bad as you'd assume from a tourist trap store with that particular name, it was still pretty bad.

The owner was a lanky dude with a long, black ponytail whose demeanor suggested he was raised on the outskirts of a swamp. His name was Ted, and 90 percent of people who met him would've pegged him as the proprietor of a strip club that catered to lonely truckers out by the interstate. The other 10 percent would've assumed he owned a vaguely racist store downtown. I truly believe he thought the store was a tribute to Native American cultures. I don't think he spent a second contemplating how he might be exploiting their lives and symbols for his own personal profit. Most of what we sold was jewelry, T-shirts, and artwork. The store could've easily been called "Looking Southwest" and lost absolutely no foot traffic. Overall it was likely a sin born in a total lack of cultural awareness. At least I hope so. Dear god, I hope so.

Looking back as a full-fledged adult and not just a dumb white kid from the rust belt, I probably should've given greater credence to my misgivings about the place. I'm not going to pretend I didn't know it was harmful to the portrayal of Native Americans. I absolutely did. I just figured there wasn't much I could do about it, and if I quit, they'd just hire some other dope and nothing would change, anyway. Every morning Ted had me haul a statue of a chief in a headdress out to the sidewalk to promote the deals within. And every morning I thought to myself, *Is this okay? It doesn't feel like this is okay.* But I didn't have much money, and since I liked eating, I didn't have it in me to walk away from a guaranteed paycheck. As I've learned in the intervening years, if you ever have to convince yourself that something is fine—it's definitely not fine. Anyway, what was once Teepee Town is now the St. Augustine Pirate & Treasure Museum, so hopefully that means we've at least inched toward progress as a society, especially since I don't think exploiting pirates is a thing.

The store itself was prime real estate—right on the Avilla Menendez across from the Castillo de San Marcos National Monument in the old town area built by the Spanish in 1565. Ted owned the whole building, which was connected to a much larger Christmas store and a tiny room in the back called The Fun Shoppe, which was mostly filled with Beanie Babies. At a majority of my previous jobs, I'd get in my truck and drive to a place where I had a stunning view of...my truck.

For this job, I got on Opie's bike at 9:30 a.m., pedaled over a gorgeous drawbridge guarded by stone lions, and upon getting to the shop was presented with a panorama of palm trees, sailboats, and a massive four-hundred-year-old stone fort. We'd open the doors on days that weren't too oppressive, and if it wasn't busy, I'd just stand there and look at the glistening water across the street wondering what the hell I was doing in a place that spectacular.

At the time, St. Augustine was basically an undiscovered redneck Key West. Quirky would be much too tame a word to encapsulate its insanity. Once a guy in a goofy hat came into the store and started browsing the jewelry. The stunning nuttiness of a guy wearing a coon-skin cap with a long, curly tail was striking, even for St. Augustine. But then again, I knew nothing about fashion. To dress for work at Teepee Town, I rotated five dress shirts I'd had since high school with the exact same pair of khakis. I didn't think much about it...

...until the monkey turned around.

St. Augustine was a place that had a few truly eccentric people and a *ton* of folks who desperately wanted everyone to think they were. I always did my best to avoid the ones who were trying too hard. I mean, if you've got to put on a leotard and skateboard around town with a boa constrictor around your neck to seem interesting, you're probably not actually that interesting. But this monkey guy was right in front of me, so I really couldn't avoid it.

The guy squatted down to examine some bracelets. "Is this real topaz?"

"As far as I've been told, yes," I answered.

He pulled a chunk of salad from his pocket and handed it up to the monkey, who enthusiastically took it and began munching. "Is it okay if Pierre gets down?"

"Uh," I said, staring at the little guy, hoping he wasn't about to throw poop or bite off my fingers. "You'd know better than I would."

And suddenly there was a monkey on the display case. Which meant I had to continue talking to this guy about topaz as if there wasn't a fucking *monkey on the display case*. I could tell he desperately wanted me to ask about it, so I didn't. Not once. Although now he's mentioned in a book, so I guess mission accomplished, sir.

If you work retail, you realize that on the whole most people are pretty friendly and reasonable. But by the time you clock out, those folks have become a faceless amalgam of polite smiles. You don't remember those people. The people you remember years later are the idiots. And in places like St. Augustine, you get a special kind of idiot—the idiot on vacation. Psychologically speaking, I'm sure vacation mentality spawns from an unconscious feeling of superiority rooted in the absence of life's daily drudgery. It's why tourists unfold giant maps in doorways when there's an entire parking lot steps away. It's why people expect their lunch 45 percent quicker than they would at the diner back home. They have places to be, damn it! Relaxing is stressful!

My girlfriend April, a feisty Marissa Tomei lookalike from Long Island, worked at the opposite end of the alley taking lunch orders at J.J.'s Café. She'd swing by Teepee Town at least once a week so we could go to dinner after I got off work. Wherever we ended up, we'd sit there laughing and chatting amongst grumbly, hacked-off people in sandals and Hawaiian shirts. Damn near every time we went out, some exasperated server would stumble toward us with an empty tray. "I'll be right with you guys, I swear."

We'd smile. "We're in no hurry. We work in this town, too."

Ninety minutes later, we'd end up with free drinks after swapping wacky stories with the wait staff about the dumbassery we had to endure that day.

Stories such as…

An exasperated middle-aged woman once stumbled into Teepee Town with her sunglasses tangled in her windblown hair. "I've been walking around for an hour," she pleaded, leaning on the jewelry case. "How do I get back to my car?"

"I'm afraid I don't know, ma'am."

Her hands went to her head. "Don't you *live* here? How do you not know how to get around town? You people are the most unhelpful…"

"Ma'am, was I in the car with you when you parked?"

"No." She snorted. "Of course not."

Five. Four. Three. Two. One…

When it dawned on her, she was so embarrassed she turned and exited the store without another word. "If you know what street you parked on, I could…"

And she was gone.

Occasionally, I got rotated back into the rainbow of completely unrelated novelty toys known as The Fun Shoppe. Diecast Dale Earnhardt cars sat next to rubber snakes and bags of water balloons. In the corner were enough Beanie Babies to cover Manhattan in a layer ten deep. On one of the unfortunate afternoons that I was besieged by all that fun, a sixty-year-old woman came jiggling into the store.

"I was told you have Mary Moo Moos!" she exclaimed.

Now that sentence might be easy to read, but when you hear it out loud, it sounds like absolute nonsense. She might as well have said, "I heard you have Blarpity Blarp Smorgs!"

I racked my brain for a polite response. "I'm sorry, ma'am, I didn't quite catch that."

"Mary Moo Moos! Where are your Mary Moo Moos?" she said with the same sense of urgency as you would when asking for defibrillators.

Once again, those syllables just didn't make sense. "Is it something we're supposed to have?" I asked. "I'm not usually back in this section."

Exasperated, she threw her hands up and turned around, pulling her glasses from her fanny pack to inspect our shelves. Finally, she came to a bunch of porcelain figurines that were, I kid you not, cows in human clothes doing human stuff. There were cows tending to their tomato plants, cows snuggling on a porch swing, a cow optometrist having a cow patient read an eye chart that had one giant M followed by a bunch of little Os—ya know, goofy shit that your aunt finds hilarious. Each piece was identified by an incredibly clever cow pun like "Udderly

Yours" and "Moovin' Uptown." Why I didn't use my employee discount to clean out The Fun Shoppe myself, I have no idea. Life is full of regrets.

When the woman located the figurines in question, she became very irritated. "Right here! You have a whole shelf of them!"

"Oh," I said, about to melt her skull with my ignorance. "The *cows*. Yeah, we have a bunch of them."

"They aren't *cows*! They are *Mary Moo Moos*!"

I did not see that verbal tail whip coming. I put up my hand to apologize. "Okay, cool. Gotcha. I didn't know they had a name."

"Say it!" she ordered. Sanity had left the room. "Give them the respect they deserve. Say you have Mary Moo Moos!"

I chuckled. Her insistence now meant there was zero chance those words were passing my lips. "Uh...no."

She stomped her foot, rattling the items behind her. "Where is your manager?"

Hearing the commotion, my supervisor, Miss Adele, a woman whose grouchy face masked an incredibly kind heart, popped her head out of her office.

"I'm the manager," Miss Adele said to the lady. "Can I help you with something?"

"He won't call them Mary Moo Moos!"

"Yeah," I sighed in the driest voice I could muster. "I referred to the cows as...cows. And now here we are."

Every minute of the thirty years Miss Adele spent in retail went into suppressing the laugh she kept down. "Oh," she said with robotic pleasantry, "I can help you. Kevin was just about to go to lunch." From then on, if Miss Adele ever said, "Kevin, you're needed in The Fun Shoppe right away," I could be 95 percent certain I was about to ring up a cow shucking corn in a top hat while Miss Adele walked away cracking up.

In some ways, the crazy people you encounter actually make your day more interesting. They're pretty harmless and then become an inside joke. The combative jerks, however...

At least once a day, someone would complain about the prices long past when I'd made it clear I couldn't do anything about it. Most times I'd politely nod and mentally tune out, but one guy just kept at it. He was one of those dudes who picked up a cowboy hat six years ago when he went to Yellowstone and now wore it everywhere even though he was born and raised in suburban Connecticut.

"Three hundred twenty-five dollars for a black opal ring?" he huffed. "What kind of scam are you running here?"

"That's the price, man."

"This is larceny. Pure and simple. You should be behind bars."

"If you say so," I replied.

"I ought to haul you out from behind that counter and straight to the sheriff."

I drew the line at threats. "Look, cowboy, do you think this is *my* stuff? This is my summer job, dude. Either buy something or go away."

My outburst startled him. "All I'm saying is I could get this stuff in Mexico for a third of the price."

"Oh, well, in that case…" The guy hopefully raised his eyebrows as if his brilliant economics lesson had me rethinking my position and now everything in the store was ten bucks. "The street right outside is business US1. Take it straight north to Jacksonville and hop on I-10 west. When you reach Texas, turn left."

His bones now litter the Sonoran Desert.

Now while being rude about prices makes you a turd that nobody likes, if you really, *really* want store employees to begin actively plotting your murder, wander into a place at 5:58 when it closes at six and browse long past when they've shut the doors, brought the signs inside, and turned off the lights in the display cases. We once had a couple sneak in the store as we were closing, then ogle everything only to purchase a cheap pair of earrings that earned me no commission at around six forty-five. Facing down my cold glare at the register, it was as if they'd awoken from a dream. "Oh, were you guys closing?"

I answered with a swift, "That'll be eight dollars and forty-three cents."

Little tip, though—if you do make the employees of a small retail store stay an extra forty-five minutes in the place they've been cooped up since 10:00 a.m., you probably *shouldn't* ask for restaurant recommendations on the way out the door.

"Two blocks north of us is Orange Street," I said with a smile. "Take it back to Riberia. Turn left on Riberia and go the whole way to the end. It's like a mile, but trust me, you'll find a hidden gem that only the locals know about. That's the place to go."

"Oh, wow, thank you," they said, walking hand in hand out the door, having no idea I'd sent them across town to the wastewater treatment plant.

Dick move? Yes. As bad as hanging out in a store for forty-five minutes after it's obviously closed? Not even close.

That summer I worked at Teepee Town from April to mid-June and then again for a few weeks at the end of August before school started, which if you know anything about calendars means there was an eight-week blip where I was unaccounted for. Now you might think to yourself, *What the hell happened? Were you just wandering around the woods all of July?* And the short answer is…yes. Yes, I was.

Why the hell I made the decision I did, I question to this day. I was spending the summer in a house near the beach with three of my best friends. I was two blocks from my girlfriend's place. No cares. No responsibilities. No worries. Outside of Teepee Town, most of my time was either spent looking at the ocean, lifting weights, or having sex. Only an idiot would leave that for any reason whatsoever, and nobody, I mean nobody in their right mind would leave it to go supervise unruly fifth graders in the middle of nowhere. Would they?

One of my good friends on the ultimate frisbee team was a stocky Marine brat named Ben. In early June, he got a desperate call from our other teammate Ryan, who was working as a counselor at a sleepaway camp in West Virginia. Somehow before the session even started, a couple of the male counselors were thrown in debtors' prison or abducted by the Mothman or something. Whatever happened, they were scrambling to find replacements at the last minute. Ben got off the phone with Ryan and immediately called me. It seemed like an interesting opportunity, but I couldn't just quit Teepee Town, leave April behind, pay rent on a room I wasn't using…

"If we say yes, they'll let us coach ultimate frisbee all morning," Ben said.

Suddenly all I could see was the face of the damn Mary Moo Moo lady. Then I envisioned myself getting paid to toss a frisbee around in the fresh air of the Appalachian Mountains. Unfortunately, that was *all* I thought about before my mouth spit out the words, "Let's do it."

"We have to be up there in five days."

"Awesome," I replied.

And so out of nowhere, I blindingly followed my ultimate buddies to a place called Camp Timber Ridge. It sat on the Cacapon River in the eastern panhandle of West Virginia and primarily catered to rich kids from the suburbs of Washington, D.C. I'd never been to summer camp myself, but what I learned immediately was that most of them have one big thing in common—they are infinitely less impressive in real life than they look in the brochure.

Now obviously they're going to put their best foot forward. If there's a big photo inlay of kids beaming smiles and showing off the friendship bracelets they made, you'll tend to focus on that and not the cracked window in the background. Their promotional materials aren't going to be filled with pictures of dead mice, runny toilets, and sports equipment that just spent ten months in a dusty burlap sack in the corner of the storage shed. But as Ben and I rolled up the gravel road toward camp and looked out over the few acres of faded yellow cabins where we were about to spend the better part of our summer, I had the distinct feeling that I'd miscalculated.

What I'd find out was that Timber Ridge had two separate complexes under the same umbrella. Camp White Mountain was right along the river where the kids could swim and fish and canoe. Everything was freshly painted and pristine. The basketball court had orange rims and white nets, the cafeteria had stainless steel tables, and the lake was blue and clear. It was an idyllic setting, the type of summer camp adults romanticize in sunny memories every time they see a kayak or a box of markers. Unfortunately, Ryan, Ben, and I were assigned to Camp Timber Ridge, which was about a mile away and connected in hypothesis only.

Our side did have some subtle advantages, however. Our kids got extra exercise when they'd miss a shot and the basketball rolled away down the hill. They could connect with their family on a tactile level by touching gum their older siblings had stuck under the lunch table years ago. And on *our* lake, they learned valuable lessons like how to fend off water moccasins with an oar. The White Mountain kids just weren't getting that.

The administration would consistently assert that the two camps were basically equal, which was like claiming that chewing an apple with or without teeth takes roughly the same effort. Even so, I can't say the experience was a total bust. Camps survive on nostalgia. It's not like a regular job where the weeks and months blend together in a swirl of gray. Good or bad, you remember something about damn near every day. And that's how they get you.

The college kids I was working with were from all over the world, placed there by an international program that allowed them to explore the USA when the session was over. Consequently, I hung out every day with Australians, Brits, Spaniards, Czechs, Germans, and folks from truly exotic places like Mississippi. On our rare nights off, we'd go play pool at a hillbilly dive bar in Capon Bridge, then come back and hang out on our tailgates at the camp entrance doing the things that you might imagine a bunch of college kids would do at night in the middle of the woods. There were some supremely good times.

The problem with being a camp counselor, though, is that you're either having the time of your life or planning your escape. Your enthusiasm meter is either at ten or zero. There is no in between. And even when you're happy, you're dead tired. Unsure if a new acquaintance has ever been a camp counselor? Ask them their thoughts on bugles and see if they growl. Ours sounded at six forty-five every morning, which was maybe four hours after we finally got the little fuckers to sleep. Combined with the fact that you were never truly alone, it doesn't take long for your brain to begin crumpling in on itself. There's only one way to avoid going completely mad—getting assigned to a bunk like cabin five, which was full of super-chill kids who hung out on their beds listening to alt rock in sunglasses, went to bed on time, and had secret handshakes with all their favorite counselors.

Unfortunately, I was assigned to cabin six.

Cabin six was where the camp dumped all the problem kids who were either totally unruly or didn't like things such as "being active" or "going outside." One kid in particular turned bedtime into a nightly war of attrition. He was a human hornet named Mack who everyone lived in fear would somehow find a box of matches. Mack was the type of kid who'd do something super shitty right in front of you and then immediately claim he didn't. The other kids hated him but were too wimpy to do anything about it, so he just got worse as the summer went on. His favorite target was Alan, a wisp of a kid who was obsessed with the number 362 and would freak the hell out if life began spilling outside the rigid parameters that guided him at home. Alan's solution to the bullying was to constantly threaten to kill Mack with superpowers he clearly did not have.

But the real wild card was a chubby, unkempt kid named Charlie with perpetually messed-up hair, giant black glasses, and the scratchy voice of an old gym teacher. He was a Tasmanian devil of weirdness who at eleven years old couldn't eat ice cream without getting it all over himself like a toddler. He'd put tennis balls under his shirt and yell, "Who wants to touch my boobs?" His favorite pastime was hopping on my shoulders and riding around barking at all the other campers. Also, he was somehow like 60 percent more obsessed with butts and farts than a typical fifth grade boy, which is *really* saying something.

One afternoon after we came back from the pool, instead of simply changing back into his clothes like everyone else, Charlie decided to dance his way out onto the front porch buck naked—which would've been odd enough even if he didn't come streaking back into the cabin in tears. Bawling, he dove face first onto his bed.

"What's wrong, Charlie?" I asked, throwing a towel over his naked ass.

Mortified, he wept into his pillow, "The girls saw my wiener!"

I was not about to provide him the sympathy he was searching for. "Remember about thirty seconds ago when I yelled at you to put pants on?"

"Yeah."

"What'd you do instead?"

"I ran outside naked and started dancing," he sobbed.

"If you didn't want the girls to see your wiener, I assume you understand where you went wrong."

"The girls saw my *wiener*!" he wailed, rejecting all possible lessons from the experience.

To top it all off, his last name was essentially Penisman. (Altered slightly, but not far off.) Which, let's face it, explains a *ton* about this kid. Nobody's given that losing ticket at birth without ending up a little sketchy.[6*]

My cabin mate was a big blond dude from Colorado who we all called Master Mike. He dated Broncos cheerleaders and flew into Dulles on a private plane because his father was an international brain surgeon. I have no idea why he was spending his summer in a mosquito-infested cabin instead of being fed grapes by his concubines, but

---

[6*] Oh my god, I just looked him up, and I'm not kidding, Charlie Penisman went on to become a nationally renowned rectal surgeon. And I wouldn't put it past the kid to have suffered the rigors of medical school just so he could get behind his patients and say, "Ha, I'm looking in your *butt*!" Well done, Charlie. I stand and applaud.

for some reason he was right there with me going gray every night as we tried to get the little jags to sleep.

"Okay, guys, lights out," Mike would say. "Three, two, one..."

DARK.

"Ow! Mack, stop kicking my bed!"

"I didn't kick your bed. I didn't do anything! You're just a wuss who can't take it when I kick his bed!"

"You just admitted it!"

"I didn't do anything!"

"Mack," I'd yell. "Quit kicking Scotty's bed."

"Cramer, Mack threw a raisin at me!"

"Alan, it's pitch black. How do you know it was a raisin?"

"Because Mack threw 362 raisins at me already today! I'm getting *fed up*! I'm going to kill him with my laser vision!"

"You don't have laser vision, you dork!"

"Guys, *shut...up!*" Mike would shout.

"It wasn't a raisin, you dorkus! It was an M&M I stole from Scotty!"

"You stole my M&M's? Cramer, he stole my M&M's!"

"I didn't steal anything!"

"Guys, go to sleep! We'll deal with it in the morning!"

And for fifteen seconds or so, there'd be silence. Right up to the point where you entertained the notion of closing your eyes. And then...

"What if the moon was a giant butt and it spent all night farting on the Earth?"

"Charlie, c'mon, dude. What'd we say about theoretical fart scenarios after midnight?"

Cue the scuttling of feet on the floor as Mack hopped out of his bed and darted everywhere like a goblin. "I'm farting on all of you dorks!"

"Jesus Christ, Mack, get back in your bed. Quit farting on the other guys!"

"Cramer, Mack farted on me!"

"No, I didn't!"

It was a great lesson in just how shaky the dynamics of authority really are. Mike and I were much bigger than all of them. We had deep, scary voices. And none of it mattered because we had zero ability to dole out real consequences. The camp needed their parents' money too badly to send them home. And the kids knew it.

"So let me get this straight. You stole a camp van, drove it out to the interstate, and stabbed a hitchhiker? Well, it seems like someone just lost fifteen minutes of swim time."

It didn't help that it was the hottest summer in the mid-Atlantic in half a century. A week of one hundred–plus temperatures pushed the rural electrical grid to its limit, and somewhat inevitably, power to the camp went out for three days. Add insufferable heat to the extreme fatigue produced by even the normal days and the whole place became an emotional time bomb. By the end of July, my capacity for reason was tapped. After some minor dustups with the administration, I was hoping a tornado would blow through and turn the whole place into a pile of splinters. For the last three weeks, I absolutely despised that place. I missed April, I missed the beach, and I missed being able to take a shit without some dweeb pounding on the door.

On the final night of camp, I was literally counting down the minutes until I could leave—right up until they gathered everyone in the fieldhouse and showed a photo retrospective of the summer. All the kids cheered when a picture of me with a frisbee slid on screen. Suddenly Mack's crying and giving me a hug and saying, "This was the best summer ever, Cramer." My ultimate kids are asking me and Ben to sign their frisbees. Charlie Penisman's begging to hop on my shoulders so he can bark at the other campers one last time. I'd walked in there wanting nothing more than to burn the place down and left with my eyes watering.

Fuckin' nostalgia.

Now that I'm over two decades removed from the stress and the bullshit and the heat, I look back on the experience much more fondly than I did while I was in the middle of it. In the end, I was manipulated cheap labor who for two months fed a machine that capitalized on rich parents' desire to leave their kids behind while they toured Italy—but at least I wasn't getting yelled at for not giving proper respect to cow figurines. In the end, I'd still surmise that there were more bad moments than good—but the good ones were *really* good, and I'm truly glad I have those memories.

And though after doing the calculations, I realized I only made thirty-eight cents an hour, I did technically get *paid* to throw a frisbee around in the mountains, so there's a lesson there, and that lesson is when you're a camp counselor, don't do something as dumb as try to calculate your hourly wage.

CHAPTER 8

Books

S t. Augustine is so beautiful that it murders your ambition. Just stabs it right in the head. The amount of people I knew that passed up decent careers in Maryland or Ohio after graduation to wait tables at the Chili's off US1 was staggering. Essentially, they said to themselves, "If that extra $40,000 comes with my hometown in February, I'll pass." Luckily for me after I collected my degree in December of 1999, I had no plan at all, thus sparing me the strain of having options to weigh. All I knew was that I was captivated by living in paradise and had no desire to leave.

I assume my experience is close to that of most American college students in that in the excitement around graduating, no one thinks to properly warn you about the earthquake that's about to hit your life. Soon after the celebration is done, you realize, "Wait, I'm just supposed to...*support* myself now?" The pure abruptness of it is disorienting. I didn't even really know what I was qualified to do. Communication degrees are just vague enough to be absolutely paralyzing. I had a little bit of knowledge of public relations, print journalism, television, radio, and film, but nothing solid enough to be confident in. Because St. Augustine's major revenue source was tourism, a majority of the openings in town were for low-wage service jobs like the one I had at

Teepee Town. Unless you wanted to run a bed-and-breakfast or open up a surf shop, you were crap out of luck. Even with a diploma, your options were pretty much the same as what was available to you before you had it—only now you had to pay back the loan you took out on the education you didn't need.

I moved into a small house with three other new graduates as we tried to navigate our new normal together. With all of us crammed into a very small place, rent wasn't much, which luckily meant I didn't have to score a high-paying job to survive. I could just drift for a while and hope something decent popped up at some point...somehow.

Although truth be told, I wasn't super concerned about finding a long-term career. I was on the cusp of fame and fortune. Without a constant litany of needless school projects to complete, I'd finally have time to finish the novel I'd been working on that would soon introduce my brilliance to the world. I mean, I was a generational talent. As soon as anyone of importance read the words I slung together, they'd immediately get on the horn to every major agency in New York. "Nobody has ever captured the human experience like this kid from Pittsburgh," they'd say in astonished cross-country phone calls. It might take a year or maybe even two, but by the time I was in my mid-twenties, I'd be jetting around the country on my book tour politely smiling at overzealous fans, working with Fox Searchlight on screen adaptations, and drinking wine with famous people in Sonoma.

And what better way to keep my finger on the pulse of American literature than by working at a bookstore? It's why I applied to the Barnes & Noble off State Route 312 just before I graduated. Less than a week later, they called and asked when I could start. All was proceeding as the gods had commanded.

Take a few seconds to imagine what it would be like to work in a bookstore. Every day you're surrounded by millions of words and ideas. The newest breakthroughs in psychology, physics, and economics, the steamiest romances, the most heroic warriors, the most terrifying monsters, all within fifty steps of your present location. It's a dream for the mentally curious.

Now picture the bookstore customers. Do they look distinguished? Are they wearing tweed jackets with elbow patches? Do they have tiny glasses on a chain that they take out to examine small print? Are they the type of intellectual luminaries who begin stories with, "I was engrossed in one of Immanuel Kant's lesser-known works when I finally understood the lesson the old fisherman had tried to impart upon me when I was young"?

Or do they ask questions like...

"Hey, my friend told me about this book on investing. It's got dollar signs on the cover. Do you have that book?"

"Do you know the author?"

"The what?"

"The person who wrote the book."

"No, why would I know that?"

"I just need some information to help narrow it down. We have hundreds of books on investing."

"It's the one with dollar signs on the cover."

"There aren't many that *don't* have dollar signs on the cover. I can take you to the investment section and maybe we could—"

"I don't have time for that! It's a really popular book! You should have it!"

And while they didn't have time to personally look for the book they so desperately needed, they *would* have time to hijack an armful of magazines and pretend the store was their living room. By the end of the day, there'd be books scattered everywhere—books that the people themselves had to have *personally* pulled off the shelves, thus verifying that they made an active choice to leave it on the railing instead of putting it back where they knew it was supposed to go. Or even worse, they'd think to themselves, *Well, this book is about the Manson Family murders. I could take it back to the True Crime section where I got it—or since I'm standing in the travel section, I could just jam it between*

"Explore Newfoundland" and "Discover Nova Scotia." Yeah, that's prob-ably the best option for everyone involved. Soon thereafter, a customer would inevitably ask for *Lots of Stabbing: The Manson Murders Revis-ited,* and you would fruitlessly thumb through the True Crime section before replying, "I swear the system says we have one."

Being honest, though, other than the minor annoyances of dumb customers, it was a really nice place to work. The space was open and bright, I was always scheduled with interesting, fun people, and being around all those books kept my mind engaged. Some jobs feel heavy. On the periodic chart, they'd be iron or lead. This one was more like nitrogen. And every day provided at least one moment that I had to rush home and tell my roommates about. Here are some of the better ones. Watch out. The last one is a doozy.

To begin, I give you a conversation between myself and a young woman as I manned the information desk in the middle of the store one afternoon. This conversation is verbatim.

"Excuse me," she huffed. "I've been looking around for twenty minutes for the books on tape. How do you not have books on tape?"

"Actually, you're in luck." I smiled, pointing to a green sign about ten feet away that said AUDIOBOOKS in big white letters. "They're right behind you."

"Uh, those are *audio*books," she snapped with a weird emphasis on the first syllable.

"Isn't that what you're looking for?"

"Hello!" she shouted, knocking on the countertop. "Audio means *visual!*"

I was too dumbfounded to be nice. "No," I replied as if talking to a small dog. "Audio means *audio. Visual* means visual."

She rolled her eyes and gave me the kind of uppity, dismissive groan you'd expect from someone who'd gotten to adulthood without know-ing basic vocabulary. My guess is when she saw that the books on tape were indeed in the audiobooks section, her first reaction wasn't, "Wow,

I've been wrong all this time;" it was, "I can't believe these people mis-labeled the whole section." If I were to place a bet, I'd wager she's no longer with us and her final words were, "Guys, everyone knows that in case of fire you're supposed to use the elevator!"

Some people aren't actively trying to be annoying; they just aren't aware of the foibles of your particular job. If you've ever dealt with the public, you know one fundamental truth. There are one or two super obvious and totally unfunny jokes that customers think are hilarious and original without realizing you've heard them five times already that day from other wannabe comedians.[7] If you've ever run a bar-code scanner, you know the joke before I even mention it. You scan the code, and due to the angle or a smudge on the product, it doesn't read properly. Say it with me now....

"WELL, IT MUST BE FREE!"

And you desperately want to reply, "No, it isn't. In fact, I'm apply-ing a shitty joke tax so it's 10 percent more now." But you can't. So you grit your teeth and say, "Ha. Good one."

There was a dude I worked with named Alex who had long blond hair and a scrubby mustache who was the only guy in the store who looked less comfortable in a shirt and tie than I did. One day we got to wonder-ing how often we heard that joke—so we created our own data set.

Sometime during the day, the scanner would go BRRRRRRRP instead of BEEEEEEP, which would inevitably lead the paunchy, mid-dle-aged chucklehead across the counter to laugh, "Must be free!"

That in turn would prompt me to yell down register row to Alex. "Six!"

"Six?" the funny guy would say with a big smile. "What's that about?"

"Oh," I'd say cheerfully. "Alex and I are counting how many times people make the 'must be free' joke today. You were number six. Record is eleven."

---

[7] "Can I get you folks anything else?" "Yeah, how about a million dollars!" (For all the wait staff out there)

I'd watch the grin drain from chucklehead's lips as he awkwardly tried to save face. "Well...glad I could help."

Then from down the counter I'd hear Alex yell, "Seven!"

The statistics are staggering. Via our experiment, we found that on average, each of us heard that joke just under twice per shift (1.85, to be exact). Right now in the USA, there are 589 Barnes & Noble stores, which works out to that joke assaulting B&N eardrums at minimum 2,179 times each day nationwide. Add in every other bookstore, Target, Walmart, Home Depot, grocery chain, and mom & pop shop in the country and that single stupid phrase is most likely vomited into existence nearly a million times a day, quite possibly making it the single most overused attempt at humor on the planet.

Although as I'd find out, customers didn't even need to be directly in front of you to be hilariously inept. Sometimes the phone calls were the best. One in particular stands out.

"Barnes & Noble St. Augustine, this is Kevin. How can I help you?"[8]*

An older guy with a scratchy voice was on the other end. "Hey, this is Chet Oldman. I just faxed over that information you needed with my signature on it. Did you get it?"

(For any younger readers, a fax machine was a device whereby information on a piece of paper could be sent from one place to another. It would scan whatever was on the first sheet and then print out a duplicate copy on a second sheet of paper in the recipient's machine. It worked through the phone lines. Phone lines used to be...never mind.)

After putting him on hold, I walked back into the break room where the fax machine was located. Sure enough there was a piece of paper in the tray, indicating that a fax had come through. I picked it up thinking I'd be able to tell the guy, "Yup, we got it. I'll get it to one of the managers." Instead, what I found was a blank sheet of paper. It wasn't fully blank, though. If you looked closely, you could see the ghostly outline

---

[8] * I answered so many calls during a typical shift that when I got home, I'd often answer my own phone, "Barnes & Noble St. Augustine, this is...my house. Damn it."

of a perfect rectangle. I thought nothing of it, assuming someone had simply left a piece of paper in the tray, so I set it on the counter and walked back through the store to pick up the phone.

"Mr. Oldman?" I said. "Unfortunately, as of yet nothing's come through. I'll tell everyone to keep an eye out for—"

"Damn it! I'm at Kinko's! I got a confirmation that you got it!"

"Hold on," I said, confused. "Maybe my manager picked it up already."

Once again, I put him on hold and trekked back through the store, this time knocking on the door to the manager's offices. "Hey, were you waiting on a fax from Chet Oldman?"

"Yes," said my manager, a skinny guy named Jim. "Did it come through?"

"He said he got confirmation that we have it, but there's nothing there."

"I'll take care of it," Jim said, picking up his phone. "Line two?"

I nodded and headed back to the registers with no idea I'd inadvertently passed Jim a nightmarish Scooby-Doo mystery.

"Yes, we have it right here," Jim said ten minutes later after walking up front to confirm we had Mr. Oldman's book order. "We just need written authorization from someone in your organization." Jim held the phone away from his ear as the guy shouted at him. "I swear we didn't get the fax, sir. Look, you can just come into the store and… Oh, you're visiting your son in Illinois? Okay, well, when you get back, just…" And more holding the phone away from his ear, this time with a finger gun to his temple.

A half hour later, Jim strode up to the registers with a smirk on his face and slammed the paper with the faded rectangle on the counter in front of me.

"We got the fax!" he snorted. "It's been here all along."

"He sent us a blank sheet of paper?"

Jim popped his tongue on the roof of his mouth. "Mr. Oldman folded up the document, put it in an envelope, and ran *that* through the fax machine."

I laughed. "He thought the fax machine was a transporter beam?"

"He thought the fax machine was a transporter beam."

That paper was pinned up on the corkboard in the break room for months.

But by far the oddest interactions came from customers who expected us to give them free stuff in return for their "suffering." To set up this first story, I have to introduce one of the four managers at the store. She was a banging-hot Russian woman named Anya who was the human equivalent of a leopard about to pounce. She had a *presence*. Gossip around the store was that we were having an affair, and it's not hard to figure out where the rumor started. One Friday morning, both of the warehouse guys called in sick—which meant they needed one of the salespeople to head into the back and carry heavy shit around all day. One guess who they immediately asked.

I was tossing boxes of books around when Anya came back to check on me. "Cramer, you're going to hurt yourself," she said in her Russian femme fatale accent. "You work up front with all the wimps. Don't pretend to be a big man."

"Anya, most of my previous jobs were in warehouses," I replied. "I know in a dress shirt I look like a skinny doofus, but I'm actually pretty jacked."

Anya prowled up next to me, tapped her fingers to her lips, and stared into my eyes. "I don't believe you."

I grinned back at her. "I'm not going to take my shirt off for you, Anya. You're technically one of my bosses. That's wildly inappropriate for you to imply."

She gave my arm a playful, dismissive shove, then bounced away toward the store, twirling her lanyard. "I don't believe you!"

These types of interactions weren't that uncommon with Anya, so I didn't think much of it. I couldn't fathom a world where my smoking-hot, *married*, twenty-nine-year-old supervisor had even a whiff of interest in me. But two hours later as I sat in the break room eating lunch by myself, Anya entered. She stopped cold by the door and stared at me as if ready to level an ambush. The energy in the room spiked.

I was in the middle of a sandwich. "What?"

She turned and peeked out the door into the hallway, then gently shut it. "Cramer, I have to know if you're lying to me."

"Probably. I lie to you all the time. Lying about what?"

"Your big man muscles."

"Oh, ha. No, out of all the lies I tell you, that's not one of them."

She crept closer. "I don't believe you."

I slid my lunch bag away. Things were getting interesting. "Do you...want me to *prove* it? Is that what you're asking?"

"I can't ask you that," she answered. "I'm your boss."

The subtext there was impossible to miss, even for a blockhead like me. It was a moment of truth. Literally anyone could walk in the door at any moment. Undressing in front of my supervisor would be extremely unprofessional. Also, I had a girlfriend who I really loved. And Anya was married. This was a request I absolutely had to say no to.

Air conditioning is really cold when you don't have a shirt on.

Anya put her hand over her mouth and squealed. She bit her lip and started patting my chest. Things were rolling into adult movie territory. Not going to lie, this scenario had happened in my mind on multiple occasions before I drifted off to sleep. (Or, ya know, other times I won't mention.) But this was real life. Oh my god, this was actually going to...

Cue the door opening.

In walked a short army veteran with a buzz cut name Mitzi who we'd hired the week before. She came through the door to see me half naked and Anya's hands on my bare chest.

Anya's eyes opened wide. "Hey, Mitzi. Did you know Cramer is a muscle man?"

"I do now."

Anya bit her top teeth down on her bottom lip and gently pushed me away. "I can't deal with this." And she turned and walked straight out the door, leaving me shirtless in the break room with Mitzi, which wasn't awkward in the slightest. Not at all.

I glanced at Mitzi and picked my undershirt off the back of the chair. "So you might be wondering what that was about."

Mitzi put up her hand. "I don't need to know anyone else's business."

"She, uh...she didn't believe, um..." I tossed my shirt over my head and desperately tried to revisit normal. "What is that you got there, a Lean Cuisine?"

If Mitzi hadn't walked in, I still think there's a 98 percent chance it leads to the exact same gentle push and Anya hustling out the door. I'm pretty sure she meant to mess with me and got an unanticipated surprise. Also, it seemed as if her marriage might've been a little choppy. But that's my one and only steamy workplace romance story, which like most things in my life came super close to amazing before getting unceremoniously interrupted and leaving me scrambled and confused.

Anyway, you'd think that if there was a singular moment that might send Anya and I into the eternal fire when we die, that'd be it. But it isn't. Everyone knows that God's down with clumsy break room encounters. I believe Matthew discusses it at length. Nope, the moment that sent us to Satan's house began as I was shelving books one afternoon. Suddenly a woman with uncomfortably stringy hair marched around the corner holding a King James Bible. "How *dare* you!" she shouted, thunder and lightning clapping behind her.

I pointed at my chest. "Are you talking to *me*?"

I'm not kidding, she literally thumped on the bible. "This is truth! Absolute truth!"

"Okay."

Avenging angels circling her head, she shoved it toward me and roared, "Then *why* was it shelved under religious *fiction*? That is an insult to believers in the one true Christ!"

"Oh," I said as calmly as I could. "People shove stuff into the wrong section all the time. I'll put it back with the other bibles unless you're going to buy it."

She wasn't about to listen. Nope, in her mind, it could only have happened due to an intentional slight by godless bookstore staff. "You'll pay the price in Hell."

"I'm going to Hell because someone else put a book in the wrong place?" I replied. "Makes sense. You want me to put it back or not?"

Anya was on her way to the offices when she witnessed this lady accosting me. "Is something the matter?" she asked.

"Yes!" the woman yelled. "You people owe me an apology!"

I shrugged. "Someone put a bible in the religious fiction section."

Anya smiled at the woman. "Would you like us to reshelve it in the correct section?"

Noticing Anya's accent, the woman's rage immediately pivoted. "Where are you from?"

Anya hit her with a cold stare. "Crescent Beach."

"Originally."

"Ma'am, that's none of your business."

"You sound like a communist. I see now. Satan works through both of you!"

I squinted. "What'd I do? I'm from Pittsburgh. I went to Catholic school."

And the woman stomped off. A few seconds later, we heard the bible slam into the proper section, which is apparently cool with Jesus. He doesn't care how you treat his sacred text, just that it's in the correct spot in the capitalist wonderland he sacrificed his life to create.

But the story doesn't end there. About fifteen minutes later, I got rotated up to the registers. It was a slow Tuesday, so I was the only one up there when the bible lady came up to pay for whatever the hell she was buying.

I scanned everything. "That'll be $42.14."

Deadpan, she replied, "And with my discount?"

"You have a discount?"

"Nobody apologized for insulting my beliefs."

"Oh, right," I said. "So with your discount then, it'll be $42.14."

"I'd like to speak to a manager."

I let out a deep breath and picked up the phone. "Anya to the front please. Anya to the front."

When the woman saw Anya stride up and walk behind the registers, the combination of disdain and disbelief nearly liquefied her.

"How can I help?" Anya said with a big, fake smile.

"I need to speak to a *manager*," the woman sneered.

"I'm the manager," Anya replied. "What can I help with?"

The woman was flustered now. "He won't give me the discount I deserve for having my religious beliefs called fiction!"

"Ma'am, nobody called your religious beliefs fiction," Anya said. "A customer put a bible in the wrong place. We offered to resolve it, and you said we were going to Hell."

"I still haven't gotten an apology!"

Anya took one step toward the counter and folded her hands. Like the coldest Siberian labor camp guard you can imagine, she said, "Will there be anything else?"

The woman stepped back and shifted her gaze to me as I rung her up. (Yes, she still paid for her books.) "You tell your manager she is the rudest communist pig I have ever met."

I chuckled. "Anya, this woman says you're smart, beautiful, and excellent at your job."

As I handed her books over the counter, the woman scowled. "You're both going to Hell!"

To which Anya, in one of history's great comebacks growled demonically, "Good! That's where I'm from...*originally*."

And you'd think that would be the best story of someone trying to randomly get free shit. But it isn't. And it's not even close.

It was a Saturday night, and the store was crowded. I was at the registers with one of the managers, a woman in her forties named Cathy. If you want to picture Cathy, just imagine your favorite aunt—the one who seems pretty bland until you're fifteen and she has a little too much wine and tells you about the year she spent smuggling peyote over the border for an outlaw biker gang. Everything was normal until a woman skipped the line and planted herself in front of the counter. And suddenly, very loudly, in an odd, I'm assuming South American accent, she squealed…

"Well, aren't you gonna *dooooooo* something?"

I was engaged with another customer, and Cathy was looking through some book orders behind the register. We both turned to see a chubby Venezuelan woman with damp hair wearing an ill-fitting black top and black sweatpants. An older woman that may well have been her mother stood silently behind her.

Very, very nicely, Cathy took a step forward. "Doing something about what exactly? We're going to need a bit more information."

The woman threw her hands in the air. With an odd shriek, she yelled, "About the *guy!*"

By now I was really struggling to pay attention to the customer in front of me as Cathy squinted and asked, "What guy?"

I have never been knocked sideways so wholly and completely by a statement in my life as I was by what the woman said next. Serious as a stroke, she howled, "About the guy running around putting butter on everyone's pants!"

Cathy's face turned into a wax statue on a hot day. "Come again now?"

"There's a *guy* running around smearing *butter* on *pants!*"

It was like an unexpected bass drop from a DJ in the sky. Reality began to warp. People's faces were distorted. Fish were swimming through the air. What the *hell* did she just say?

I thought to myself, *Okay, maybe there was a mishap and one customer accidentally dropped a buttered muffin on another. We do have a café, after all.* Not really our problem, but a feasible scenario. But when this woman backed up and pointed down at her sweatpants, I kid you not, they were covered hip to knee in *gobs* of butter, a few that were damn near racquetball sized. There was more butter on her pants than would go into most shortbread recipes. It would be weird to see that much butter on someone in a bakery. But we were in a *bookstore.*

The world in front of me was a funhouse mirror. WHAT. THE. FUCK?

Cathy couldn't handle it. As soon as the woman backed up, Cathy collapsed to the floor in the type of giggling fit you only see when toddlers are being tickled. Desperately trying to breathe, she looked up at me. "Kevin, you have to…I can't…my god, I'm crying. I'm crying!"

I shifted over. "Ma'am, were you in the café when this happened?" I asked.

"No!" she exclaimed. "I was reading a book in one of the chairs!"

"Is the guy still in the store?" I asked. "What did he look like?"

"I don't know!" she yelled back. "He's a guy!"

"What color shirt did he have on? Shoes? Hair color? Anything that can help."

"Well, I didn't *see* him!"

Below me on the floor, Cathy was now convulsing. Stone faced, I shuffled over toward the Venezuelan woman. "So let me get this straight. A guy walked up to you and smeared—what is that—two pounds of butter on your pants and you didn't see him do it or notice anything about him?"

"He was *sneaky!*" she shrieked.

I was about to make Cathy's heart stop. "Wow, that is one devious butter bandit."

And this is where it gets even more confusing. The next thing the woman said was, "I think I should get something, don't you?"

"You want to be compensated for your ruined sweatpants?"

"At least fifty dollars. These were good pants!"

I just stared at her. She was dead serious. "Let me talk to my manager."

"Oh, hell no," Cathy said through her tears, now laying in a snow angel position. "There is no way we're paying for her sweatpants."

I nodded. "Apparently, that's against store policy. But if you tell us something about the guy, we can try to make sure it doesn't happen again."

As soon as I nixed her request, the woman and her mother turned and silently walked out of the store. I watched them until they hit the parking lot, then held up my finger to the customer in front of me. "Excuse me."

I collapsed to the floor next to Cathy, who grabbed my wrist so hard it left a temporary mark.

"Do you need some oxygen?" I asked her.

"He was *sneaky!*" she cried.

I laughed. "I don't know if I'm ever going to recover from this."

I've since gone over the situation in my mind hundreds of times like a detective with a corkboard full of photographs. There are only two possibilities here. First, a dude really was running around the store buttering pants, chose that oblivious lady as his first and *only* victim, then ran out of the store before we caught him yellow handed, or that insane butterpants thing was her scam. Which, if true, I can't imagine the plans she rejected. A Druid stole her shoes? A priest burped in her ear? Nope, a ninja put butter on her pants. That won. You've got to admire the sheer audacity of it. Looking back, I sort of wish we'd have just given her ten bucks. She definitely earned it.

Barnes & Noble wasn't the last time I'd have to deal with customers, but it was the final time I'd work in a retail setting. It was a good job. I liked the people. But when you got home, it's not as if you felt like you'd accomplished anything. You put books away, ran credit cards, and occasionally put up holiday displays. I needed something a little different. I just didn't know what yet.

CHAPTER 9

Clearcut

In May of 2000, April and I had a dumb fight about something I don't even remember, thus proving exactly how inconsequential the genesis of the argument was. We were too young, too in love, and too volatile to just take a breath—so we broke up. I couldn't fathom tottering around the same town, awkwardly running into her once a week, so in mid-June I said goodbye to everyone at Barnes & Noble, packed up my things, and headed back to Pittsburgh.

After spending six months as a very small cog in a giant corporate machine, I really wanted something different, something where even if I wasn't making a ton of money, I was at least making a difference. Which is why when I saw a classified for positions with the Sierra Club, I nearly sprained my ankle leaping toward the phone. I probably wasn't the tree-hugging hacky-sacker they were used to, but I liked forests. Forests were where you could fish and sit in the shade and throw rocks and not have anyone ask if you were busy. Forests were awesome. And I was going to protect them. Somehow.

I'm not certain what I thought the job was going to be. I guess I imagined heading up into the mountains to rescue birds and stand in front of bulldozers and shit. It was amazing in my mind—as most jobs are before I actually start them.

The job was actually for PENN PIRG (The Pennsylvania Public Interest Research Group), a nonprofit that was subcontracted by larger nonprofits to carry out national objectives at a local level. They invited me to come down to a four-story brick building just off the campus of the University of Pittsburgh to check out the operation. I sat in traffic on the Parkway East for forty-five minutes trying to get there, then shelled out fifteen bucks to park in a dirty, concrete hell that was the exact opposite of the forests I hoped to protect. But I made it up to the third floor to find a lively space full of ambitious twenty-somethings like me. I'm sure everyone wasn't actually wearing a tie-dyed shirt and hemp necklace, but that's what my memory produces.

"Welcome," said Mookie, the twenty-six-year-old director who I'm positive *was* actually wearing a tie-dyed shirt and hemp necklace.

I looked around. "I'm Kevin. You guys told me to come down and check the place out."

"Right on. Glad to have you."

There was a chaotic energy in the space—young people on the phones spoke enthusiastically about clean water propositions while others folded pamphlets and tossed around mini frisbees. It was like someone put a senatorial campaign office inside a lava lamp. I felt at home right away. The whole thing was incredible except for one thing...

My entire job was to ask strangers for money. And I despise asking strangers for money. Hell, I hated asking them for cash in exchange for the dreamcatchers at Teepee Town (which I knew for a fact did *not* catch dreams). I realized immediately the experiment that was about to happen. Could the atmosphere and the people provide enough good vibes to counteract the fact that my employment depended on doing the one thing I hated doing the most? Was I such a terrible salesman that I couldn't even sell something I was passionate about? I was about to find out.

The Sierra Club's campaign at the time was fighting clear cutting in national forests, a practice whereby logging companies wiped large chunks of habitat bare, thus scarring the landscape and negatively affecting local watersheds. We'd spend the morning rehearsing our pitches, a thirty-second assault of facts about how clear cutting a forest in Alaska affects your pocketbook in Allegheny County. We discussed rising carbon levels and tipping points and endangered owls and native fish populations and, "Could you spare five, ten, twenty bucks to help the cause?" Then we'd pile into old minivans that hadn't seen an oil change in the equivalent of two trips around the planet and head off to some quaint suburban neighborhood to be dropped off for the afternoon.

On my first day, I was assigned to shadow a girl named Mari, an unassumingly fierce and intensely cute twenty-one-year-old who could knock on a door and smile twenty bucks from the wallet of a gruff, retired cop. She made it look so simple. I fell head over heels in love with her in about five minutes, which was only amplified when a huge thunderstorm popped up and, with no shelter, we had to huddle together in a downpour underneath her tiny red umbrella like we were acting out the final scene of a cheesy romantic comedy. Laughing and drenched, we circled the neighborhood and brought in over $300, which the entire office voraciously applauded upon our return. In the van on the way back, "American Pie" came on the radio. We all sang at the top of our lungs as the city rolled by, and holy hell, I'd found a home. I loved it.

Right up until the next day when I had to do the whole thing myself.

Certain things are much more difficult when you're not a cute girl. Getting people to fork over money is one of them. I'm pretty sure Mari could've been working for an organization that flung pandas into space and people would be like, "Sure, here's fifteen bucks. Fuck pandas." I could've been collecting money for their nephew's liver transplant and they'd be like, "Please leave."

After knocking on a hundred doors a day, the job started to wear on me. You begin to realize that nothing you say truly has any bearing on the endgame. Before you ever stepped on their porch, the people who lived there either had the resources to give you some extra money or they didn't. They were either an environmentalist or they weren't. In the end, you were just an extension of the fanny pack you kept the cash in.

Incredibly, I didn't have any bad experiences. Nobody pulled out a shotgun or screamed at me. No cursing, no voices raised—just a lot of indifference. When you're wandering alone around a neighborhood you're unfamiliar with, you have a lot of time to think about the futility of what you're doing. Each house begins to feel less and less like an opportunity to make a difference and more and more like confirmation that the human species is on its way to the exits. It's quite discouraging. Especially if, say, you're a twenty-two-year-old who's now living back with his parents and even the sunny days are cloudy.

In the end, though, what ended my tree-hugging career was my first paycheck. Weirdly, organizations dedicated to saving the planet rely a lot more on youthful idealism than compensation to retain their employees. I spent half of what I made each day just for the privilege of parking my truck in the city. As much as I wanted to be a champion of the environment, I first needed to be a champion of paying back my student loans. So they thanked me for the couple hundred bucks I'd managed to ferry in from the suburbs during my few weeks of canvassing, and I drove home jobless once again.

In many ways, the next job I picked up was the inspiration for this book—a job I'd keep going back to like a familiar ex who you swore you could make it work with *this* time despite all of the trauma of the past. It was grueling, boring, exciting, and disillusioning all wrapped in one atrocious package. And once I was in, it took me over a decade to truly escape.

My dad's buddy casually mentioned that his son was working as a car prep for Emerald Rental Car, driving customers home and cleaning vehicles once they were returned. It was a job I didn't realize existed and didn't seem too bad considering it seemed like you might spend a good portion of the day cruising around listening to the radio. And since my dad was about to make me start cutting the grass every two hours just to make sure I wasn't being a bum, I needed something immediately. So I applied.

Getting the job was a rigorous process. I walked in, they asked me my name, looked at my application, noticed I hadn't checked the box about felonies, and said, "We need a guy out in Irwin. The job is yours if you want it."

Emerald's Irwin Branch occupied the first floor of an office building on Route 30 and sat within a mile of four large car dealerships. Connected to the back of the office was a garage where I spent a lot of time vacuuming crumbs off floor mats, checking oil levels, topping off washer fluid, and scraping bugs off windshields. With me most days was the other car prep, a small Italian guy named Vic. To picture Vic, all you have to do is imagine that Mario from the Nintendo games got old. Vic wasn't real chatty, but he was pretty efficient for a guy in his sixties who apparently needed six bucks an hour to supplement his railroad pension.

"So what do I need to know?" I asked him on my first day.

"You know how to worsh a car?" he replied.

"Yup."

"Well, that's what we do," he answered, scuttling off to find some rags, which I believe he located by jumping up and punching through a square of floating bricks above him.

Before I started at Emerald, I, like most people, assumed that all rental car places had a giant fleet of cars just sitting idly in some lot waiting to be driven—even when the place clearly only had fifteen spaces available in front of the branch. Admit it, when you show up to rent a car and there's only three vehicles in the lot, your first reaction isn't, "I bet they only have three cars right now." It's, "Oh, there must be an asphalt sea of Toyota Camrys just around the corner here." The thought of how massively unprofitable that would be never registers. For the managers, the whole thing is a hellish juggling act of locating and getting rid of cars based on each day's demand. For the car preps, it often meant being jerked in seventeen directions at once.

There were hang tags for each car, which provided a checklist meant to reassure customers that we'd diligently inspected every aspect of the vehicle before it was given to them. In addition to washing and vacuuming, car preps were supposed to clean the interior windows, wipe down the dashboard, clean and sanitize the instruments, thoroughly wipe the cup holders, shine the tires, check the tire pressure, inspect the belts and hoses, and hand dry the whole thing to prevent water spots. This whole process would be fine if the demand for rental cars happened at evenly spaced intervals throughout the day.

It did not.

When you clean rental cars, 80 percent of your work happens Monday morning and Friday afternoon as people prepare for and return from business trips or start/end their insurance claims. Monday morning cars were "good enough" if they were given a quick, haphazard squirt off and weren't filled with potato chips and dog hair. Mondays I'd wash sixty cars and drive a hundred miles around the city in an eleven-hour blitz of go-go-go chaos that left me stumbling to the couch when I got home. By Tuesday afternoon, Vic and I were playing cards in the garage.

But by far the oddest part of the whole experience was picking people up or driving them home. No matter how many rides you give, being alone in a car with a stranger never gets to the point where you think, *Well, this is pleasant.* Sometimes you'd luck out and they just returned from a relaxing trip to Niagara Falls. But mostly it was a lot of grumbly folks whose alternator blew on the way to work that morning.

In the end, though, customers only fell into two categories that mattered:

1. Considerate folks who'd be mortally embarrassed to fart in the car with you, and

2. Explanation unnecessary.

Check that. There was a third category: people that were so strange you'd have actually preferred to be fartboxed. Case in point, there was an older guy we had to pick up every Friday. He had a little yippy dog that apparently would've turned to dust if left alone for a half hour, so every week I got to listen to, "Bubbles, quit yapping. Bubbles! Quit. That. Yapping!"

His request was always ignored.

But one time halfway back to the office, the dog quit yattering. The silence was angelic. Maybe Bubbles had a breakthrough and now fully understood her owner's previously futile requests for silence. Maybe she...

...wait, what's that slurping sound? Oh no, no, no...

Do not look into the passenger's seat. You do not want confirmation on this. At all costs, just stare straight ahead and—Oh my god, he's making out with his dog. I'm trapped in a moving prison with a man who is tongue-tapping an animal.

At that point, I'd have honestly rather have been sitting next to a hitchhiker whose jacket I just realized was stained with blood. As we exited his subdivision and turned onto Route 30, the yapping began again, which meant the dude's mouth was once again free to make small talk.

"Supposed to get some rain later," he said nonchalantly.

I nodded like a zombie and stepped on the accelerator. "Rain. Yeah. Sure."

We zipped through an intersection. He turned to look out the back windshield. "You *do* know that light was red when you went through it?"

"Yes, I do."

The manager at Irwin was a dude in his mid-twenties named Andy who was always sporting a grin like he'd just set a prank in motion. The branch was profitable and he knew it, so half the day he'd just be in his office with his feet up on his desk flipping a stress ball in the air or doodling on his calendar. Add in the assistant manager, a former college basketball player named Mark, and the management trainees, an

Army Reservist named Justin, and a big dopey dude with floppy hair and sideburns named Gary—I basically went to work every day in a frat house.

We were all young and truly, truly, truly dumb. Anything went. I once found a thirty-inch wooden baseball bat in one of the cars. On the first of every month, I'd use it to blast all the unclaimed garage door openers over the hill and into the woods. It's definitely satisfying to watch a Liftmaster 3000 become a tiny black speck as it sails off beyond the trees. Someday archaeologists are going to stumble upon the valley behind the office and create bizarre hypotheticals about why they discovered ninety-seven mangled garage door openers in a random pattern three hundred feet from any other structures.

One day, I'd just gotten done with batting practice when Andy strolled out into the parking lot. "Cramer, I need you to come with me. We got a special mission." He took two steps and turned around. "Bring the bat."

I didn't ask any questions as I hopped in an F-250 with him and headed out to some housing plan in Penn Township. As the residential homes passed by, he leaned forward, squinted, and began to slow down. Seeing his target, he rolled the truck to a stop in front of a split-level house, blocking the driveway. Parked in front of the garage was a Ford Taurus with a green E sticker on the back.

Andy turned and looked at me. "I don't need you to do anything except stand behind me with the bat." Next thing I knew, we're headed up the front walkway. For the first time since I'd known him, his sly smile faded into something cold and serious. He rang the doorbell. A few seconds later, the door opened to reveal a woman in a slobby, oversize T-shirt. Kids were shouting behind her.

"Yeah?" she said.

"Is Mike Machusko here?" Andy asked.

The woman's eyes tracked past Andy and focused on the baseball bat I was meticulously tapping on my shin. She instinctively backed up and put her hand on the door. "Can I ask what this is about?"

"We're from Emerald," Andy snarled. "We need our car back."

Nervous now, she spun around and yelled up the stairs. "Honey!"

Apparently, my uncle Bob used to accompany some guys who may or may not have been in the mob when they went knocking on doors back in the seventies. He was a burly guy with crazy eyes, and my dad thinks he may have done it to clear his bar tabs. As we waited there on Mike Machusko's porch, the thought briefly occurred to me that I, like my uncle before me, was presently a hired goon.

A six-dollar-an-hour hired goon.

The guy we were there to squeeze crept down the carpeted stairs toward the door, trying to figure out who we were. One thing was obvious: he wasn't super happy we were on his porch. He and his wife had a brief conversation before he took an angry stride across the linoleum landing and reached for the storm door. I'm pretty sure he was about to open it and start shouting at Andy until he also noticed the bat in my hands.

"Whoa, hey, I don't want any trouble here," he said, remaining inside.

"We don't, either," Andy replied. "Just need the car you were supposed to return three weeks ago. And the four hundred sixteen dollars you owe us after cancelling your credit card."

"I don't have the money right now," he pleaded. "The keys are under the floor mat. It's unlocked."

Andy turned and pointed at the car. "Cramer."

I was going to turn and sprint down the stairs, then realized that hired goons don't typically look like gleeful eighth graders headed to recess, so I quashed my instincts and took them one at a time. I opened the car door, lifted the floor mat, located the key, and held it up for Andy to see. Without saying another word, Andy turned and walked methodically down the stairs as well. I'm not certain I've ever felt as bad ass as I did the moment we pulled out of that driveway after strong arming some third-rate car thief.

We returned to the office conquering heroes, getting high fives from Mark, Gary, and Justin. "You actually got the car back from Mike Machusko?" Justin asked. "The guy who's told us to fuck off a hundred times on the phone?"

Andy giggled. "I had Cramer stand behind me with a baseball bat. The dude caved like a hole in the ground."

"Wow," Justin said. "I'd have thought for sure he would've tried to fight you."

"Nah." Andy laughed. "I knew he was all talk."

"Yeah," Justin said in response. "But what if he wasn't?"

For the first time since I walked up the guy's stairs, I truly considered what we'd just done. "Yeah, dude," I said to Andy. "What if he tried to fight you? Was I supposed to crack his skull? Cause I'm pretty certain I could go to jail for that."

Andy choked back a gulp and forced a grin. "We got the car back!" And he pumped his fist and moonwalked into his office.

After that incident, we ditched the bat. Andy just had the dealerships cut duplicate keys so we could get into the cars ourselves. A few times we went on heart-palpitatingly fun runs to steal our own cars back, a process whereby I'd picture myself as some suave international criminal sneaking a Maserati out from under a crime syndicate's nose rather than what I actually was—a car washer making a panicked thirteen-point turn to squeeze a Toyota Corolla out from behind some deadbeat's firepit.

On the whole, though, most people returned their cars on time. They didn't always return them unscathed, however. Because I was often in the parking lot, I was typically the first person that a nervous customer would spot after spending a sleepless night trying to create a believable story about why the crumpled fender wasn't their fault. The best excuse, though, by far came from a professional woman who looked like she'd been running seminars all day. She returned a car one night in late November just after it got dark.

"Hi," she said calmly. "So I'm sure this happens all the time, but I hit a deer the other night, and I'm not quite certain what to do. I know this is their mating season or whatever, so they're everywhere. I mean, you can't avoid them. I was on Brush Creek Road and *boom*. Leaped over the guardrail and into the right headlight. Unavoidable. I felt so bad watching it hobble into the woods. It's a terrible experience knowing you injured an animal. But I know you guys check the cars for damage when they come back, so I wanted to be up front and let you know what happened."

I nodded and walked toward the right headlight, which was mostly missing. The plastic casing that remained poked out from the rubber seal in jagged pieces. Behind it, the fender was collapsed inward and pointing back toward the door panel at a nearly perfect right angle. Damn. That deer was deader than a…

As I squatted there in the dark, a car rolled down Route 30, its headlights briefly illuminating the damage. Alongside the cavity in the fender were four or five orchid-colored scratch marks. This lady was full of shit.

I grinned as I stood up. "You hit one of those purple deer?"

She gasped. "I, well, I, um… What do you mean? I hit a…deer. On Brush Creek, um… Why do you think I, um…?"

I almost felt bad for her. She'd obviously smashed into a parking garage pillar and was too embarrassed to admit it. "Hey, I just wash the cars. I don't care," I said as a shadow in a coat and tie came out the front door. "But you might want to have a better story for Gary."

Fifteen minutes later as we were leaving for the evening, Gary and I walked out the front door together. "Hey," I asked him. "Did that lady stick with the deer story or not?"

"The lady whose husband crashed his golf cart into our Chevy Lumina?"

Silent applause filled my head. "Yes, Gary," I replied. "The woman whose husband crashed his golf cart into our Chevy Lumina."

"What do you mean about a deer?"

"Have a good night, buddy."

As you may imagine, washing rental cars in the Midwest in the spring, summer, and fall isn't all that unpleasant. You're outside or outside adjacent on a lot of nice days, and when it's unbearably hot, the water from the hose cools you off. Winter, however, is brutal. I'll go more in depth in future chapters, but all you need to know for this story is that in order to combat the cold, we had a single industrial box heater mounted to the wall in the corner of the garage. When we cranked that thing up, it could melt stuff. Unsurprisingly, Andy and I often spit loogies into it just to watch them catch fire and drip to the ground like lava. The thing got so hot that after about two hours it felt better to just turn it off and deal with the eighteen-degree weather.

One particularly chilly day, Vic and I shut the garage door and turned the heater on for the last hour. We were washing a car when a woman in her sixties with a somewhat tall beehive hairdo wandered in from the office. Vic saw her and clicked off the vacuum.

She gave a nervous wave. "I was told there's a restroom back here."

"Yup, bathroom," Vic answered. "The white door."

"Don't mean to interrupt your work," she laughed, "but when you gotta go, you gotta go, ya know?"

She spotted the door and skirted around the front of the car, an innocuous few steps that should in no way be seared into my mind decades later. Unfortunately, those steps took her directly under the heater. Don't get ahead of me.

It was the exact same sound that happens when you light the burner on a gas stove.

FOOOF!

Vic's face contorted as if he'd been tasered in the nuts as we both watched a tiny blue flame rise from the top of the woman's beehive. *Holy crap.* There were three people in the garage. Two of us knew that her hair was on fire. Panicked, I did the first thing that popped into my head.

With the help of a tiny puff of water from about a foot away, the flame dwindled to almost nothing. I stood ready with an apology for "accidentally" pulling the nozzle trigger, but she had a big coat and scarf on and a lot of hairspray in and didn't seem to notice getting misted. The woman simply walked into the bathroom and closed the door. Vic and I got absolutely no work done as we stood there in silence, staring at each other wide eyed and waiting for the tortured screams of a woman who finally recognized that her scalp was burning.

We were still in the same positions four minutes later when the door creaked open. She walked out with a smile. "Much better," she said. "Again, sorry to interrupt."

"No worries," I answered, deftly attempting to get a good look at the back of her head. It wasn't engulfed in flames or even lightly smoking, which seemed like a good sign. She tried to walk back around the car the same way she'd come.

"Uh," I said quickly. "Why don't you walk around the other side? I don't want you to trip over the hose."

"Safety first." She laughed, making her way past Vic, whose face had all but frozen.

Just as the woman was about to enter the office, Gary threw open the door. "Hey, what's the ETA on this Malibu?" He sniffed and took a repulsed step back into the archway. "What is that smell?"

"Smell? I don't smell anything," I replied. "Vic, you smell anything?"

If you've ever seen Super Mario run into a Goomba, you know what happened to Vic when I pulled him into the conversation. "I gotta get the vac done," he mumbled, diving back into the car.

Gary sniffed again. "It's like burning hair."

I leaned on the door of the car and looked Gary directly in the eyes. "Gary, you *don't* smell anything. Trust me."

He paused and let the woman slip by him. "Okay."

Once she was safely back in the office, I pointed at the heater and mimed the lady's hair going up in flames to which Gary mouthed the words, "No way."

Then from the office rang Andy's voice. "Does anyone else smell something burning?"

"Nope!" Gary said, shutting the door. "Andy, you don't smell anything!"

But nothing sums up my time in Irwin more than one afternoon when Vic and I were cleaning a Chevy Lumina. Like usual, he was scrambling around the interior with the vacuum and I was slopping soapy water on the roof with a giant brush. It was just like any of the other cars we cleaned together those few months. Until it wasn't.

Most mid-size Chevys at the time had pockets sewn into the upholstery behind the front seats. People would always forget to check them when they returned the vehicle. Mostly you'd find used Kleenex or some kid's homework or a half-done book of crossword puzzles—stuff that would go directly in the trash. But on this particular afternoon, what Vic found in the pocket very nearly killed me. Well, indirectly.

I saw Vic playing with something and paid it little mind until I heard something along the lines of *buzzzzzzzzzzzzzzzz click buzzzzzzzzzz click.*

I turned to see Vic filled with curiosity and confusion at the object in his hand. "Hey, Kev," he said jovially. "Look at this crazy hoosamawhatsit. It buzzes. It's a buzzy little sword. Maybe my grandson would…"

I recognized what it was immediately. "Vic, that's a vibrator."

You haven't lived until you've seen an old Italian man in the first stages of realizing he's holding a stranger's vibrator. His face essentially went out of focus with dismay. He stumbled backward into the washer fluid containers as the vibrator left his hands like he was releasing a dove. I can only see the next part in slow motion as it flipped over and over—a giant wingless dragonfly buzzing through the air, eventually landing on its side and rolling into the corner.

"A *dildo*! Aaaagh!" he screamed. "I touched a *dildo*?"

I swear the music from when Super Mario falls into a bottomless pit blared through the garage as I fell to the ground, physically incapable of continuing to wash the car. Vic dove for the bathroom. He used at least half the soft soap in a ten-minute germ exorcism as I laughed so hard I damn near threw up.

But our real problem came when he finally exited the bathroom. We stared at this thing as it lay idly in the corner all by its lonesome, yearning for a lover it would never see again.

We spent a good minute scratching our heads to the tune of its helpless buzz before I spoke up. "I mean, should we put it in the lost-and-found box?"

"I ain't touching that thing again," Vic snapped.

"That would be really funny to have in there. People digging around looking for their mailbox key or a pair of sunglasses…"

"I ain't touching it again. These hands don't play with dildos. That don't make me gay."

"I'm no expert, Vic, but I don't think that's technically a dildo. I don't think dildos have a mechanical component."

"It don't make me gay."

"Do you think someone will come back to claim it? How boss would you have to be to come back for it?"

"Just forget about it," Vic grumbled.

"Okay," I said.

Buzzzzzzzzzzzzzzzzzzzzzzzzz…….

In the end, the batteries died while we were out delivering cars. When we returned from our respective trips, neither of us wanted to touch it, so we just left it there. Summer turned to fall and fall to winter. There it remained. We'll find out in four hundred years whether the archaeologists uncover the vibrator or the garage door openers first— and what hypothetical link they'll build between the two.

CHAPTER 10

Confederacy of Dunces

When I was fifteen, a kid named Bradley sat behind me in English class. He was one of those annoying pests who'd say things like, "Duh," a million times and kick the back of your chair over and over. It was how he made himself relevant in the cesspool of hormones that was our sophomore year of high school. One afternoon Bradley decided to throw a fake punch at my face, cackling when I flinched. Though I was a good athlete, I was also a skinny, acne-faced geek, so I endured this shit all the time. But in this particular moment, something inside me snapped.

I glared at him. "If you actually touch me, I will kill you." Since I was essentially made of straw and pipe cleaners, Bradley ignored the "threat." Laughing, he smacked me across the back of the head, daring me to respond. At that point I knew I had two options: back down and subject myself to a lifetime of harassment or...

There's a scene in *Jurassic Park* where the conniving lawyer is sitting on a toilet in a rainstorm and looks up to see a Tyrannosaur towering above him. In our reenactment, Bradley played the lawyer. I was the T-Rex. He offered minimal resistance as I picked him out of his seat by the neck and chucked him across the aisle into Misty DeMitro's armrest. The entire class froze. The dork had gone ballistic. Bradley got up woozy and embarrassed with red impact lines crisscrossing his face. He wasn't the type of kid who ever expected let alone knew how to deal with the consequences of being a douche, so he just meekly sat back down—and never annoyed me again.

After that, I realized there was a direct correlation between acting slightly insane and getting picked on less. I started breaking stuff for no real reason and hanging out with the devil-worshipping burnout kids who nobody really liked but nobody really messed with, either. I began getting In School Suspension. On my first day, to keep the bullies guessing, I set the rug on fire. I was angry, resentful, and supremely unconfident, which I now realize is par for the course at fifteen. I needed a fresh start before I turned Penn-Trafford High School into a pile of smoldering ruins. So my parents scraped together the money to send me to the Catholic high school over in Greensburg for my junior year. I may have been leaving the daily demolition of my self-assurance behind, but I was also venturing into a new, uncharted world.

And I was terrified.

A majority of the kids at Greensburg Central Catholic were rich, preppy, and good looking—all things I was not. For the first month, I defaulted back to my old habits. It worked. Rumor had it I was dealing drugs and had done time in juvie. Other than the occasional kids who'd nervously ask if I could hook them up with some weed, I barely interacted with anyone. I'd done what I'd set out to do. Nobody was picking on me. I was being left alone. But I also didn't have any friends. It was lonely. Incredibly lonely.

Enter my guidance counselor, Mr. Devlin. He was a tough man with a military background and a big heart who saw potential where no one else did, encouraged me to come out of my shell, not be so combative all the time, and give Greensburg Central a chance. He quietly asked the cross-country coach to encourage me to join the team and persuaded a group of seniors to invite me to sit with them at lunch. He created an atmosphere that gradually allowed me to quit walking around all day with my fists clenched. By my senior year, I'd completed such a turnaround that he put me of all people on the peer leadership team. I was one of the students chosen to help the lonely kids who weren't fitting in. With responsibility came confidence. For the first time in years, I felt like I belonged somewhere. I wasn't just existing. I was thriving.

Mr. Devlin's support meant everything. It's not hyperbole to say he carried me up the mountain I'd tumbled down. Other than my father, there's no other man in my life who had such a large impact on the person I am today. For that I will always be eternally grateful.[9*]

So what does all this have to do with washing cars? Well, not much except that my mom recognized I wasn't happy living at home and getting up to go to a minimum wage job every day at twenty-three years old. So she asked me a philosophical question.

"Who are some people you admire? What do they do?"

The very first person I thought of was Mister Devlin. Could I be a…guidance counselor? Was that a thing I was even eligible to do? So much of what I'd done in life had to do with mentoring kids. I'd coached youth basketball at the St. Augustine Recreation Center. I taught frisbee skills at the Special Olympics. Hell, if I hadn't spent a summer as a camp counselor, chapter seven would've been a lot shorter. Evidence suggested that perhaps I'd missed my calling. For the first time in a good long while, I had a direction, a real goal. Guidance counseling. Hell yeah, I'd be good at that.

The big obstacle was that my undergrad degree in communication hadn't afforded me the education and psychology credits that most graduate programs in counselor education required. In order to get them, I was going to need a transition semester, which I'm sure I could've easily done at Pitt or Duquesne or Westmoreland County Community College. But those places were just as cold in January as it

---

[9*] He passed away of a heart attack in 2016 after a day of fishing with his boys. Losing your mentors hurts.

was at my parents' house. Luckily, I knew where the temperature was much more pleasant.

The University of North Florida.

In order to pay for the credits I needed, I was going to have to work during the semester. So I asked Emerald to transfer me—which they did—to a brand new office located in the plush Omni Hotel in the heart of downtown Jacksonville. Having put in eight months in Irwin, I thought I knew what to expect. But though the jobs were definitely related, they were at best estranged cousins. First of all, we only had four spaces in the front of the hotel, so all of our cars were stationed up on the tenth floor of the parking garage next door. Six minutes and forty right turns later, I'd finally be up to our wash station. Unlike Irwin, it wasn't across from a Sunoco and an apartment complex that got condemned due to mine subsidence. I got to look out over Water Street at the St. John's River and the traffic zooming along over three different bridges. It was absolutely gorgeous at sunset.

The other car prep was a dude named Reggie who looked and acted like the hype man for some famous rapper. Dude had a gold tooth and didn't give a *shit*. Whereas Vic got nervous the minute you acknowledged him, Reggie was a human party. He'd blast the radio in one car while we washed another, turning the wash station into an outdoor nightclub while describing in vivid detail the steaks he was going to grill up that night, the seasonings, the sauces—and how his girl was going to react to his charcoal prowess.

"Everything's going to sizzle at Reggie's tonight," he'd howl as he grooved his way around a Kia Forte. "Ev-ry-thaaaang."

On Valentine's Day, we were sitting at a light on Turner Boulevard when suddenly Reggie jumped out of the driver's seat, handed a guy on the corner some cash, and hustled back with a batch of giant, heart-shaped balloons.

"Cramer, help me get these in the car," he ordered. "Reggie's getting it onnnnnn tonight."

It takes more effort than you'd think to cram ten giant love balloons into a Ford Focus. We were nowhere near ready to go when the light turned green. Cue the honking.

"Go around!" Reggie yelled at the other cars. The balloons crinkled beside my ear as I tried to shove them inside the car with my forehead, shoulders, and knees without any of them popping. It was like trying to wrangle anti-gravity toddlers.

"Reggie," I said with balloons punching me in the face from the breeze. "I think we're going to have to roll the windows down."

"I'm in agreement with your conclusion, Cramer," he answered as the horns became a demonic flock of ducks. "Go *around!*"

Reggie's smile was as wide as a tunnel as we cruised back to the office trailing red and pink balloons behind us like a dragster equipped with the sport's most ineffective parachute. We were impossible to miss rolling through the hood north of the city with the bass thumping. I believe it's the most gangsta I've ever felt.

Up on top of the garage, Reggie and I were a ten-floor elevator ride from the office, so the suits had to commit to five minutes outside their air-conditioned bubble to check on us—which they almost never did. So we were free to rock. Often, we'd glance across Bay Street toward the forty-story headquarters of SouthTrust Bank to see some dissatisfied accounts manager pressing his forehead to the glass, yearning to switch spots for just one day.

"Freedom," he'd say, his breath fogging the glass. "Sweet, sweet freedom."

What the dejected SouthTrust guy couldn't see, however, was the blond buzzkill we were desperately trying to avoid up there. Her name was Allie, and she'd just been given her first branch manager position when the new Omni office opened—a position that turned her into a neurotic, stressed-out mess.

Truthfully, the crew she was given didn't help. Along with Reggie and I, our driver was an old dude we referred to as Cautious Walt. For him, safety was paramount—to the detriment of literally everything else. "Okay," he'd say as we'd slide into a car for a four-minute trip to the body shop. "Driver's mirror. Up a smidge. Up a...smidge. Whoops... too far. Down a...smidge. That's good. Now the passenger mirror. Up a smidge...whoop. Gotta...get it jusssssst right. And...good. Driver's seat needs to go back a..."

"Walt, you know Allie's glaring at us through the window, right? She told us to leave five minutes ago."

"Dang it, took the seat back too far," Walt would chuckle. "Gotta come in a bit." And the seat would ZRRRRRRRRR, ZUP, ZRRRRRRR ZUP, ZUP, ZUP, ZUP ZRRRRRRRR. "Oops, shoulda done that first. Side mirrors aren't where I need them anymore. Up a smidge..."

Because Allie didn't have any control over Walt or Reggie, she tended to focus her stress-induced irrationality on me. One time I had to toss some keys onto Allie's desk in the tiny little break room that doubled as her office. Back at Irwin, Andy bought pizza for the office every Friday as a token of appreciation. Well, it was Friday and there was a half-eaten pizza on the break room counter. I'd been gone delivering cars to the airport and stupidly assumed that I'd missed the announcement that Allie had bought lunch for everyone. I was super hungry, so I picked up a slice and walked back into the office.

A few moments later, Allie came striding in from the parking lot and stopped cold right in front of me. "Where'd you get that pizza?"

"Thanks for buying us lunch," I said, licking cheese from my fingers. "I was starving."

She looked at me like she'd caught me urinating in the corner. "I bought lunch for me, Courtney, and Latisha for meeting our sales goals. That's not for you! That's stealing! I could fire you for that!"

The speed at which I'd gone from grateful employee to immoral thief was dizzying. Her allegation rendered me mute. I shrugged and offered her the half-eaten slice.

"Eeew," she said, slapping my hand away. "Just eat it now! God!"

Allie muttered something under her breath and moved over behind the computers, watching me eat the rest of the slice with a glare that suggested we were married and she knew I was cheating on her. It was decent pizza, but I made sounds that suggested the taste was sending blood to my groin. This marked the beginning of a cold war between us that would last for weeks before eventually exploding. Stay tuned for drama!

At the time, Emerald had a promotion called the Weekend Special, which let people rent cars on Saturday and Sunday for a discounted price in order to keep them from sitting idle in the parking lot for two days. In a slick advertising tactic, they featured the phrase "From $9.99 a day" on all their banners and sandwich boards, which was true…sort of. You could indeed get a car for less than ten dollars a day plus tax, but that car was essentially a Hyundai Atom or a Chevy Mite. You still had to pay a reasonable amount for bigger vehicles.

One day a happy family of ten walked into the office rolling suitcases behind them. It was a mom, dad, I'm assuming an aunt, and seven kids. I held the door as they sauntered in. A four-year-old girl wearing a Minnie Mouse shirt looked up at me as she dragged her little backpack though the doorway.

"We're going to Disney World!" she said with the exact inflection you'd expect from a little girl on her way to Disney.

"Oh, you'll have so much fun!" I said. "Do you think Cinderella will be there?"

"Yes!" she shrieked. "It's where Cinderella *lives!*"

They seemed like a relatively normal family heading on a fun-filled trip to the Magic Kingdom. Allie was behind the computers, so I leaned on the counter. "What do you need me to bring down? That Dodge Caravan?"

Allie squinted. She slowly looked up from her computer to see a group of people that barely fit in our office. "Um, hold on," she said, holding up her finger. She looked at the guy in the striped golf shirt in front of her. "Are you the Katz family?"

The father was a dude in his late thirties with rosy cheeks and a subtly vacant stare. "Yes. We are the Katz family. Disney Trip 2001."

"Um," Allie said, making faces that suggested a computer malfunction. "You made a reservation for the $9.99 weekend special?"

"Yes."

Allie blinked. "Sir, you realize that's for our economy-size car."

"If it can get us to Disney, we'll take it!" he answered with glee.

Allie's eye began to twitch. "We do have a minivan available and ready to go," she said. "With the weekend special, it'd only be $27.99 a day. With taxes it'd come out to barely over…"

With the cadence and inflection of a man who'd been brainwashed by a cult, the dude responded, "We'll take the $9.99 car."

Allie and I shared an alarmed glance and retreated back to her office to look at the pegboard of keys. "Bring down this Nissan Sentra," she said. "That's the smallest thing we have. They'll realize they can't all fit and I'll upsell them into the minivan."

"Allie, they obviously have another car," I said. "Half of them are going in this one and half are going in whatever they drove here."

She grabbed my wrist and exhaled. "Oh my god, I thought they were all going to cram into an economy class! I feel so much better."

I brought the Sentra down from the garage and parked it on the curb in front of the office. Allie walked around the car marking scratches and dents and then handed them their pink receipt. This should've been the point when they began giving each other hugs and saying things like "be safe" and "we'll see you down there." But there was none of that. Just suitcases and backpacks being jammed into the trunk. The luggage they couldn't fit got tossed in the back seat. When they opened the doors, nobody walked away. My god, nobody was walking away. Allie came back into the office to see me at the front window watching the horror unfolding on the curb.

Five kids and the aunt piled into a back seat that comfortably fit three. With totally oblivious smiles, the mom and dad slid into the front, holding the smallest two. No car seats, just kids packed on top of each other and a shit-ton of gummi bears.

"Allie, I was wrong," I said in awe. "They're going to clown car it to Orlando."

What I'll always remember is the oldest kid. He was ten or eleven—old enough to know his family was failing him but not old enough to truly resist. Pressed between his aunt and the door, the side of his face smushed into an involuntary half smile against the window, his eyes pleaded for rescue. Were his immobilized lips able, they'd have uttered the phrase, "I'm going to Disney World," in the exact inverse tone as a quarterback who'd just won the Super Bowl. I never saw them return the car, so I can only assume they pulled out of the lot and happily drove due east into the ocean.

Now while that scenario was just plain ridiculous, this next story delves into some serious issues that America has been wrestling with since the 1600s. I've met a lot of people in life and found that in the end, most of us are just trying to exist, just attempting to get through the damn day so we can get another one tomorrow. All the shit that the people in power concoct to divide us is irrelevant when you're cleaning six pounds of dog hair out of a Kia Sportage. But sometimes no matter how hard you try you can't avoid the past. Especially in a place like Jacksonville. Which is stuck there.

One night I gave some customers a ride to a body shop way over in Orange Park and didn't get back to the office until well after six. It was always a race for me if I didn't get out of there on time because I was paying for the meal plan on campus at UNF and the cafeteria closed at seven. So when Allie asked me to do one more pickup after I returned, I knew I was fucked.

I grunted. "Allie, you know I need to get back by seven or I don't get to eat tonight."

"I guess it's your call if you want to leave a family stranded on the side of the road," she replied.

My stomach rumbled, wondering if I could make it all the way to breakfast the next morning. "Fine."

"They're in a brown Chevy Blazer broken down at First and Main."

"Any way you could order me a—"

"If you say pizza, I'm going to scream."

"I'm just saying it'd be nice considering—"

"Go!"

As with most of my interactions with Allie, it ended with me sighing heavily and walking out the door. She was a pretty blond machine devoid of empathy, and no matter how hard I tried to connect, our worldviews would always divorce at free pizza.

My dinner plans rebuffed, I hopped into a car and peeled out onto Bay Street, taking the left on Main, going north at sunset through some of the rougher sections of town. Along the way, I passed the Shell Station that did all of our oil changes. Twice a week, Reggie and I would be sent to grab a car at the airport, but before getting on I-95 we'd stop there and chill for twenty minutes with Reggie's boys from the neighborhood. It was honestly hard to tell who worked there and who was just hanging out. Things on the north side of downtown moved at a different pace than I was used to—a pace one standard deviation faster than Cautious Walt and thirty-three slower than Allie's demands. I loved it.

The first time Reggie and I rolled up to the Shell Station, I was confused. "Are we picking up a car here?" I asked. "I thought we were on our way to..."

Reggie laughed. "Nah, man, we're just gonna sit a spell. I need a smoke." Like I said, Reggie didn't give a *shit*. "Yo," he said to the guys hanging around outside the garage. "This is my boy Cramer."

You could tell that since I had Reggie's approval, they were much less skeptical of some dopey white kid walking up on them than they otherwise would've been. Almost immediately an older guy with a white beard laughed. "Cramer, you ever hear the story about when Ozzie fell in the river?"

A younger guy who was obviously Ozzie threw his hands up. "Man, you don't need to tell everyone we meet about the time I fell in the river. It was five years ago!"

I laughed. "Wait, *you're* Ozzie? Yeah, I heard that story." I laughed. "Up in Pittsburgh before I even moved down here."

The old guy slapped his knee and almost tipped his chair over. "See, everyone knows! You're world famous. Ozzie that fell in the river!"

"Maaaaaan," Ozzie said, walking back into the garage. "Y'all killing me."

I'm not going to pretend I truly became one of the boys or anything, but it was definitely interesting to be recognized and accepted by a bunch of chill Black dudes at a Shell Station in north Jacksonville. We were all just guys working on cars in an attempt to feed ourselves and have a place to stay. Sometimes the work was hard. Sometimes it wasn't. The similarities overwhelmed our differences. On a micro scale of day-to-day interactions, those differences, while apparent, didn't factor at all into our interactions. We talked about cars and laughed about the dumbasses we met because of them.

I only mention the guys at the Shell Station because of the family that Allie sent me to pick up at six thirty that Friday night. The sun was disappearing as I rolled up on the inoperative Chevy Blazer at the corner of First and Main. A dude with a camo hat was standing in front of the tailgate with his wife, who was holding the hand of a skinny six-year-old boy. The giant Confederate flag hanging from the back window and casually racist bumper stickers let me know this probably wasn't going to go smoothly.

Of all the places in Jacksonville to sputter to a stop when your vehicle is sporting a window-size Confederate flag, the last place you want it to be is at the corner of First and Main—even if you're making it abundantly clear that you have a gun. By the shaken looks on the rednecks' faces, it was obvious that the locals had already voiced a few strong opinions on their vehicle's accessories.

I stepped out of the car and muttered to myself, "Motherfucker."

"You from Emerald?" the redneck asked.

"Yup."

"That our car? I said I wanted a Suburban."

I was not in a customer service mood. "This is the car we have, man. You want it or not?"

He smacked the tailgate. "Damn it, fine. Give me the keys."

"Dude, I have to drive you back to the office so you can fill out the paperwork," I said. "We don't just hand people car keys and let them drive off."

"I ain't going nowhere until the tow truck shows up," he growled, gesturing to a small crowd gathering nearby. "You know what these people will do if I just leave it here?"

I let out a long, heavy sigh—longer than the one I'd given Allie when she refused to buy me a pizza for doing her this shitty favor. "Look, dude, you either come with me right now or you don't get the car."

"We ain't going nowhere," he said, hand on his pistol.

His wife tugged on his sleeve. "Jimmy, I think we should…"

"We ain't going nowhere."

Any other day and I'd have already been eating a cafeteria cheeseburger. "I'm gonna back the car up fifty feet so nobody thinks I'm with you," I grumbled. "You got two minutes to decide."

Truthfully, if it was just him, I'd have left his ass right there. But I couldn't do that to his kid, who still theoretically had a shot at growing up to be a decent human. I got in the car and slowly backed it up, then got out and sat on the hood, watching the couple argue. By now there was a definite gathering on the periphery of folks who were not appreciative of the symbolism displayed on the Blazer. It got very tense very quickly. I swore my heartbeat was making the car bounce.

Then suddenly I heard a voice from beside me. I tensed until I realized it was one of the guys from the Shell Station. I'm not positive, but I think his name was Desmond. "Emerald, what the hell are you doing with these fools?" he asked.

My heart rate immediately dropped. I was no longer alone. "Fuck, man, the office sent me to pick these dickheads up. I'm not here voluntarily."

He snarled at the rebel flag. "You best tell these folks to get up out of here."

"I'm working on it."

As I spoke, a guy I didn't know walked up beside us. He was a ripped dude in a tank top and skull cap that I did not want to mess with.

"The hell is this shit?" he said, taking a step toward the Blazer. Then he looked back at me. "Who the fuck is this?" he said to Desmond.

Desmond waved him off. "He's cool, man. He's boys with Reggie. His name's Collins or something…"

"Cramer."

"Yeah, Cramer," he said. "He's just at work. He ain't with them."

"I'm just trying to get home, man," I said. "Hell, I'm not gonna get to eat tonight because of these assholes." I looked toward the arguing redneck couple and tapped on my wrist. Their two minutes were up.

"Tow truck ain't here yet!" the redneck yelled.

And that was my cue. I gave a fist bump to Desmond, slid off the hood, and hopped in behind the wheel. I started up the car and prepared to pull back onto Main Street when the redneck's wife hustled up with her son in tow. She reached for the back door, threw it open, and slid in.

I stared at them in the rearview. "Once I pull out of here, I'm not turning around."

"Just get us to your office, please," the wife said. "Jimmy's staying until the tow truck shows up. Oh god. Is he going to be okay?"

I wish I'd have replied with something clever like, "Depends on how fast he can run," but the six-year-old in the back seat was obviously terrified about leaving his dad behind. Most likely, the redneck I currently despised was the guy who was teaching him how to hunt and fish and ride four wheelers—a guy who probably snaked drains or put up gutters for a living just like some of the dudes currently yelling obscenities in his direction. And yet here we were because his whole life someone told him that differences in pigment mattered more than all the similarities in our mutual daily struggles. "Probably," I answered as diplomatically as I could. "As long as he's not too attached to that flag."

I have no idea what happened. I didn't have a TV at my apartment and thus never saw the news. Maybe they snatched his flag. Maybe he got pushed in front of a bus. Maybe they held him down, tickled the hell out of him, and all walked away friends. Most likely the tow truck showed up soon afterward, and other than the yelling, the whole thing petered out. I don't know. But what I did learn is that it always pays to be cool to people. You never know when you're going to need someone to vouch for you.

Mad love to the boys at the Shell Station.

I don't know a single person who hasn't dreamed of telling their boss, "You're an idiot, this company sucks, and I'm done." You think it'll be a glorious vindication of your autonomy, a moment that gives the higher-ups the painful realization that they never fully appreciated the value you provided. But more often than not, the whole thing is dumb, you walk away feeling massively uncertain, and they replace you like a dirty air filter and keep going.

We sometimes rented cars to the Federal Reserve of Jacksonville, this giant concrete building that looked like it housed the National Dullness Museum. When they rented cars, there was no such thing as "good enough." They were apparently carting around bankers in $15,000 trousers, so these cars needed to be showroom clean. We'd typically spend over an hour on whatever Buick or Cadillac they'd requested.

It was late April, and I was only a week away from heading back to Pittsburgh for the summer when Allie had me go to another branch to pick up a white Buick Regal, which was not treated particularly regally by the previous customer. I brought it to the top floor and took more care with this car than any other car I'd ever previously cleaned. Working alone, I spent forty-five minutes wiping, drying, and polishing until this thing was shining so bright it was distracting astronauts. I was toweling it off when Allie came bursting out the door from the parking garage elevators. I expected her to say something along the lines of, "Wow, Cramer, that looks great. Thanks for working so hard on it," which is what anyone without icicles up their ass would've said.

Nope.

Instead, she immediately fixated on a dime-size spot of dirt next to the license plate and yelled, "Have you not even started yet? What the hell have you been doing for the last hour? God, why do I even pay you?" Then she got down on her knees in her little red business suit and leaned in to inspect it at fine-print range. "They're *waiting* on this car!"

Should I have waited until she'd backed up to squirt off the dirt? Probably.

The backspray from the license plate caught her right in the face. She turned and scowled at me with a drip hanging from her nose, too angry to scream. She just wiped her eyes and walked around to open the door. I think at that point, she realized the rest of the car was spotless but was too irate to care.

"Keys!" she yelled.

I took them from my pocket and handed them to her. The glare she gave me before she drove away almost shattered the window. I started on the next car, knowing full well that at some point before the end of the day I'd be taking the full brunt of Allie's wrath. Sure enough, about a half hour later the door to the tenth floor flew open. I heard her before I saw her.

"Hey, asshole!" She came roaring across the top deck of the garage with flames behind her. "You wash fucking cars. It's not like I can't easily replace you."

"Don't fucking swear at me, Allie."

"Or what? You'll quit? How will we ever get by without a prick car washer who thinks he's better than everyone else?"

The only thing I regret is that I didn't hose her down on the way out. We were locked in a stupid battle of egos and cuss words, and I'd quit thinking clearly. Instead, I just dropped the brush. "Fuck off, Allie. Do the rest of them yourself."

I know she got some last word in, but I wasn't listening. I got in my truck and drove off. Really, my satisfaction came in the rearview mirror watching her have to pick up a brush and slop soapy water onto the Ford Festiva she needed.

All in all, I found that saying fuck off and quitting was much less vindicating than I anticipated. You realize that in a big corporation, no matter how hard you work, you don't truly matter. They will swear up and down that you are an important piece of the puzzle, but in the end, it's all hollow platitudes. You matter as much as one bee does to the survival of the planet. Sure, we need bees, and if they all went away, we'd be screwed. But that one? We'll find another bee.

So I'd angrily quit a job for the first time and found the experience more aggravating than freeing. But just before I quit, I found out that I'd somehow gotten into one of the top counselor education programs in the country. I was on my way to something bigger and better than cleaning cars.

But first I had to clean a bunch more cars.

CHAPTER 11

Day

L uckily for me, Emerald is separated into a bunch of regions that operate more or less independently and seemingly don't communicate whatsoever. It meant that hypothetically let's say…you soaked your boss in Jacksonville, human resources in Pittsburgh probably wasn't going to find out. Which is how I ended up cleaning cars at Day Chevrolet off of Route 286 in Monroeville.

Day Chevy was yet another totally different experience doing virtually the same thing. The office itself had three desks crammed into a room that was smaller than some of our minivans. Our wash area was in the back of a crowded parking lot next to a garage door that led into the dealership's repair shop—a spot where the mechanics often parked cars because it was convenient for *them*. These were dudes with mullets whose idea of humor was to announce at the end of the day that it was "time to go home to the *ol' ball and chain!*" Every time they parked in my space, I'd have to aimlessly wander the garage and ask them to move their car. Of course no one knew who parked it there or where the keys were and "I've got *important* shit to do here, fella."

I'd been there about two weeks when I rolled up behind one of the mechanics just as he was parking an old ambulance in my spot. He got out and passed in front of me on his way to the garage.

"Hey, buddy," I said, cracking my door open. "There's like ten open spots. This is the only place my hose and vacuum can reach. Any way you can…"

"Not my problem," he replied as he walked inside.

But wouldn't you know, there was in fact one other spot my vacuum and hose could reach. About two minutes later, the jag who'd parked the ambulance was trying to pull another car out of the garage, presumably to clear space in one of the bays. He was not pleased to find his exit blocked by the lowly car washer cleaning a Saturn Ion.

Freight trains going through an intersection don't blow their horn as long as this clown did. HONNNNNNNK! "Hey, asshole!" he yelled. "Move your fuckin' car!"

I shrugged and pointed to the ambulance.

HONNNNNNNNNNNNNNNNK! "Hey, asshole!" he repeated. "I can't get out!"

He'd set me up as beautifully as I'd hoped. "Not my problem," I yelled back.

My spot was free the rest of the summer.

Anyway, there were four employees in a really crammed office, so we spent a ton of time together that summer. The manager was a beautiful twenty-five-year-old Korean named Cindy, who was somehow more uptight than Allie was—but with one crucial difference. Cindy had the ability to recognize when you were working hard and subsequently use phrases like "thank you" and "I appreciate it." It's amazing the amount of insanity those sentiments can mask. Whereas Allie's constant ungratefulness encouraged my vindictive side, I'd have done anything for Cindy.

It also helped that Cindy was massively unlucky, and I was always around when the disempowering gypsy curse she was subject to dished out its evil magic. That summer, being around Cindy was slapstick comedy gold. Consequently, she was convinced that any illusion of authority over me had disappeared. Once we were alone in the office when she reached up to open a cabinet only to have a random tub of ranch dressing and a stapler tumble out. The ranch dressing burst upon hitting her forehead. The stapler damn near knocked her cold. Her legs buckled, and she sat on the floor in shock.

Sitting on the ground in a small pool of runny white liquid, she clenched her fists and closed her eyes. "*Why* is there *salad dressing* in the *cabinets*?"

I stared at her, trying to figure out if I'd imagined that or not. Ranch dressing and a stapler? I *had* to have made that up. But a tiny cut on her scalp and the slime in her hair said otherwise. I extended my hand to help her up. "Good news is that 90 percent of the crap running down your face right now *isn't* blood."

She wiped some ranch from her skirt, took my hand, and upon standing immediately resumed tearing apart the office for the file she needed. "I don't have time to bleed," she replied. "Ugh, where is this *file*?"

But that was far from Cindy's most ridiculous moment. What I'm going to henceforth refer to as "Cindy's Terrible, Horrible, No Good, Very Bad Day" fully encapsulates what I'm certain were the stresses of being a young professional trying to prove your worth in a company whose business model relies on chewing up and spitting out postgraduates desperate for management experience.

Cindy's Terrible, Horrible, No Good, Very Bad Day began with two nearly simultaneous phone calls. The first let her know that one of our Buick 300s had been impounded by the city of Pittsburgh after being abandoned in a ditch in Homewood. The second informed her that the Cadillac she'd planned on getting back that afternoon wasn't returning until the next day because the lawyer who'd rented it was stuck with clients in Ohio. This left her without the luxury car she needed for a delivery at eight the next morning to our biggest corporate client, Westinghouse Electric. At this point, an EKG on Cindy's brain would've registered as mid-seizure.

I walked in to see her at her desk, rubbing her temples and trying not to shake. A deep breath calmed her down as she opened up a small cash box, pulling out a roll of twenties, which she threw in her purse.

"Cramer, drop what you're doing. We're going for a ride," she said.

At the time, the Pittsburgh City Pound was in a post-industrial wasteland underneath a railroad trestle off of Penn Avenue in the Strip District. After the thirty-minute ride, I followed Cindy into a trailer where one gruff dude with neck tattoos stood behind a faux wood–paneled counter surrounded by fading pictures of hot chicks on motorcycles. It was about as welcoming as a federal penitentiary—although I suspect that's not exclusive to Pittsburgh. I doubt the motto for Milwaukee's city pound is "Your friends and neighbors since 1966!"

"We're here for the Buick 300," Cindy said to the counter guy, digging in her purse for the bills she'd taken from the cash box.

This dude didn't care a lick that we were standing in front of him. He glared at us before typing something into the old PC on the counter. "Emerald Rental Car?"

"Yes," Cindy answered.

"One hundred forty-two dollars."

Cindy looked the guy in the eye for the first time since we'd entered. "That's insane."

"Been here three days."

"Nobody called until this morning!" Cindy yelled back.

Even the biggest proponents of capitalism would have to agree that it allows certain businesses to run totally legal schemes based on your desperation. Our entire healthcare system comes to mind. Also in that same asshole cartel? Impound lots. What's a fair price to get your car back through their fence? We'll never know because nobody in America has ever paid a fair price to do so.

The guy just silently waited for Cindy to break and slide the money across the counter. Which she did. Her neck was throbbing as he handed her the keys and a few papers to sign. "It's out back," the counter guy said coldly, turning to watch TV without giving us any further instructions.

The sky was darkening as we clomped our way down the wooden ramp and along a tall fence topped with barbed wire. "I need you to drive this Buick back and get it ready for Westinghouse," Cindy said as we looked out over the jumble of cars crammed behind the trailer. "We need it first thing tomorrow morning."

The wind started to kick up as deep gray rain clouds began rolling over the downtown buildings two miles to the west. No matter, we'd be on our way by the time the storm…

Our car was completely blocked in. Cars on both sides. Car in front. Car behind.

The keys involuntarily dropped from Cindy's hand. "Are you kidding me?"

"Oh damn. That sucks."

"Can you go talk to the guy? I can't deal with him again." She turned and yelled at the back of the trailer. "You can't charge me for days I didn't know our car was here! That is soooo unethical. Oh my god, this isn't happening."

As amusing as it was to hear the manager of a rental car branch bitching about the ethics of other businesses, I could see the storm coming and knew I had to act quickly. I hustled back to the trailer to find the guy with the neck tattoos seemingly trying to kill things with his mind.

"Hey, man, our car is blocked in," I said. "What's the protocol for getting it out? Is there a guy back there we have to find or…"

The fucker just shrugged.

"Buddy, I make six bucks an hour and I'm trapped here with my neurotic boss who is about to have a stroke. Some idea of what we need to do would be appreciated."

I still remember him disinterestedly reaching up and flicking some keys on the pegboard. "Looks like you need a tow."

"If you give me the keys to the car behind it, I'll just—"

"Liability," he replied with zero empathy.

I'd have told him to go fuck himself, but it seemed like he fed on conflict, so I just turned and walked out the door, wondering whether I'd be sleeping at the impound lot that night. When I got to Cindy, she was staring into the open trunk of the Buick with the same expression she had after getting bonked with the stapler. It was filled to the brim with wrinkled clothes, hangars, Burger King bags, empty liquor bottles—seemingly everything from the last renter's life. With the wind howling and the clouds blowing in, she quickly gave me instructions.

"Cramer, I know this car is trashed, but when we get back, I need you to empty it. Find some trash bags and throw this guy's crap in them. I don't care if you're nice about it. We desperately need this car for tomorrow morning. What did the guy inside say?"

I sighed, knowing I was about to cripple her mind. "Apparently, we need a tow truck."

"Really?" she said, trying not to hyperventilate. "*Really?*"

I walked around to the front of the car. It was then that I decided to wreck her day completely. "Hey…Cindy?"

"Oh no, what now?"

The right front tire had been replaced by a sorry-looking donut, and the front bumper was half on the ground. "You might want to consider a different car for Westinghouse."

"We don't have another…" And she hustled over to see exactly what I saw. She snorted and looked to the heavens just as the rain began to fall.

I squatted next to the destroyed fender. "Gonna be honest here, this thing isn't getting back with a bumper scraping the Parkway."

"This sucks!" Cindy exclaimed as the drops became waves. She opened the door and ducked into the car to get out of the rain, reclining the driver's seat to try and destress while her car prep attempted to rip off a bumper in a driving rainstorm.

After a few unsuccessful attempts, I realized that I could indeed pop the bumper out, but only if I had it at a certain angle—which required someone else to hold it. Cautiously, I knocked on the passenger window, which Cindy reluctantly rolled down.

"What?" she said fearfully.

"I, uh…need your help if I'm going to…"

"Don't make me come out in the rain. It's so dry in here."

"I just thought—you made it seem like we're on a time crunch here."

She sat up and pressed her forehead to the steering wheel. "We are," she whined, reluctantly opening the door and stepping outside into the tsunami. The rain was coming down so hard we could barely see each other on opposite ends of the car.

"It's stuck on something underneath," I yelled over the roar of the storm. "I need you to unhook it while I pull or it's just going to keep…"

Cindy's sigh briefly parted the waterfall as she realized what I needed her to do. I was in a mechanic's uniform and old cargo shorts, clothes perfectly designed for getting greasy, wet, and dirty. Cindy was in a light blue business suit that was designed to project power and sophistication—and probably cost like two hundred bucks.

"Are you kidding me?" she whined for the ninth time since we'd arrived.

"I mean, I can do that part, but then you'd have to deadlift this bumper. If you'd rather…"

Cindy disgustedly shook her head and crawled underneath the car, squelching in the cinders, the mud, and the random windblown trash to unhook this piece of mangled plastic from the undercarriage as I pulled and kicked the bumper until it popped loose. Mission accomplished—except for one thing.

We were still stuck.

The soaked, dirty, disheveled mess I knew as my boss wrenched herself out from under the car and stared at the bumperless Buick that had quite literally wrecked her plans. As mascara streamed in purplish zigzags down her cheeks, it seemed as if she was contemplating existence itself and whether the prevalence of evil left any room for good in this awful, awful world. Just then, a tow truck from some local wrecker service bounced through the gate. It was one of the old ones with just the hook and winch. He pulled in behind us and sat there to wait out the storm.

One thing I'll say about Cindy was that even at her most frazzled, she had the ability to recover quickly and do what needed to be done. Her lips quivering, she strode through the falling ocean and gave a hearty knock to the tow truck driver's door. The dude inside peeked his window down to see a frantic, soaked Asian girl with wet garbage in her hair wearing what was now a half-blue, half-brown business suit. To the guy peering down at her, she had to have looked like she'd just escaped a shallow grave.

Cindy pointed toward the Mitsubishi Galant that was blocking us in. "I need you to tow that maroon car for me."

The dude peered through a tiny sliver of open window, blinking as the rain splashed into his eyes. "I don't move cars for less than fifty bucks."

Undeterred, Cindy turned and splashed past me, heading for the Buick, throwing the door open, and digging around in her purse for what cash she had—which due to the unexpectedly high price she paid to get the keys from the front desk was…eight dollars. She slammed the door and sloshed over. "Cramer, how much cash do you have on you?"

"You sign my paychecks. You know it ain't much."

She was not in the mood for jokes. "I'll pay you back." And she put out her hand.

I pulled out my wallet and peered inside. "Looks like, uh…eleven bucks."

She curled her fingers, inviting me to put the two wet fives and crumpled one into her palm. From there she marched over and forcefully knocked on the door of the tow truck. Once again he crept his window down.

"We have nineteen dollars," Cindy said. "Please."

I don't know if she managed to beam some sort of drenched puppy dog eyes through the rain or if the guy just felt sorry for the undead girl begging him for help, but just before he shut his window, he muttered, "As soon as this storm rolls off."

Fifteen minutes later, the Buick was free and the dude with the tow truck was nineteen dollars richer. I hopped in the Buick and backed it out, drying off with a random shirt that had been covering the shifter.

"Get it back to the branch," Cindy yelled as she was running away. "I have to see if Wilkinsburg has a luxury car we can use!" And she hopped in the fully functional car we'd driven to the impound lot and sped off, leaving me behind in the mangled Buick.

Now normally the first thing you do when you pick up any car is check how much gas is in it. But after all the insanity, I'd completely forgotten. The first time I glanced at the gas gauge was right as I was pulling onto the Parkway. It was also the first time I noticed the glowy orange dot next to the E. How long had that been on? Uh-oh.

Every second was an hour. Every rotation of the tires I thought to myself, *Well, that's a few feet I won't have to walk.* Nine miles, eight miles, seven miles... Cars were shooting past me as I crept along like I was in a construction zone no one else could see. Six miles, five miles, four miles... I was constantly looking ahead for places on the shoulder where I could roll to a stop. Three miles, two miles... I pulled off the Parkway. There were now only four traffic lights between me and Day Chevy—but they were all backed up at 5:24 on a Thursday afternoon.

I sat in traffic for twenty minutes unsuccessfully trying to will the lights green, chewing on my knuckles, certain I was going to have to pull over and turn on the hazards. But to my shock and surprise, that plucky Buick had exactly enough gas to glide within fifteen feet of a parking space at the dealership.

Gary, the floppy-haired frat boy I'd worked with at Irwin, was now Cindy's assistant manager. He'd just gotten done checking in a return, so I yelled over to him. "Hey, Gary, can you help me push this car into one of these spots?"

He nodded and moseyed over. "This the one from the pound?"

"Yup. Had enough gas to make it to right here."

"Oh hey, random question," Gary asked as we slowly guided the car into an open space. "Did you take my ranch dressing? I had it up in one of the cabinets where the girls couldn't reach it. You're the only other person in the office tall enough to find it."

I laughed. "Don't mention that to Cindy."

"Why?"

"Just trust me." I chuckled. "Also, aren't you supposed to refrigerate ranch dressing?"

"Nah, it's like ketchup. You can leave it out."

I squinted. "I don't think that's true, dude."

Anyway, when I entered the office, Cindy was still a mess but a much drier mess with hair plastered to the sides of her head, little black specks of mud on her face, and a suit that was definitely going to need a good dry cleaning. But through it all, she'd persevered.

"Cramer, I sweet-talked Tay at Wilkinsburg into giving us a Lincoln Town Car," she said in a giddy voice. If she was the type of person who did victory spins in her rolly chair, she'd have done ten. "Their car prep is in the back cleaning it up. He should be just about done, but maybe you can go check on him. Help if he needs it?" She let out a satisfied breath. Despite the rain and the mud and the money, she'd pulled it off. She'd worked a miracle. Everything was...

There was a four-way stop right outside the office where the main alley running behind the dealership met the access road that came in from Route 286. I worked there four months and legitimately had to stop for another car *once*. I only mention this tiny intersection because we haven't yet reached the summit of Cindy's Terrible, Horrible, No Good, Very Bad Day.

"Thank god Wilkinsburg had that Lincoln," Cindy said, smiling as she typed into her computer. "I don't know what we would've done without—"

SCREEEEEEECH! BANG![10*]

[10*] You may think I exaggerated the timing on this for comedic purposes. If I did, it was by fractions of a second.

I turned to look out the window. In the intersection, Cindy's Lincoln Town Car had challenged a box truck. And the box truck won.

The look on Cindy's face was the same as a teenage girl who just realized the creepy phone calls were coming from inside the house. She locked eyes with me. "Cramer, please tell me that wasn't the Lincoln."

To that point in my life, I'd never broken a woman's heart. I wouldn't be able to say that anymore. "Uh, *one* of the vehicles involved wasn't the Lincoln."

Cindy gasped and kicked her chair into the filing cabinets. She hustled outside and threw her hands over her mouth. At that point, I don't know how she didn't fall to her knees, look at the sky, and scream, "Why, God, why?" Instead, she sullenly turned away and sulked back into the office. "Can you guys deal with that?" she said. "I'm going into the bathroom to cry."

Long story short, I tore off my second bumper of the day, Gary and I stayed until after eight o'clock to go pick up the Cadillac from the lawyer who'd been trapped in Ohio, and Cindy murdered Wilkinsburg's car prep, stuffed his body in the Buick, lit the whole thing on fire, and pushed it off a bridge.

Remarkably, Cindy's Terrible, Horrible, No Good, Very Bad Day wasn't the most insane thing to happen at Day Chevy that summer. I was cleaning a car when Gary parked a Toyota Camry behind me and hopped out. "Cramer, when you're done with this one, we're going to Murrysville," he said, ambling into the garage to bullshit with the mechanics. A few minutes later, I headed inside to find him leaning on a metal workbench that was scattered with tools. "Division champs. You heard it here first, boys," he said, thumping his chest and chuckling his way outside. As he walked in front of me, it was impossible not to notice a black streak on his khakis that definitely hadn't been there before.

"Dude, what's on your pants?" I asked.

"What?" he answered with alarm.

"Your pants. You got shit all over your pants."

Gary awkwardly tried to turn and look at his own butt, which he soon realized wasn't possible without the side mirror of the Toyota. What he saw in the reflection horrified him. There was a dirty black line from his inseam straight up his butt cheek. "Cramer, there's shit all over my pants!"

"That's what I just told you."

Unlike the butter bandit, the culprit was pretty easy to figure out. Blinded by his football predictions, Gary sat down on the workbench without first checking to see if it happened to be spattered with engine grease. Chagrined, he shuffled back into the garage. "Why didn't any of you jags tell me I was sitting in grease?" he squawked with his arms out like an oblivious sitcom dad. "I didn't know any better, I'd think yinz were Ravens fans!"

As Gary laughed his way through his mortification, a pudgy hillbilly appeared from one of the bays like a possum emerging from a holler. "Ya got grease on 'em slacks?" he said, shaking up an aerosol can as he walked toward Gary. "I got somethin' take 'at right off 'air for ya."

And before Gary really knew what was happening, this dude was spraying bubbly chemical foam on his pants. "Whoa, buddy, I didn't know we were this close," Gary chuckled uncomfortably.

The hillbilly handed him a rag. "Give it a minute, then wipe 'er off."

Gary followed the dude's instructions, and much to his amazement, the miracle foam worked to perfection. Minutes later, there was zero trace of the grease he'd sat in. I was just as astounded as he was. Gary's pants were clean. Totally clean.

"You're a life saver, man!" Gary yelled happily, flipping the rag onto the workbench as we exited. "I owe you a Miller Lite. Maybe two!"

We'd just pulled onto the road when the pre-cell phone walkie talkie thing all the managers carried around beeped in the cup holder. Cindy's voice echoed through the car. "Hey Gary."

"Yeah?"

"Nikki isn't back from Westinghouse yet. I'm going to need you and Cramer to take a quick detour to pick up Mrs. O'Malley. Right next to Plumline Nursery."

"On our way," he said, looking for a place to turn around.

And so we picked up Mrs. O'Malley, a nice woman in her early seventies who was renting a car to go see her sister in Altoona. She hopped in the back seat, and the always chatty Gary asked her about her grandkids and her golf game as we headed back down the hill.

"Oh, we mostly play Cloverleaf if we can," Mrs. O'Malley said. "We play from the senior tees now. But I'll tell ya, I played from the men's tees until I was fifty-five."

"The way I'm playing right now, I might have to join you on the senior tees." Gary laughed. Then suddenly his eyes jolted open. He sucked in a deep breath and began to twitch around in the driver's seat. "I, uh...never played (shift, squirm) Cloverleaf myself, but I hear (grunt, suppressed hiss) good things."

Waiting at the light to turn left onto Route 286, sweat began to bead on Gary's forehead. He started biting down on his finger as if he was in the middle of a colonoscopy.

"You okay, bud?" I asked.

He didn't actually answer. It was more of a rapid, unconvincing nod. As Mrs. O'Malley regaled us with tales about her latest round with the gals, Gary was quite obviously trying to hover above the seat as if it had suddenly become lava. When the light turned green, it looked like we were going to make it, only to have the car in front of us stop on yellow.

"Ah, come on," Gary choked, giving an anxious slap to the steering wheel.

It was like watching someone who just had an alien egg hatch inside their intestines and begin feasting.

"...within two feet of the cup! Two feet!" Mrs. O'Malley beamed.

"Yeah," Gary grunted. "Golf. Ha ha! (Deep exhale) Golf is *fun*!"

Three minutes of pure hell later, the light turned green and we eventually pulled back into Day Chevy.

I got out to open the door for Mrs. O'Malley. "Cindy will take care of you inside," I said.

"Thank you," she said before leaning down to wave at Gary. "Have a good day, Gary! Keep it in the fairway!"

He tried to say something back that came out as more of a chicken cluck than actual words. I hopped back in the passenger seat as Gary locked eyes on the front door. As soon as it closed and Mrs. O'Malley was safely inside, he popped off the seat, bumping his head on the dome light as he wildly fumbled at his belt.

"Jesus Christ, Jesus Christ, Jesus Christ," he repeated.

"Gary, what the hell is..."

And he ripped his pants down, exposing his butt like he was about to moon the parking lot. "Aaaahhhhhhhhhh."

"What the fuck are you *doing*?"

"My asshole is on fire. Oh my god," he said, worming around. "Cramer, level with me, does my ass look burned? It feels burned."

"I'm not looking at your ass."

"Cramer, please."

"I'm not checking your ass, Gary!"

He started rolling around in agony. "What the *hell* did they spray on my pants?"

It finally hit me what was happening. "Oooooohhhhh."

Since we were still parked in front of the door, he pulled his pants halfway up and awkwardly crawled over the console into the back seat. "You gotta drive. Oh Christ, it's like a firework went off up there. If Mrs. O'Malley wasn't in the car, I'd have stripped naked at that red light and run into the forest. I'm not kidding. Oh god. My asshole is poisoned, Cramer. *Poisoned!*"

That was pretty much how our drive to Murrysville went. Three miles of Gary moaning about his bum. Somewhat unbelievably, he was able to pull it together long enough to pick up the van we needed and drive back. He parked it in the wash bay and immediately tore around the corner into the garage. His incredulous screech echoed off every socket wrench.

"What the *hell* did you spray on my pants?"

I dropped the hose and sprinted in because, let's face it, I needed to know why I'd been unceremoniously exposed to Gary's naked butt. The hillbilly guy strode over with the aerosol can and handed it to Gary, who read it and nearly passed out.

"Brake cleaner?" Gary exclaimed. "You sprayed *brake cleaner* on my ass?"

The hillbilly nodded. "Got ridda 'at grease, dint it?"

Gary's hands went to the sides of his head. "I'd rather have grease on my pants than..." He was having trouble finding words. "Than..."

"A brake cleaner enema?" I interjected.

"A brake cleaner enema! Thank you, Cramer."

Gary's sarcastic tone went completely over the dude's head. "Well, you need it again, you know where to find it." And he walked back to the car he was fixing.

From then on, every time Gary got frustrated, I'd ask, "Is it worse than..."

"No," he'd answer before I'd even finished. "Not even close."

After four months at Day Chevy, I was finally off to my graduate program in counselor education two hours northeast of Pittsburgh in the ridges of central Pennsylvania. At Penn State, I had classes on statistics, counseling techniques, and a bunch of other stuff that I'd later find had almost no relevance to actually being a school counselor. Needing money to pay for the cheese sandwiches and apples I was surviving on, I once again returned to a familiar place. And honestly, looking back, I'm surprised at the complete lack of chaos emanating from Emerald's State College branch. It was mainly just nice drives through the mountains to pick up PhD candidates from the airport and changing tires for random travelers on I-80.

And that was about it. In mid-August, I scrubbed my last car[11*], and for a few years at least, things would take a more serious turn.

---

[11] * So I thought.

CHAPTER 12

Witch

O n the night before Thanksgiving in 1928, a farmer named Nelson Rehmeyer was beaten unconscious with a piece of firewood, doused with kerosene, and set ablaze in his own home. By most accounts, he was a quiet, religious man who grew potatoes in a secluded hollow in southern York County, Pennsylvania. But soon Rehmeyer's death at the hands of three men—John Blymeyer, Wilbert Hess, and John Curry—would capture the attention of the nation.

Now you may ask yourself how the murder of a simple farmer in a place so rural it's still hard to locate a century later came to briefly captivate the entire country. For the answer, we need to rewind a little over two hundred years and head up to Salem, Massachusetts. While many of us have never heard of Nelson Rehmeyer, most of us have indeed been regaled with tales of the hysteria spawned when a town went mad fearing the occult and executed nineteen souls who'd been found "guilty" of witchcraft—*in 1693*.

But this was 1928, the year of the world's first successful Trans-Pacific flight. It was the year penicillin was discovered. Hell, they'd already been playing the Rose Bowl for twelve years. All four of my grandparents were alive. And Nelson Rehmeyer was killed *for being a witch.*[12*]

[12 *] Blymeyer had recently had a run of bad luck and blamed it on a hex that Rehmeyer had supposedly cast upon him.

All of this is to say that southern York County is a place where the devil is still very real. How do I know? It's where I ended up.

I'd gotten an eye-opening introduction to school counseling during a year-long internship at Mountaintop Middle, a school in central Pennsylvania that might as well have been in eastern Kentucky. Fifteen percent of our students didn't have electricity, and 5 percent lacked running water. On my first day, a twelve-year-old girl came into the guidance office complaining that her leg hurt. When we finally convinced her to show us what was wrong, she rolled up her jeans to reveal an infected *tattoo* that her mom's boyfriend inked on her calf while drunk. We had to call Children and Youth Services.

I'd been there fifteen minutes.

Back on campus, my classmates would say things like, "The kids in the idyllic little town where I'm assigned are so cool and creative. Counseling is amazing! Kevin, are you loving it as much as I am?"

I'd answer, "Well, today I had to reach into a urinal to fish a handful of discarded pills from a lake of piss so the cops could do a toxicology report after a seventh grader stumbled into our office in the middle of an Oxycontin overdose. On the plus side, our kids aren't smart enough to use an actual toilet to get rid of the evidence, so we quickly figured out what we were dealing with. What's not to love?"

But while Mountaintop Middle forced me to drink on weekends so I could mentally escape the Appalachian trauma, it also beat the inexperience right out of me. By the time I started applying for guidance jobs, I'd already dealt with more chaos than most suburban counselors had in their first decade on the job—which put me far ahead of most other recent graduates.

Hoping to return to St. Augustine, I uploaded my resume to the St. John's County Schools website. I had visions of living the sea breeze life I'd left behind three years prior but this time with (gasp) financial stability. Much to my delight, they contacted me about an opening at Murray Middle School. So down the East Coast I went.

The principal at Murray Middle was an African American man who you could tell was stern but caring. Positive energy radiated from every square inch of him. Meanwhile the assistant principal was a gray-haired woman wearing a turquoise necklace who brimmed with excitement as she gestured to the colorful art projects and musical instruments surrounding us. I felt comfortable the moment I sat down.

Murray Middle served a part of St. Augustine that was literally on the other side of the railroad tracks from the ritzier places in town. A majority of students fell into the same socioeconomic class that I'd experienced at Mountaintop. Plus, it was a creative arts magnet school. At Penn State, I'd written my thesis on healing trauma in middle schoolers through writing and imagination. To top it all off, while at Flagler, I spent two years coaching rec league basketball for kids who lived in the exact neighborhoods the school served. I couldn't have been more perfectly aligned for any job in the country.

Whatever questions they threw my way, I had three-part responses that built on relevant statistics as well as my personal experiences. I was *on*. To this day, it's the best interview I've ever had for *anything*. I nailed it, and I knew it. As I shook their hands and prepared to head out, the principal gave me a smile.

"Kevin, you're by far the most impressive candidate we've interviewed," he said. "Thank you for coming down from Pennsylvania."

"No problem," I said, trying to stifle a grin. "I could imagine myself here very easily."

"Well," he replied, "I can't officially welcome you to Murray Middle but..."

The assistant principal smiled. "You'll be hearing from us."

"Safe travels and we hope to see you soon," the principal said.

It was a long drive home, but I didn't care. I'd done it. I'd managed to get myself back to my favorite place on earth—this time with a legitimate career. I just had to wait for official confirmation.

A week. Nothing. Two weeks. Nothing. I was starting to get nervous. I mean, I had to move and find a place to live and... Three weeks.

Still nothing. Finally, a full month later, I got a letter from the St. John's County Schools.

Dear Mr. Cramer,

Thank you for your interest in the guidance counseling position at Murray Middle School. There were many qualified candidates…

Fuuuuuuuck.

I'll always wonder what happened between the principal's handshake and the typing of that letter. Who worked there that I pissed off in college? Or more likely, whose nephew needed a job? It's one of those things you can only hope to find out in the afterlife.

"Before we guide you to the great beyond, Kevin, do you have any questions?"

"Yeah, what the hell happened at Murray Middle School? Also, what was that weird metallic disc I saw hovering above the Turnpike when I was thirteen?"

So my dream job in my dream location mysteriously evaporated. I still have no idea why. Unfortunately, you don't always get the answers. It left me scrambling. I was still jobless in the middle of July when I got an email from Stateline High School in York County, three hours east of Pittsburgh. I drove out there just to have a stilted and awkward interview with the principal that I was certain I bombed. Depression crept in. It was getting damn close to the school year, and after spending all that money to get my degree, I was still unemployed. What was I going to do, go back to cleaning rental cars?

It was a colossal shock when Stateline called to say I got the job. It may not have been my first choice, but it was a job in my field— and with a contract that included full benefits and $33,472 a year, it meant I could support myself like a real adult. I could fill up my gas tank without inversely rationing my meals to compensate. Plus, I could do totally insane things like go to the dentist and get new glasses. My last name might as well have been Vanderbilt. I got a townhouse in a giant complex of similar townhouses that, like everything else in York County, was across the street from a megachurch surrounded by cornstalks. And I began my new life as a professional educator.

The whole experience didn't begin as the stuff of nightmares. The other counselors were extremely nice in a folksy, plucked from a Midwestern novel sort of way. Albert was a jolly man with thinning gray hair and a pot belly who was in charge of all the students with last names A-G. He was the type of guy who'd give you a big smack on the back if you were close enough when he laughed. Albert was a year from retirement and mostly drank coffee and wandered around. Stacey had all the kids with last names Q-Z. She was a farm girl in her mid-thirties who had freckles and wore knitted cardigans featuring leaves and pumpkins. The guidance secretary was a woman named Deb who looked like she probably made the best cherry pie this side of the Susquehanna River. We all got along just fine. I genuinely enjoyed their company.

And though the bright spots were few and far between, it wasn't a total loss. I got put in charge of the gifted program, which allowed me to get to know and help some incredibly talented kids. I resurrected the "School to Work" pipeline, helping set up internships in nursing, automotive, and electrical for students whose future plans didn't include college. Through a network of employers, I helped at least a dozen kids land good-paying jobs right after graduation. Plus, I was hired to be the junior varsity baseball coach. I got paid an extra $2,400 to spend every dry spring afternoon hitting ground balls to fifteen-year-old baseball dorks. It was awesome.

My dad spent his entire thirty-year teaching career in one district, so I assumed that would be my path as well. Unfortunately, the universe had other plans. What followed was hands down the worst experience of my working career. All because of the egotistical mania of one man. In fact, the story of my time at Stateline comes down to a head to head battle—a battle I was always destined to lose.

The principal at Stateline was a man whose ill-fitting suits you swore hid scales. He was an upright lizard of a human being with a bad combover and an absolutely brutal need for power and control. His name was Mr. Snook, and someday when he finally dies, I will drive hours to urinate on his grave.

It started out okay. I mean, he was the administrator I interviewed with as well as the one who called to congratulate me on getting the job. But even those first encounters were peculiar. Being in a room with him, you felt like the walls were teeming with spiders. He was the human equivalent of a beat laid down by a toddler learning the drums. You just never felt comfortable. At faculty meetings, he'd constantly be making "jokes" that in reality were just massively confusing statements.

"Kids are still congregating in the halls after the bell," he'd say. "Get them inside your classrooms and ready to learn." And then he'd tip down his reading spectacles and say something like, "Don't make me call Richard Nixon." And he'd glance toward the assistant principal, who would then chuckle, which was a sign to everyone else in the room that what he'd just said was apparently comedic—which meant we all had to laugh, too. I've since realized that if you're in a job where you're forced to laugh at things that aren't funny, you need to get the fuck out immediately. Just grab your shit and run.

Anyway, my first real hint of what was to come happened about a week before the students arrived for the first day of classes. One of the sophomores assigned to me was a kid named David who had a directive known as a 504 plan. Kids with diagnosed emotional and educational needs have arrangements known as IEPs (Individual Education Plans) that address specific areas of concern for the student's overall development. Often these children are put in smaller classes designed to give them more support. IEPs are implemented after rigorous testing by professionally trained staff who give recommendations to the school as to what daily strategies would best assist the student in question. They are absolutely necessary to foster learning and development.

Five hundred four plans, on the other hand, are essentially shady black-market IEPs for kids who the professionals decided didn't qualify for special attention but have wacky parents who see it as the school's job to raise their child for them. David absolutely didn't need extra help. He was quiet but incredibly smart. In fact, he was smart enough to play as stupid as possible knowing that his divorced parents would blame any and all of his failures on the school, allowing him to coast through life playing video games. I'm not kidding, they once requested that his plan be amended to require me to search through his locker each morning, find his homework, and turn it into his teachers *for* him. It took everything I had not to ask them if they needed me to hand feed him his lunch as well. I only didn't because I wasn't 100 percent certain they'd say no.

"He's too distractible! If you let him feed himself, he'll shove Fritos in his eyes!"

The first time I met David was during a crucial meeting with his parents and Mr. Snook about the contents of David's plan. Which was... lengthy. I was responsible for something like 230 students who had last names H through P. And I'd end up spending a good 16 percent of my time dealing with this one goddamned kid. For no real reason.

Before the meeting, Albert came up to me holding his customary cup of coffee. He'd usually whack you on the back with a fair amount of jolly aggression, but this time he just put his hand on my shoulder. "In this meeting, you agree with whatever Snook says."

"Oh, okay. So if—"

"I need you to understand me," he interrupted. "Don't speak unless spoken to. If the parents ask you a question, you defer to Snook. If you're forced to speak, say as little as possible. Snook is in charge. That's just the way things operate here." And he walked off to get more coffee.

As if to reinforce Albert's warning, when I met Snook in his office before the meeting, he grabbed a folder, stood up, and said, "These people are dangerous. You leave all the talking to me."

"Yes, sir," I said nervously, following him down the hall. He burst through the door of a classroom and turned a desk around to sit in front of David's parents, who were already seated. I pulled a desk over and sat next to him. It was August, but it was *cold* in that room. Not air-conditioning cold, either. The type of cold you only feel on tours of abandoned prisons.

"This is Mr. Cramer, David's new guidance counselor," Snook said. "He'll be your contact point with the school this year."

I just nodded and waved. I didn't say hi. I wasn't supposed to speak. Hell, I wasn't certain I was allowed to wave or nod. Oh shit. I fucked up already.

Parole hearings are more cordial than that meeting was. David's parents ranted about what they wanted. Snook countered. David's parents would issue threats of legal action. Snook would tell them why their threats were ill advised. I sat there trying to be invisible.

Halfway through, David's dad tried to get all buddy-buddy with me. He turned and made eye contact. *Ah, crap.* "I want to know what Mr. Cramer thinks," he said.

"He agrees with me," Snook answered before I could speak. "Next item…"

It was the most contentious thing I'd ever been a part of. When the meeting was done, we walked back to Snook's office. "Excellent work," he said, sitting down in his throne-like rolly chair. I'd maybe said eight words the whole time—the implication being, *"You're a good little employee as long as you stay perfectly in line at all times and never express an opinion of your own."*

Which as you may have realized by now isn't really my jam.

Honestly, the first eight months of the school year went fine. I was far from perfect at my job, but I was learning. And the community seemed to like me. I got a lot of positive feedback from parents whose kid I helped through one situation or another. Along with the regular hormonal and academic stresses, there were some genuine crises as well. A former teacher committed suicide; a kid in a neighboring district who was close with a bunch of our students got killed in a domestic dispute; one of our seniors got into a serious car wreck. There were drug and alcohol interventions, evidence of abuse, and the new ability for kids to bully each other online through social media. I did my best to help as many students as possible while still adhering to the strict guidelines imposed by Mr. Snook. It was a stressful tightrope.

Looking back, there was definitely foreshadowing as to what was on the horizon. One morning I was counseling a kid whose grandmother had passed away the night before when Snook came in the door, interrupted the session, and ordered the kid back to class.

"He should be studying, not down here rambling," Snook commanded.

"Sir," I said, trying to process such callousness, "he's really sad about his grandma, and I'm trying to get him to a place where he can manage his grief so..."

Snook glared at me. I'd dared to question him. "I don't like how many students keep coming down here to dilly dally. Are we clear?"

I sighed and nodded. And sent the kid back to *homeroom*.

But none of that was what ultimately sunk me. The incident that started my descent into hell was the most innocuous moment possible. The day before PSSA testing started, we had a meeting in the auditorium with all the sophomores. The objective was to somehow pump the kids up about spending the next three days in the library using a number two pencil to fill in bubbles on a standardized test that had literally no bearing on their future. Me, Albert, Stacey, and Mr. Snook were standing at the front of the stage getting ready to engage all of the gathered students when the afternoon announcements came on. In the auditorium, they were a bit more garbled than in a regular classroom, especially with the din of all the kids in there.

Earlier in the day, I'd sent a note to the main office that baseball practice was cancelled since the field was soaked from overnight rains. The afternoon announcements were typically how my players found out. But over the auditorium intercom, it sounded like, "Practice canc *(static)* for *(static)* noon *(static)* as follows. Field hock *(static)* varsity base *(static)* V base *(static)* oftball, and BUZZZZZZZZZZ..."

When the announcements were done, one of my players in the third row raised his hand. "Coach, I didn't hear. Is practice cancelled?"

I stepped forward to answer him. "Yeah, the field is still wet, so just be ready for the game at Hanover tomorrow."

When I turned around, Mr. Snook was at the podium behind me ready to speak. He sneered at me. I contritely raised my hand and filed back in line with the other counselors. What I didn't realize was that in Snook's mind, I'd just taken a giant dump on his shoes. After we delivered our pep talk and all the sophomores filed out, Snook curled his bony-ass finger in my direction.

"Where's my apology?" he demanded.

I cracked a brief smile, assuming it was one of his weird jokes. It wasn't.

"Do you think interrupting me in front of the entire auditorium is funny?" he scoffed.

"Oh," I said, now aware he was serious. "One of my players asked if practice was cancelled. I honestly didn't know you'd moved to the podium. Yeah, sorry about that."

"I shouldn't have to demand an apology," he growled. "Your response should've been immediate. For everyone to hear."

"I...didn't realize it was such a big deal, sir."

"A first-year teacher cutting off the principal in front of an entire auditorium doesn't seem like a big deal to you?" he snapped.

I didn't know how to react. "Again, sorry," I replied without the cowering he apparently desired.

I can't say for sure that's why everything spiraled out of control, but after that incident, there was a stunning, abrupt, and disorienting change in how I was treated by the administration—like a switch had been flipped. And the lights definitely went from on to off. But I didn't fully comprehend what was happening until a few weeks later.

Sometime in April, one of my students got caught drinking. She was in a clique of goth kids who sometimes came in to chat about music and life during study halls. For me, it was a good way to keep tabs on the collective mood of the spooky vampire kids who were mostly ostracized by the faithful Christian teens they shared the hallways with. In high school, I'd been a trashy metalhead myself, so they felt more at ease talking to me than, say, Albert or Stacey, who I'm sure would've stared at them in stupefied horror as soon as they opened their mouths.

Anyway, because she'd been busted for underage drinking, this girl was mandated to have three sessions with a counselor from the York County Intermediate Unit. The counselor from the IU was a short, chunky woman with frizzy black hair who was an absolute affront to the profession. She'd burst into our office and expect everything to screech to a halt as if she was the superintendent and not some rando from an outside agency. Before she took the IU job, I'm pretty sure she travelled the country trying to scam bookstores out of money by smearing butter on her pants. Although truthfully, we had an okay professional relationship until she served as the catalyst for my demise.

"Kevin, I need your help with Sarah," she said, entering my office in a huff after her counseling session. "She says she talks to you a lot."

"How can I help?"

"She told me she practices *Wicca*?"

I nodded. "Yeah, that makes sense. Not totally surprising."

"What is this Wicca? Is it something you know about?"

Unfortunately for me, via a girl I'd dated at Penn State, I could produce a wealth of information on the subject off the top of my head. "It really depends on how Sarah's using it," I answered. "In actual practice, it's an earth-based religion that's mostly about aligning your spirit and connecting with nature. But it's really misunderstood. A lot of kids will use it in a darker way, trying to cast spells, summon demons, stuff like that. Honestly, they mainly do it to seem scary so other kids will think twice about picking on them."

The lady's jaw dropped. She desperately clutched the cross pendant she wore around her neck. "Well, I'm a Christian, so I wouldn't know anything about it." From there, she asked me a couple more questions, which I answered without reservation, hoping she'd use the information to, I don't know, help Sarah deal with her alcohol situation, which my dumb ass assumed was the point of the whole thing. Until I got called into Snook's office after dismissal. Going in there, I had zero idea why he wanted to meet with me, so I assumed it had something to do with testing or scheduling. It didn't.

I knocked and entered. Snook glared at me and gestured to the seat in front of him. "Sit down," he grumbled. A billion guesses and I couldn't have predicted what came out of his mouth next. "What's this about you doing spells in the woods with the kids?"

"Uh...*what*?"

"I know all about it," he snapped. "The woman from the IU was very upset. She said you're teaching them to do Satanic rituals. She marched down here and told me right away after you admitted it to her."

"That's not what I said to her at all. Not even kind of."

"You're on probation," Snook asserted. "It would be best if you resigned at the end of the year. I will not have that type of person on my staff."

"Wait," I responded. "You're trying to fire me because you think I'm a *witch*?"

Snook pointed toward the door. "You're dismissed."

And you thought I brought up the York County Hex Murder of 1928 for no damn reason.

I didn't know what to do. Was this going to end my career? Was I going to owe tens of thousands of dollars in student loans to obtain a degree I'd no longer be able to use due to one man's vindictive, buffoonish pettiness? Truthfully, I should've just resigned and told them all to screw off. But I also knew I hadn't actually done anything wrong and thus thought the universe would eventually set things right. You can't be punished for things you didn't do, can you? Especially when the case is built upon a totally unproven claim that you're dabbling in fucking witchcraft. What was next?

"The janitor told us that you're helping the Martians build a nuke. I know all about it."

Unfortunately for the administration, they had to have a certain number of consecutive poor performance reviews in order to terminate me with cause. And every review to that point had been supremely positive. I decided I'd come back the next year and do such a good job that there'd be no way they could fire me. At twenty-six, I still believed there was justice in the world, so instead of simply washing my hands of the whole situation, I came back determined to prove myself. I'd rise above it all and succeed anyway.

And that's how I found out how the world *really* operates.

The next year I was actually better at my job because I'd gotten more comfortable with my role. For the first nine weeks, I put my head down and plugged along, doing everything I could to show them I was a vital piece of the school community. When my first review came up, I felt great going into it. I knew they didn't have a thing to complain about, and even if Snook didn't particularly like me, in order to give me poor marks, they'd have to just make shit up—which I was pretty certain they weren't allowed to do.

I walked into the office of the assistant principal, a tiny man in a giant neck brace named Mr. Dodson. In over a year, I'd never had a single problem with him—until he stiffly reached over his desk to hand me my review.

"Let's cut to the chase," Dodson said. "You're doing an incredibly poor job. On a scale of one to five, you don't have more than a two in any category. Professionalism, organization, preparation, it's all unsatisfactory."

I almost fell out of my chair. Apparently they *were* allowed to just make shit up. "Where are you getting this information?" I asked. "You haven't observed me all year. How are you reviewing my performance when we've barely interacted?"

"I'm seeing enough," he answered. "And I'm talking to people."

"Who are you talking to?"

"That's not for you to know."

I leaned forward. "So you're telling me that all of my reviews last year were fours and fives, then suddenly, out of nowhere I quit having any idea what I was doing?"

He rocked back in his chair, knowing the next thing out of his mouth was going to strip him of all credibility. "Yes."

No wonder he wore a goddamned neck brace everywhere. Doctors opened him up to check for a spine and didn't find one.

I marched out of there and went straight to our union rep, a middle-aged home economics teacher who was sympathetic to my plight but ultimately didn't help at all. She set me up with the district's union lawyer who met with me over lunch one day. I told him the whole story, about how I was essentially being run out of town because I'd once accidentally interrupted the fool in charge—a fool who seemed to be losing his grip on reality.

Surely the lawyer understood my plight and knew exactly how to handle it. Assuredly the law was on my side here. And he'd know just what cases to site and how to bring the hammer down. "This mirrors *Gonzales vs. Whipplecorp*, 1972," he'd say. "Our case is ironclad."

Instead what I got was, "Maybe you should wear a tie."

This stooge was my last line of defense? I was screwed, and now I knew it.

For my second review, Mr. Dodson was out on medical leave, so the other assistant principal Mr. Sandal got assigned to it. He was a younger guy who to that point I'd gotten along with incredibly well. We even played basketball together after school every Tuesday afternoon. While far from a friend, I definitely considered him an ally. And then he looked me dead in the eye and told me what a poor job I was doing.

I held eye contact with him. "Connor, you know this is crap."

He shrugged his shoulders and pointed at the paper. "You need to sign the bottom."

"I'm not signing this."

"That's a bad idea," he responded. "It could be taken as insubordination."

"What's it matter?" I grunted as I stood up. "You guys are running me out of town whether I sign it or not."

He gestured for me to sit down. "This meeting isn't over."

"Yeah, it is," I said, turning and heading out the door.

I walked into the hallway knowing I was absolutely, truly alone. No one was going to step up to help. Until Stateline, I always thought if I worked hard and did the right things, I'd eventually be rewarded. That vision of the world was now annihilated. Now obviously, many people in this world have had their lives shaped by far worse situations than mine. But in a lot of ways, Mr. Snook and Stateline High School stole my sense of self. It would take me a long, long time to get it back.

The meeting to decide my ultimate fate was held at the superintendent's office. Dr. McSorley was a tall, droopy, and mercifully reasonable man. He sat between Snook and I, attempting to negotiate a truce between what he suspected was a good employee and a curmudgeon who was slowly going mad.

I'd come prepared. I spent the morning doing nothing but printing out positive emails I'd received from parents. It was an impressive stack of papers. Reading them narrowed my eyes. I'd almost started believing the crap the administration was spewing—that I wasn't particularly competent at my job. But right there in my hands was confirmation that I was being gaslit.

Snook slithered into his chair and handed Dr. McSorley my performance reviews. "Here are his latest evaluations. I recommend termination at the end of the semester if he doesn't willingly resign."

In response, I handed Dr. McSorley my bundle of emails. "This stack of papers contains 105 separate communications from the parents of seventy-seven different students, all of which say some version of 'thank you for what you've done for my child.' The sources vary from my regular H through P students, to my gifted students, my school to work students, and my baseball players. I highlighted the relevant passages for your convenience."

Snook obviously didn't expect me to have evidence on my side—especially hard evidence that was going to contradict his story, expose his scheme, and make him look like an asshole. He exploded. "You don't work for the parents! You work for *me!*"

"I think the taxpayers of this community would disagree."

I didn't think. I just said it. If I'd have planned it out, I'd have stuttered. But damn, that was the most satisfying verbal bitch slap I've ever given anyone. It unhinged him. If he could've gotten away with lunging over the table and putting his hands around my throat, he would've.

"You are untenured staff! Where do you get the nerve?" he erupted, thrusting his finger toward me. It was pure insanity. The guy wasn't even trying to hide his psychopathy right in front of his own boss.

Dr. McSorley's forehead wrinkled. He turned to me. "It says here that you've been doing Satanic rituals with the students? What is, um... where is this coming from?"

I sighed. "The lady from the Intermediate Unit asked me a question about one of my students, didn't understand my answer, and made up a bunch of nonsense."

He squinted. "So no spells?"

"Look," I answered, "if I really was a witch, Snook would've been dead months ago."

Now obviously, that was what I *wanted* to say, not what I actually said. In reality, I just replied, "No. Of course not," and McSorley accepted it and moved on. Thus ended my time in the realm of sorcery.

When the meeting was over, Dr. McSorley dismissed Snook, who slammed his files on the table, tried to stare me down, and grumbled away. I watched as McSorley briefly thumbed through the emails I'd printed out, obviously realizing that I was being bulldozed.

"Kevin," he said, leaning forward and choosing his words carefully. "I am in a difficult position here. These positive emails are more indicative of what I've heard about your performance from the greater school community. I have only heard negative things from one source." He rubbed the bridge of his nose. "But that source is your principal, and due to variables that are in many ways beyond my control..." he stopped. "You could appeal this, but I assume you don't want to continue to work in that type of environment."

"That's a correct assumption."

It was clear he did not want a fight. Also, it was obvious that he knew with competent representation (i.e. not the local union lawyer), I probably had a case if I wanted to pursue it. "What I can offer you is my personal recommendation for any job you apply to in any other district," he said. "In state, out of state, I will keep Snook away from the process. You don't have to worry about that."

I audibly exhaled.

"I don't want this to ruin your career," he said. "I believe you're a good counselor. Unfortunately for us, you need to be a good counselor somewhere else."

I nodded and asked him the proper way to type up and deliver my resignation letter. He sent me to the human resources department to square away my retirement. And that was that. A few weeks later, the school board approved my resignation. I worked my final day, said goodbye to nobody, got in my car, drove off, and never looked back. Not even when I put up my middle finger.

I don't have any specifics on the matter, but by the end of the following year, Snook was no longer the principal of Stateline High School. I can only hope that I played a small role in his downfall. And I shouldn't say more.

CHAPTER 13

Redemption

More often than not in my career, I've been the victim of absolutely wretched timing. But occasionally, events align that rupture my skepticism and genuinely cause me to wonder if a coincidence is part of some greater cosmic plan. As January of 2005 rolled around, I returned to Stateline from Christmas break knowing that I'd be jobless by the end of the month. But I couldn't go back to Pittsburgh because the lease on my apartment continued through mid-August. I was trapped in a place I didn't want to be with two months of financial cushion at best. For weeks I'd lie awake at night, staring at the ceiling, wondering how the hell I was going to make any of it work.

Then one day as I was sitting in my office at Stateline, I got an email from the girl I was dating at the time. She was an unassumingly devious ultimate player named Julie who I'd met when we were both hammered on the beach in New Jersey that summer. Julie was in her final semester before graduating with a degree in British Literature from Gettysburg College over in Adams County and was acutely aware of my current stress level—which was why the title of her email was…

HAVE YOU SEEN THIS?!!!!!!!!!!!!!!!!!

It was a link to the open positions in the Central Adams School District. According to the website, they needed two janitors, a lunch cashier, and—*wait, a guidance counselor at the middle school?* There was no way the school six blocks from my girlfriend's apartment needed a counselor the Monday after my final Friday at Stateline. Things don't work out like that. Usually it's, "Here's a great opportunity but it's on an onion farm in Belarus and you need to sacrifice a finger." I had to jump on this immediately. I stayed after school for an hour to fill out the online application, using Stateline's resources to help get me the hell out of Stateline. When I was done, I hit send, and the next three days can be summed up with the thought, *Hmmm, I haven't opened my email in at least thirty seconds. I better check just in case.*

Finally, after seventy-two hours of nervous fretting, I returned from bus duty to find an email asking if I was available to interview at Buford Middle School at one o'clock the next Tuesday.

I felt like answering, "If you need me to interview on Jupiter in fifteen minutes, I'll be there." Instead, I just confirmed. And began to breathe again.

That Tuesday morning, I walked into Stateline in a full suit, alerting everyone as to why I'd used a half personal day for the afternoon. Upon seeing me wearing a tie, the administration immediately apologized, begged me to stay, and offered me a significant raise.

"Alas, your overture comes too late," I replied. "Good day."

Anyway, that afternoon, I drove through a snow squall, greeted the office staff at Buford Middle, and waited for the principal to wrap up a meeting. The only thing I was nervous about was answering the inevitable inquiry about why I was available. I was pretty sure that nobody else applying for the job at that moment had my experience, so I was already ahead of the pack. But I knew I could easily blow this chance if I didn't correctly navigate that flytrap of a question.

The principal at Buford looked like a sergeant who'd just walked in from barking at new army recruits up at Fort Indiantown Gap. He'd have also needed a step stool to look me in the eye. His name was Mr. Lippert, and he was basically a jacked, middle-aged elf. You'd have nearly understood if he became a power-obsessed bully like Snook in order to compensate. But he wasn't. As we began talking, he seemed strangely...competent.

"Well," Mr. Lippert said, leaning forward. "Our sixth-grade counselor is taking an unexpected medical sabbatical for the rest of the year. Which leaves us in a bit of a bind. Looking at your resume here, it seems your experience is at the high school level. Sixth grade would be a much different world."

"To be honest, sir, that's what excited me," I answered. "I interned at a middle school, and it was a much better fit than the high school I'm at currently."

He tapped my resume on his desk. "Counselors with your experience aren't typically available at this point in the year. What's the real story?"

Oh, that's what an arrythmia feels like.

I wanted to reply with spooky sounds and say, "Prepare yourself for a frightful tale of witchcraft and betrayal," but instead I just ninjaed around the question. "If you talk to my superintendent, he'll tell you the same thing. Just not a good fit," I answered, desperately hoping I didn't have to elaborate. Any more probing and I'd have probably just caved and said, "Look, man, my principal is a dickhead. I don't know what else to tell you."

He folded his hands. "I talked to Dr. McSorley in preparation for this meeting, and that's exactly what he relayed to me. He said you're an excellent counselor, but you'd probably be better in a middle school setting." Mr. Lippert sized me up across the desk as if he knew I was holding something back but also realized he had no other options and less than two weeks until he was one faculty member short. "You realize this is only a temporary position," he said. "Just until the end of the year."

"Yes."

Mr. Lippert tapped on his desk. "We'll get a contract drawn up and get it to you. Welcome to Buford Middle School."

It took everything I had not to dance into the parking lot. Scoring another job meant I could continue to eat prepackaged meals in my sparsely furnished apartment instead of, I don't know, trying to make a go of it in the woods. And so at the end of January, I left Stateline one Friday afternoon and showed up at Buford on Monday morning. I thought I'd take the first week to get acclimated to my new surroundings—new policies, new students, new colleagues. I'd ease into it. Which I did on Monday. Then on Tuesday a drunk driver crossed the center line and crashed head-on into one of our school buses. None of the kids were injured, but it did mean that a bunch of them saw a dead woman on their way to school. And away we go…

At Buford, teachers were grouped in teams that met once a week to discuss classroom strategies and how to best support their students. In an attempt to nip minor problems before they became major disruptions, they actually encouraged kids to visit my office and scheduled times for them to do so. The administration supported their efforts. It had to be a mirage. I kept waiting for reality to kick in. But as the weeks went on, they kept meeting and kept caring and kept laughing. After my time at Stateline, it seemed flat-out bizarre.

What really helped was that just after I arrived, Buford got a new assistant principal. Mr. O'Connell was a skinny, balding man with glasses and a soothing Fred Rogers voice. Having arrived at more or less the same time, we formed an immediate bond. His philosophy was to look beyond a student's offense in an attempt to pinpoint the root cause of the behavior instead of simply doling out punishment. After Stateline, however, I wasn't in a trusting mood. I was certain that it was only a matter of time before he showed his real face.

Then Tommy happened.

Tommy was a rambunctious kid with spiky hair who loved dirt bikes. When he was in a good mood, the secretaries would call him a sweetheart, and it was impossible to tell why he was assigned to the special education classroom. Then something would inevitably set off his hair-trigger temper, and he'd absolutely lose his shit. If he didn't understand the directions on his math worksheet, he'd get so frustrated he'd toss his shoe across the room, start eating his paper, and run around jumping on other kids' desks like an insane goblin. Then when the tantrum was over, he'd crawl under the computer desk and tangle himself in the wires so nobody could get to him. Which meant I'd get a call from Miss Tipton.

Miss Tipton was the sixth-grade special education teacher. She was a distractingly attractive marathon runner, and because of Tommy, we might as well have been married forty hours a week.

Seeing the extension on my phone, I'd answer. "Hey, Katie. Where's he at?"

"We just started a lesson on pluralization, and he didn't understand, so somehow it meant he needed to wedge himself behind the filing cabinet," she'd say with an audible sigh. "And he refuses to come out. Hold on. Eddie, leave him alone! Do your worksheet!"

"I'll be up," I'd say, rushing out of the guidance annex.

I'd get in there to find Tommy wedged in a crevasse that champion spelunkers would've considered off-limits.

"Hey, buddy, what happened?" I'd ask.

Tommy's mouth would be too smushed against the cinderblocks to annunciate properly. "Wee me awone!"

I'd sit there for a half hour trying to convince him that if he came out, he'd be able to take a full breath, which was somehow never the cookie I thought it'd be. Eventually we'd convince him to reemerge, only to have the same thing happen again a few days later. Katie and I had multiple meetings with Tommy's parents and Mr. O'Connell as we desperately tried to combat a problem that was rapidly getting out of hand. We moved the filing cabinet three times, making it nearly impossible to get behind, and still the little spider managed to get back there—until one day when Mr. O'Connell saw me in the hallway as I hustled toward the special education classroom.

"Do we have an emergency?" he asked, beginning to walk with me.

"One guess." I laughed.

He shook his head. "We're stopping this today." When we arrived, Katie was trying to teach a massively preoccupied class who knew one of their peers was jammed in a space that an octopus would've had trouble reaching. "Tommy, this is Mister O'Connell," he shouted. "Your father said if you do this again, we have his permission to remove you physically. Now I don't want to do that, so why don't you just come on out?"

"Noooooo!" Tommy shrieked.

Mr. O'Connell nodded to me. "If you could pull the cabinet out from the wall."

What followed was like trying to get a cornered raccoon out of your garage. Tommy thrashed around, snarling and shouting, banging on everything, until Mr. O'Connell managed to grab him by the shirt and yank him into the open.

"Mr. Cramer, if you could secure his feet," he said in a voice as calm as a beach umbrella despite the wiggling, hissing kid desperately trying to squirm out of his grasp.

As instructed, I grabbed Tommy's ankles. Together we hoisted him up and walked him out of the classroom like battlefield medics. Outside, one of the sixth-grade classes was lined up in the hallway waiting to head down to the art room. Seeing their counselor and assistant principal carrying a human wolverine brought all of their conversations to an abrupt halt.

If my hands were free, I'd have waved. "You guys headed to art class?"

Tommy kicked me in the stomach. "LET GO OF ME, YOU ASSHOLES!"

"Yeah," answered the stunned kids in line.

I nodded. "Making anything cool?"

"I'm gonna punch EVERYBODY!" Tommy shrieked.

"We're doing, um...nature collages."

"Sounds awesome. Can't wait to see them."

"Let me fuckin' GOOOOOOOO!"

"All right. Have fun," I said, smiling. "Be good for Mrs. Logan."

On our way into my office, Tommy grabbed the doorframe, refusing to let go—screaming like we were taking him to the guillotine.

Finally, after some maneuvering, sweat, and leverage, we got the little brawler back to my office where he promptly scrambled under my desk.

Mr. O'Connell took off his glasses and rubbed the bridge of his nose. "I was actually on my way to a meeting when I ran into you. Should be about twenty minutes. Maybe thirty."

"No worries," I said. "We'll get it figured out."

"His father said to call him if it happened again."

"Will do," I answered.

"NOOOOOOO!" Tommy yelped. "Don't call my dad! I won't be able to ride my dirt bike this weekend! I'll be in so much trouble! Don't call my dad!"

Tommy's father was a no-nonsense truck driver whose voice through the speakerphone conveyed the frustration of a man who wished he could just ship his kid off to work in a coal mine. When he showed up a half hour later, Tommy and I met him in Mr. O'Connell's office where it was made very clear that the next step was a move to off-site alternative education. As Mr. O'Connell spoke, the mood in the room was heavy with Tommy's dad grinding his palms together and Tommy staring directly at the floor. But unbeknownst to them, Tommy and I had a little surprise. I'm not naïve enough to overlook the fact that it was most likely to help mitigate his punishment, but while we were waiting in my office for his dad to arrive, Tommy began opening up. Consequently, we ended up with a few straightforward strategies to deal with his frustration before it went volcanic. After the insanity of the past few weeks, having a blueprint was a giant win. Once Tommy and his father left, Mr. O'Connell and I sat there in his office trying to catch our breath like two hockey players that had been trapped in the defensive zone for minutes on end.

Mr. O'Connell leaned back in his chair. "You said Tommy helped you come up with that plan? You got him out from under the desk and talking rationally?"

"It took a while, but yeah," I said. "He needs to know exactly what our expectations are and what specific consequences will follow if he fails to meet those expectations. Who knows if it'll work in the real world, but at least he understands we care, and that's the biggest part."

Mr. O'Connell rolled his chair forward and leaned his elbows on his desk. I'll never forget what he said next. "You know, you're very good at your job."

After all I'd been through in the past few months, those eight words meant everything. They meant I wasn't crazy. They meant I really did get bulldozed at Stateline. It was vindication. Not only did he give me the freedom to do my job the best way I knew how, he followed it up with support, thanks, and respect.

I'd have run through plate glass for that man.

Anyway, the first thing I did when I got back to the guidance suite was head to the bathroom a few steps from my office. I shut the door, thankful to have a minute to myself. After I flushed, I headed to the sink to wash my hands, amazed at how much of a breakthrough we'd had with Tommy. He was going to be all right. We'd probably have some flare-ups the rest of the year, but now that we had comprehensive strategies to help him with...

In order to get him out from under my desk, Tommy and I struck a deal. He could use the guidance bathroom, but when he returned, he had to sit in a chair and talk to me. As I glanced at the mirror above the sink, something caught my eye. Crammed in the bottom corner was a message written in soap suds by someone who was obviously between four and five feet tall.

Fuckyo

u Ass

holes!

I just blinked, dried my hands and laughed my way across the hall. I was in my office giggling when Katie knocked on the door.

"How'd that go?" she asked. "How long did it take to calm him down?"

"You have to see something," I said, leaping out of my seat. I hopped the three steps to the bathroom, threw open the door, and flicked on the light.

She made a skeptical face as if anticipating seeing something gross in the toilet. "I don't know if I—"

"Yes, you do," I interrupted. "Look at the mirror."

Her hand went to her forehead immediately. "Oh my god, Tommy. Really? I'm sorry." She put her hand on my shoulder. "You spend so much of your time with my kids. I feel like I'm doing a terrible job. It's just this group—no matter what I do they're just…"

"Shut up." I laughed. "Look how he pluralized assholes."

Her eyes lit up. I swear her ponytail bounced around like it was attached to a happy puppy. "He pluralized assholes right! And used correct punctuation!"

"And you think you're doing a terrible job." I put my hand up for a high five. We smacked palms, and she skipped into my office to go over the plan that Tommy and I had devised. And that's teaching in a nutshell.

The coolest and most exhausting thing I got to experience while at Buford was a program where the sixth graders all spent a week of school at an outdoor camp next to the Appalachian Trail. Half the students participated one week and half the next. The good part was that my office was a cabin in the woods. I was surrounded by fresh air, trees, and birds instead of cinderblocks covered in encouraging posters. In exchange for the peaceful surroundings, however, I ended up on duty 106 straight hours in back-to-back weeks.

Homesickness was a huge deal. All of the kids were assigned to cabins run by high school seniors from the leadership council. Anything the seniors couldn't mediate on their own they brought to me. Most things were minor disputes resulting from kids who couldn't get away from each other, but there were a few students who'd never spent a night away from their family and subsequently freaked out. I had to sit with one girl named Chloe for almost two hours the first Monday as she begged me to call her mom to come get her.

"Can you get through tonight?" I asked. "Just one night?"

"I don't think so," she said.

"Okay, let's try this. Can you make it to dinner? Oooh, and there's a cool concert after dinner. It's a steel drum band. Everyone will be dancing and having fun. I don't want you to miss that. Do you think you can get through that?"

"Maybe."

"Okay, that's our plan. All you have to do is make it until then. Cool?"

She nodded. "Okay."

And then I hustled around camp meeting with her senior counselors and a couple of the girls in her cabin. I gave them a secret mission to help Chloe stay. And truthfully, after the concert, it seemed like they'd accomplished the goal. We handed out late-night snacks, and Chloe followed her roommates back to their bunk. All of this meant the day was finally over and the teachers could retire to the faculty cabin where one of the math teachers had hidden a case of Coors Light up in the rafters. After running around all evening and not eating a ton, the two beers I consumed in quick succession gave me a slight, comfortable buzz.

Just before midnight, we were all about ready to turn in when there was a quiet knock on the front door. We froze.

"Shit," said Mr. Ruderman, the teacher who'd brought the beer. "It might be one of the high school kids. Hide the cans." For a moment, we resided in the upside down as a bunch of teachers ranging in age from their mid-twenties to early sixties scrambled to hide alcohol from what we assumed was a teenager.

Mr. Ruderman walked over to open the cabin door. Luckily, it was just the school nurse. "Is Mr. Cramer here?" she asked.

Oh no.

"Oh, hey, Pam," I said, trying not to wobble as I stood. "What, uh… what's up?"

"Chloe is in my office. She said she really needs to talk to you."

"Okay," I said. "Give me a minute to, uh… I should brush my teeth."

A minute later, I found myself wandering down the gravel path between the cabin and the old farmhouse where the nurse was stationed, desperately trying to sober myself up in those fifty yards. I entered to see Chloe with tears in her eyes next to her senior counselor.

"I can't do it," Chloe said, weeping into her hands. "I want to go home."

I nodded with compassion. "It's weird not sleeping in your own bed, huh?"

"Yes," she replied. "I don't like it, and I want to go home."

"Well, what's your home phone number?" I asked. "Are you sure you can't do it? Just imagine how proud of yourself you'll be on Friday."

"I'm sure."

"Okay," I said. "You know what you can handle. That's fine." She told me her phone number. The nurse gave me an outside line, and I dialed. What I didn't tell Chloe was that I actually dialed my own number and got my answering machine.

"Oh, man," I said after a few rings. "No answer. They must be asleep."

"Can you try again?"

"I guess so. But let's think about this. It's almost midnight. And it's going to take your parents at least an hour to get here. And then another hour to get back. So that puts you home after 2:00 a.m. When do they have to get up for work?"

"When I get up for school."

"What is that? Seven a.m.? Man, it doesn't sound like they'd be happy about that."

Chloe sunk in her seat, knowing there were no good options. "No."

"Well, I don't want you to get in trouble," I said. "So I guess what we need to do is devise a plan to make sure your parents don't get mad at you. But what could we do?"

"I could…stay the night."

"Now that's an interesting idea," I said with a smile. "I bet you could do it. Let's try that. That's a good plan."

I put my fist out. She gave it a reluctant bump, and her counselor escorted her back to her bunk. And I wandered back to the teacher's cabin having successfully counseled a student while kinda drunk. One beer a night from now on.

I couldn't contain my excitement when I saw Chloe at breakfast the next morning. "Chloe, you did it! I knew you could!" And I skipped and jumped around like I was celebrating a game-winning goal. The girls in her cabin all gave her supportive hugs. And while Tuesday was still a struggle and I thought I was *actually* going to have to call her parents, at dinner she approached me and said, "Mr. Cramer, I think I'm going to stay again tonight." By Wednesday, she was running around smiling with her new friends and having the time of her life. On Friday when we were about to leave, she came up and gave me a huge fist bump that was nowhere near as reluctant as the one in the nurse's cottage Monday night.

"Thank you," she said with the type of sincerity you don't expect from a sixth grader. "I had such a great time." And she scampered off to the bus. As a teacher in a world that tries to squeeze every last ounce of energy from your body and mind, it's the little wins that keep you from walking out the door and never coming back. That was definitely one of them.

I felt bad for the kids in the second week because it rained most of the time—which definitely made the astronomy lesson kind of lame. "Well, if you could see through this cloud bank, Cassiopeia would be right about here." In the end, it was a lot of work and not much sleep, but it definitely broke up the monotony of the semester. Plus, the science teacher and I spent late afternoons fishing for brook trout in a clear mountain stream. There are worse ways to earn money.

But if you truly want to know what being a middle school guidance counselor is about, nothing encapsulates the heaviness and humor of the position like one afternoon the week following our return from the mountains. Just before lunch, a girl showed up at my door. I'd just recently gotten to know her because she was a big part in helping Chloe get through camp. The girl's body language made it clear that something was troubling her. Something big.

To respect her privacy, I won't detail much, but she sat down and revealed that she'd been sexually abused the previous summer by a community member the family had trusted. For a counselor, this is a nightmare scenario. Other than a student dying, there's not much else where you're so needed yet feel so helpless. I had to call her mom, knowing full well that I was about to crush her with the news. It's still the hardest phone call I've ever had to make. The second hardest was to the police. What followed were three hours of soul-draining revelations as she described the abuse to the policeman and to her mother. There were tears and strength and darkness and light as she genuinely seemed to have released a ten-month burden by revealing what happened. I was amazed at her bravery. It was incredible that a sixth grader had amassed that amount of resilience.

When the process had wrapped and the police had left and her mother had taken her home, I was tapped. I hadn't eaten lunch. Time had skipped forward. I had almost no strength left to get through the last half hour of the day, desperately hoping I could just shut the door and eat my sandwich while messing around on the internet. I staggered out of my office to ask our guidance secretary if there was anything I needed to catch up on before I disappeared to realign my brain. Having seen the mom, and the cops, and my haggard face, she knew I needed a break. But there was also a kid waiting patiently to see me.

"Robbie wants to talk to you, Mr. Cramer," she said. "I told him you had a lot going on, but he says it's very important and can't wait until tomorrow."

I sighed. I couldn't deal with another crisis. Not now. I was beyond empty. But this was my job. This was what I'd signed up for.

"C'mon back, Robbie," I said.

Robbie was a redhead with freckles and a big cowlick who was always in trouble but never for being a jerk—just for being a curious little dude with a motor that never stopped. But this time he looked forlorn. It seemed serious, like I was about to be presented with another emergency that would drain what little energy I had left, causing everyone to wonder where I'd gone and what that pile of ash was doing in my chair.

"Hey, buddy," I said. "What's going on?"

Robbie took a deep breath. Here it was—the next loadbearing, soul-crushing bit of proof that the world is pure evil. I readied myself.

"Tyler said I farted, but I didn't fart."

It took everything I had to suppress the laughter that raced up my throat. Now to that kid at that particular moment, being framed for someone else's butt song was the most important thing on the planet. But for me, the hilariously sixth-grade triviality was a massive relief. And the dichotomy of the situations always struck me as a perfect representation of the job.

"Okay, buddy. We'll deal with it."

Over those five months, Buford Middle School felt more like home than any place I'd ever worked. I loved the teachers, my fellow counselors, the office staff, and most amazingly the administration. I went to my students' Little League games and church plays, developed an afterschool ultimate frisbee program, and overall felt like a vital part of the school and the community. Unfortunately, I was only a substitute. Those five months were all I was allotted. In June, I went out for my last bus duty, did my final fist bumps, and the kids went home for the summer.

My final day was the following Monday, an administrative half day for teachers to tie up loose ends from the year and decompress without the kids in the building. We had one last faculty meeting where Mr. Lippert presented me with a Central Adams umbrella, which is apparently what you get for five months of service. But truthfully the best present they gave me was the caring atmosphere they created and a reaffirmation of my faith in other humans. No material object could possibly compete with that. I shook hands with Mr. Lippert and Mr. O'Connell, thanked them for everything, got in my car, and headed out.

The story doesn't quite end there, however. The eighth-grade history teacher, a burly guy named Mr. Calloway, was throwing an end-of-the-year party for the faculty at his house a few miles out of town. The teachers themselves had all left at lunch time to head out there, but I had to stick around to do some paperwork—which meant I arrived at the party three hours late. I figured I'd go in, have a drink or two, say my goodbyes, and be back home before dark. I was wildly mistaken.

I pulled up expecting to see people milling about, casually eating burgers and discussing politics or sports, the kind of small talk you'd hear in the faculty room at lunch. But I will never forget what I witnessed the minute I opened the front door. The seventh-grade teachers were crammed into the kitchen with a city of alcohol bottles on the table in front of them. They'd had an awful year, as it was pretty universally agreed that the seventh-grade class was Buford's most horrid collection of little pricks in thirty years.

As I stepped into the kitchen, a normally patient and serene English teacher in her early fifties held up a shot and yelled, "Danny Petrosky! Fuck you, you little weasel. I hope you get hit by a train this summer!" And all of the teachers cheered and downed their shots. This continued until they'd killed off like nine more kids—who, admittedly, the world probably wouldn't miss.

"I come bearing good news," I said, strolling in. "My sixth graders are the best group of kids on the planet. You'll love them."

"Mr. Cramer!" they shouted. "Welcome to summer!" They handed me a shot of bourbon, and we all drank to the awesomeness of the sixth-grade class.

It wasn't the biggest party I'd ever been to. Or the loudest. But it was damn near assuredly the rowdiest. You want to know how to party? Go watch some teachers let loose at the end of the year. There's really no other profession where the entire staff goes on vacation at the same time, so it's pretty unique.[13]* Mr. Calloway had a small house with

---

[13] * And if you're one of those dopes who thinks that teachers get too much time off, trust me, if they didn't, there'd be nobody teaching your kids. NOBODY.

a huge backyard. And we tore that shit up. The motherly fifty-year-old English teacher was passed out in the bushes before five o'clock. There was an intense beer pong tournament, drunken football, some food I think, and capping it all off, Mr. Calloway busted out the hose and turned his hill into a muddy Slip 'N Slide. After a few runs, the gallery began chanting, "Naked, naked, naked!" to everyone at the top of the hill. Knowing I probably wouldn't see many of these people ever again, I obliged, tore off all my clothes, and flexed to a giant roar from the teachers who were still upright.

And I dove down the hill.

In a microcosm of our year and our relationship, Katie Tipton came screaming down the hill after me, and we bashed heads in the mud puddle hard enough that blood was spilled. As I was giving naked, bloody high fives to my drunken colleagues, I heard our gym teacher over by the fire laughing with one of Mr. Calloway's neighbors. "If you want to know anything about Buford Middle," he said, "that's our sixth-grade guidance counselor."

A lot of people made a lot of bad decisions that night. I think Mr. Calloway was forced to burn his house down to rid the world of the evidence. And was probably happy to do so.

So ended my time as a school counselor. I'd used my degree for exactly two years. What came next was the most insane journey of my life—a journey that took me the entire way across the country in a valiant attempt to live out my dream.

CHAPTER 14

Hollyweird

When I was eight years old, my mom came across a bunch of blank storybooks, the kind where a giant illustration square sat atop three entire lines dedicated to text. I was always a kid whose imagination canceled out reality, so these things were like gold. I distinctly remember my first book being about my friends, and I discovering a secret military base behind our elementary school from which the French were going to launch an invasion of America.[14*] None of our teachers believed us (presumably because they understood real world geopolitics), so it was up to me and four other intrepid third graders to use our cunning wits and surprising knowledge of military technology to drive the croissant-munching invaders back across the Atlantic. I got to fly an F-15. On the last page, Ronald Reagan gave us medals. It was the first of what would become an entire filing cabinet full of stories.

As I got older, the imagination fountain I had as a kid never went away. When I wasn't teaching, playing ultimate frisbee, or partying, I was writing. So when Julie, the girl who'd alerted me to the Buford Middle School job, showed me a packet for the graduate program in

---

[14*] And you knew they were French because in all the pictures I drew, they had mustaches.

Writing for the Performing Arts at the University of California-Riverside, I was intrigued.

"This is where I want to go," she said. "They have one of the best British Literature departments in the country. You could apply for the writing school and we could go together."

She wrapped her arms around me and batted her eyelashes in a way that pretty much signed the application check right there. Though interested, I also realized I wasn't in any way prepared for grad school...again. At that point, I had like nine hundred bucks and two other degrees to pay off. Also, one of my fellow counselors at Buford announced her intention to retire after the following year so if I could just hang on for twelve months, the real-world interview I was presently acing nearly assured me a full-time position at the school I loved. There were already rumors that the district to the north needed someone to cover a year-long sabbatical at the high school. Career-wise, things were lining up nicely.

Truthfully, I only applied to UCR because Julie had gone to all the trouble of printing everything out, and I wanted to keep having sex with her as long as possible. I knew the most likely scenario was that she'd get in, I wouldn't, and we'd end up shedding some tears before she inevitably left for California without me. I filled out the packet, sent them my undergrad transcripts and some screenplays to read, mailed it off, and immediately forgot I'd done it.

A few weeks later, Julie and I broke up after an ill-fated ski trip—which is why when I returned home from my second week of outdoor camp ready to pass out until Sunday morning, I was stunned at one of the thirteen voicemails on my machine. In between a slew of folks peeved that they'd misdialed the Best Western off I-83 was a very unexpected message.

"Hello, Mr. Cramer, this is the graduate school in creative writing at the University of California-Riverside. Just letting you know you've been accepted into the program and we'd like to offer you some financial assistance. We'd love to hear from you. It's Monday at about two Pacific Time so..."

Again, after Julie and I broke up, I'd *totally forgotten* that I applied. "Huh." I chuckled, flopping on the kitchen floor with an astounded grin. Now obviously I wasn't going to leave solid job prospects in Pennsylvania to follow a silly dream two thousand miles to a school I'd never heard of. And no matter how much assistance they gave me, I assuredly wasn't going to be able to afford it anyway. But it was cool that they liked my writing enough to accept me, and ignoring them seemed rude, so I called them back, told them I'd been on the side of a mountain all week, and asked them to send me the information.

I'd just returned from lunch duty the following Monday when I checked my email to find a message from UCR. I was busy with sixth-grade shenanigans and had a million other things on my mind, so I meant to quickly scan it and read it more thoroughly after school. But the title caught my eye...

"Congratulations, you've been awarded a distinguished fellowship." *Uh, what now?*

I scrolled down to the next page where it outlined the financials. Inside a couple boxes were numbers with dollar signs beside them. One was a significant stipend amount. The other was a box that said, "Tuition owed by student - $0."

"Hey, Deloris," I yelled out to the guidance secretary, in no way comprehending what I was looking at. "Could you come in here a second?"

She poked her head through the doorway. "What can I help with?"

"Read this and tell me what you think it means."

She scanned the email and nodded. "Seems to me like someone got a full ride to college. What do you think it means?"

What I was presented with was a choice between living a relatively stable life in a job I liked in a community that I loved and flying forward into a void of unknowns to attack my dream. UC-Riverside needed an answer by the end of the week, so I didn't have time to agonize over it. I made a snap decision. Though it was the rockier path, I knew I'd always kick myself if I didn't follow it.

"I think it means I'm going to California," I answered.

That September, I packed everything I owned into my two-door Chevy Cavalier and headed west with my father. At fifty-eight years old, he saw the Mississippi River, the Rocky Mountains, and the Pacific Ocean for the very first time. It was the best five days of my life. When we finally got to Riverside, he helped me move into a new seven-floor prefab apartment building, and suddenly I lived in the sprawling suburbs an hour east of Los Angeles—right where the smog hits the mountains and relaxes. The air looked like what everyone in California *thinks* the air looks like in Pittsburgh, a sort of hovering industrial fart that gradually blurs the horizon. For a couple weeks in the spring when you could see the snowcapped mountains and everything was flowering and smelled like oranges, Riverside rivaled St. Augustine as the most gorgeous place I'd ever lived. But most of the time just glancing around made me thirsty.

My two years at UCR were amazing. I learned from nationally renowned playwrights, screenwriters, and authors. My scripts got tighter and better as I began to understand higher-level concepts about how stories work. My time there not only gave me a second (completely unnecessary) master's degree, but also provided a needed buffer between landing in Southern California and trying to make a go of it in Hollywood. I came out of it ready to roll.

My first job after graduating was as a do-everything grunt on an independent film directed by one of my professors. Chuck was a laid-back dude in his mid-forties who looked desperately out of place if he wasn't holding a coffee. A decade prior, he'd interrupted a burgeoning screenwriting career to join the Navy, after which he wrote an acclaimed play titled *Adopt a Sailor*, loosely based on his experiences. Now the play was being turned into a film starring acclaimed actors Bebe Neuwirth and Peter Coyote as a bougie New York couple who invite a sailor from rural Arkansas into their home for one life-altering night during New York Fleet Week.

The main set for *Adopt a Sailor* was a ritzy house in a development of similarly ritzy houses in a gated community in Palm Desert. It was the home of the film's producer, a retired New York fashion model named Kim, and her husband, a former Olympic skier named Jon. They, uh, had some cash. And since they were staying with Chuck on set, it left their *other house* across town unoccupied—which, for reasons I never questioned, was given to the director's assistant and her sweaty boyfriend.

The aforementioned director's assistant was a hyper-intelligent girl from Wyoming named Jessi who looked as if a reality show had given a librarian a punk-rock makeover. She'd arrived at UCR after having a play she'd written performed at the Kennedy Center, which suddenly made all of my accomplishments look small and cute. Somewhere along the line, the long-distance relationship with her girlfriend in Denver dissolved, we started hanging out, and long story short, we now have two kids and a mortgage. We'd only been dating a few months when we got to spend the majority of the summer in a million-dollar home with every amenity you can imagine. We'd come back after twelve hours of work, relax in the saltwater pool, and stare up at the stars, hoping none of the neighbors saw us and called the cops on the imposters next door. It was unreal—and gave us a massively warped and unrealistic sense of what the future might hold.

During the day, Jessi's main jobs were to take notes and hand Chuck his coffee. I did a little bit of everything from moving heavy shit to unloading heavy shit to driving a box truck into LA to pick up a bunch of heavy shit that needed moved and unloaded. Being a small film, the shoot itself was allocated only twelve days for principal photography. By the end of day eleven, everyone was cranky and frazzled. (Did I mention that it was *August* in *Palm Desert*?) I was out in the garage stacking equipment crates when suddenly Jessi burst through the door.

"You are needed immediately," she said, urgently tugging on my wrist.

My assumption was that something heavy needed to be moved. How wrong I was. Apparently while I was in the garage, absolute bedlam had descended on set in a chain of events that crippled the production in the dumbest way possible. Jessi quickly ushered me into the living room where she pointed to a big tear in the wallpaper at the very top of the wet bar. When we'd first arrived on set, the back and sides of the bar were giant inset mirrors, which needed to be covered so as not to catch reflections of the lights and cameras. One of the first things I did during set prep was wallpaper over it with a brown-speckled pattern that the production designer had picked out to match the decor of the room.

Anyway, as the electricians were moving one of the lights, a piece of gaffer tape accidentally caught the wallpaper up near the ceiling and ripped it, creating an ugly and noticeable continuity error in the background of a critical shot. And because nobody on a film shoot is ever expected to do anything at a reasonable pace, the production designer—a delightful gay man named David—frantically rushed into the sunroom to find the few extra strips of matching wallpaper he'd stashed away in an antique desk. In his desperation, David bumped into one of the two Roman pillars I'd had to move out of the corners of the dining room to create space for the camera before filming the shot. This wouldn't normally be a big deal. But unfortunately for him, the tops of the columns were ordained with giant fake acorns. And with his accidental hip check, one of these forty-pound squirrel treats tumbled off the pillar, nailed him in the back of the head, and knocked him the fuck out. It was like hell's version of Sir Isaac Newton and the apple. To repeat: the entire shoot ground to a halt because the production designer got knocked cold by a *decorative acorn.*[15*]

As it turned out the wallpaper strips weren't in that desk anyway, and with David now woozy and unable to relay where else he might've

---

[15*] Everyone who's ever worked on a film shoot is currently giggling and saying, "I can top that."

put them, it set off a mad dash around the house by the production assistants to find anything that might match the color scheme enough to fool the viewer's eye into thinking the wallpaper was uniform. Which was why I snickered when Jessi handed me their solution: a picture cut from a magazine.

"You're the only one tall enough to reach it," she said, quickly sticking a tape donut to the back of it.

I was *certain* they were pranking me. "Is this a *hamburger*?" I laughed, unaware that the events of the past few minutes had frayed the nerves of everyone inside.

The assistant director was a normally chill guy named Jim. But in that moment, his voice boomed across the room. "Don't fuckin' chuckle! Just put it up and get the fuck out!"

I turned and tried to stab him with a glare only to see all of the actors looking back with stressed, unhappy faces and the camera pointing at me like a gun barrel. The tension in the room felt like a hostage was about to be killed. So I reached over my head, taped this hamburger patty to the wall, and stormed out through the garage door into the driveway to cool down. As I was sitting there looking up at the stars, one of the PAs, a flirty Iranian girl named Shirin, came out and sat next to me.

"If you're wondering, the picture was from a Wendy's ad in some local magazine. I cut it out myself," she said. "It wasn't even the good Wendy's one. It was the crappy comparison hamburger."

"So wait." I laughed. "You're telling me there are paintings and sculptures on loan from prominent art museums all over the walls in there, and what saved the whole production is a crinkly picture of lousy meat?"

Shirin just nodded and laughed. "Yes, that's what I'm telling you."

Something in the absurdity of the situation activated an unstoppable laughter in me that I hadn't experienced since my parents tickled me as a toddler. I was straining my abs trying not to ruin the audio inside. And the laughter was contagious. Shirin began trying to stifle her own howls as well. There in the dark in this ritzy Palm Desert neighborhood, we laid in the driveway clutching our stomachs, trying not to cackle too loud in our delirious haze.

I laid my head back to the concrete. "I'm taping a drawing of a burrito up there tomorrow and nobody's going to stop me."

The next night we had a wrap party. And that was it. The stars of the film all left, the PAs went back home, and I stayed behind for an extra week to move all the heavy shit back where it came from. Unsurprisingly, with the on-screen talent and Chuck's poignant script, *Adopt a Sailor* screened at festivals all over the world. As of the writing of this book, it's available on multiple streaming platforms. If you ever get to watch it, look really close in one of the critical scenes and you can see my beefiest work.

Los Angeles, California, is a baffling place to try and exist. It's a sprawling expanse of everything and nothing, a paradise for the self-involved where entire days are devoured by traffic and beautiful people ignore each other at outdoor cafés as they pose for some imagined studio executive who might happen to amble by and say, "My god, doll, you're too good lookin' not to be in the motion pictures!" In a city whose main export is a theoretical version of itself presented to folks thousands of miles away, it's harder than you'd think to figure out what's fake and what isn't. And most of it is fake.

My friend Rob and I moved from Riverside into a converted guest house in Pasadena with no heat and no air conditioning. In September, it was so hot in the house that I couldn't run my computer until after dark or the internals would fry. By February, it was so cold that I had to sleep in double hoodies underneath four blankets and still shivered myself to sleep. The good news was that the driveway was lined with grapefruit and orange trees, so there were literally free nutrients just lying in the yard when we inevitably got sick.

And so with no real plan, Rob and I attempted to make it as writers in a city where thousands of other wannabes just like us were all fighting for the same scraps. Rob was a human bear from Niagara Falls who loved to drop ecstasy and dance the night away listening to trance music. Over the summer, Rob scored a coveted internship at Village Roadshow Pictures, the production company behind the *Matrix* trilogy among countless others. For three months, he drove his shitty minivan from our condo in Riverside two hours into Studio City to learn the particulars of the industry from well-connected professionals. When we got to Pasadena, it led him to an incredibly prominent job working the counter at Starbucks.

With no money coming in, I was mainly eating these tiny, unfulfilling frozen dinners you could get at Von's for a dollar a piece. The meals consisted of six chicken nuggets the size of quarters, five fries, a scoop of vegetables, and a chocolate sponge that always managed to rise up and envelop some of the corn from the neighboring pocket. No matter how you aligned the tray in the microwave, three of the nuggets served as ice packs for the burns on your tongue you got from the other three. And that was dinner. Sometimes Rob would bring home a few bags of expired sandwiches from Starbucks and it was like Christmas.

I had just turned thirty years old.

But even though my stomach was constantly agitated, I ended up involved in enough interesting shit to keep me from giving up entirely. Once I got a call from an old high school buddy named Luccy. He was a tall, thoughtful guy who I'd always race to the finish line at our cross-country meets to see who'd finish nineteenth. Oddly, he was also in LA trying to make it as a writer. Unlike me, however, he had a plan. Luccy was going for broke, investing most of his savings into a ten-minute short film he wrote, hoping to get it into Hollywood festivals where he could hobnob with people that could help launch his career. But in order for all that to happen, he first had to get the film done. And in order to get the film done within his budget, he needed to get creative. Which was where I came in.

Short films tend to be set in simple, easily accessible locations like restaurants or public parks—places where paperwork isn't involved.

Which was what I expected. Until I rolled up to the address Luccy gave me to find a behemoth abandoned hospital off the 101 in East LA. As I got out of my car, he strode over to meet me. After a handshake and some pleasantries, he handed me a flathead screwdriver. "Can you help me get the front door off?"

I looked down at the screwdriver and then up at the wooden double doors. "We have to take the door off the... Are we allowed to be here?"

"I don't know that we're *not* allowed," he answered, casually working on the top hinge. "I didn't ask anyone."

I nodded. "Good to know."

"But, uh, there's a security guard that comes around. And *I'm* really bad at bullshitting," Luccy said, the implication being that I *was* somehow adept at creating the little untruths that help you tiptoe around authority. I mean, he wasn't wrong. Back in high school, he'd watched me Jedi my way out of multiple detention-level offenses.

"Understood," I said, sliding the door screws into my pocket for safe keeping.

My second task after removing the door was to wander this lonely old hospital to try and locate a wheelchair for the upcoming scene. There weren't any on the first floor, so I cautiously pushed the doors to the stairwell open and headed into the basement, knowing full well that there was a 30 percent chance I was about to be stabbed by a junkie or murdered by ghosts. There were literally patient files scattered on the floor as if one day in 1983, the doctors, nurses, and administrators all said fuck it and left. Computer monitors, stretchers, biohazard containers, and other medical devices were strewn underneath cracking, graffiti-covered drywall. My curiosity and my instinct for survival were in a raging battle as I peeked around every doorway until I finally spied a bunch of wheelchairs folded up behind what I assume was an old nurse's station. I grabbed one and quickly headed upstairs, peering over my shoulder every few steps just to make sure I was still alone. Cause I'm not going to lie—it felt like I wasn't.

Anyway, in order to get anyone to pay attention to his film, Luccy knew he had to get a "name" actor in the lead role. Psychologically, we tend to associate familiarity with quality, which means an audience is infinitely more likely to gravitate toward an unknown product if it contains an actor they recognize. Such is how I found myself holding cue cards for Ian Ziering.

Ian Ziering was best known for playing a hunky rich kid in the popular nineties television series *Beverly Hills 90210*. How he ended up involved in Luccy's project, I have no idea. But there he was. It was a critical scene, the moment the main character unleashes his world-shaking new philosophy on an unprepared populous. Due to Ian's schedule, it needed to be filmed *that day* or it simply wouldn't get done. Everything was ready to roll. The assistant director was writing the take number on the slate. Luccy was making last-minute adjustments to the camera.

And that's when the security car drove up.

Luccy turned and threw me a look that I interpreted as, "If you decide to murder the guard and store him in the basement of the hospital, I'm okay with it." And I replied with a look that said, "Well, maybe I should talk to the guy first." And he gave me a look that said, "Murder might be easier." And I gave him a look that said, "I'd rather not take the life of a stranger today." And he gave me a look that said, "Fine, but if he gives you shit, don't rule out the murdering." And I gave him a look that said, "Cool." Now Luccy is a guy with an incredibly gentle demeanor. He's one of my few friends that I can't for the life of me picture in a fight. But in that moment, I saw the panic in his eyes as he imagined his career and his finances burning, and I understood exactly how good people can commit atrocities.

As I walked toward the security car, I waved. The guard rolled down his window. He was obviously talking to someone on the radio about our presence, which was not a good sign.

"Hey, man," I said as I strolled up. "Just want to make sure it's cool if we—"

"You have a permit?" he interrupted. "I called it in. They're checking."

This scenario required my bullshittiest bullshit. "We're, uh…not actually filming. We just brought the camera to our location scout to see how everything would look through the lens," I said, trying to block his view so he didn't see the boom microphone that would've given away the lie. "Obviously we'll get a permit when we come back with a real crew. I mean, there's only, what, six people here?"

He pointed to his radio. "They tell me you don't have a permit, you either leave or I call the cops."

"Understood," I answered. "I know you have a job to do. I've worked security, too. We just gotta look through the camera a couple times. Five, ten minutes tops."

He sighed and began to roll up the window. "Next stop on my rounds is a warehouse down the street. You're still here when I get back, I'm bringing LAPD."

"Not a problem," I said with a smile before hustling back toward Luccy.

He took a few steps toward me so as to be out of Ian's earshot. Last thing he wanted was to look like a hack in front of his star. "What's the situation?"

"We should get this done quickly," I said, leaping toward the cue cards.

Luccy's eyes bulged out like he'd sparked some jumper cables. He spun around. "Okay, let's get rolling!"

Aware of the looming catastrophe, Luccy and I subtly began looking around for cop cars every time Ian slightly flubbed a line and stopped to gather his thoughts. Somewhere around eight minutes had passed and we were on our sixth take when Ian had his first clean run. Luccy breathed a sigh of relief. It was in the can. All was…

Ian shook his head. "I know I can do better. I want to hit the line about not being who you think you are with more emphasis. I want to punch that up. You are *not* who you think you are. You are *not* who you think you are…"

"Yeah," Luccy squawked, trying to mask his skittishness. "Let's, um...do it."

"Hospital take seven," said the assistant director. And she cracked the slate.

Through the entire take, every sound in the background made me want to drop the cue cards and run. Not only did we not want the star of the film to suddenly realize the straw house the whole production was, we still had to put the front door back on—something the guard miraculously didn't notice as he drove by. If we didn't get to it and the security guy came back with the cops, I had all the screws in my pocket. That seemed like pretty damning evidence. I didn't have the money or contacts to deal with a misdemeanor trespass let alone a felony for breaking and entering. Whether or not I spent the night in a holding cell in East LA was presumably dependent on the acting prowess of a pop culture icon from fifteen years ago.

Every word Ian spoke in that forty-second monologue became the footstep of a monster walking away. Each utterance, each syllable, each emotion delivered made my hands desire to tremble a little bit less. Three sentences, two sentences, one last sentence and...he smoked it. Oscar worthy? Maybe not. Good enough for the situation at hand? Absolutely.

Ian cracked his back and shook out his arms. "That one felt good," he said to Luccy. "You want to get one more just in case?"

"Unnecessary," Luccy exclaimed. "You delivered on that one. Let's wrap up here and head to the next location." Luccy turned and gave me an awkward thumbs-up as he gathered the crew and began herding them toward their cars. Their backs now turned, I hurriedly chucked the wheelchair back inside and grabbed the screwdriver. It's amazing how fast you can put a door back on its hinges when you're trying to avoid getting the shit kicked out of you by gang members all night. I casually waved at the security guy as he pulled in—just as I was driving away.

That afternoon, we got the final scene done at a paycheck-cashing place on Crenshaw Boulevard in South Central. Afterward, Ian shook our hands and drove off into a lucrative tornado full of sharks. As for Luccy, he got the film into a few targeted festivals, more or less executing his career plan. He now writes for a super-popular one-hour drama on ABC. He's kind of a big deal. And I think it's quite obvious he owes it all to my bitchin' screwdriver skills.

My state of mind during this time was, um...not good. I knew I had talent but zero idea how to go forward with it, and the excitement of scrapping and fighting to start my career in Hollywood was quickly morphing into a sense of ambient futility. I didn't have much time before I was forced to crawl back home a failure. I needed a break. And I needed it quickly.

Beginning in 1955, the Samuel Goldwyn Foundation began giving out five monetary prizes each year to up-and-coming writers attending one of the ten schools in the University of California system. The application process included sending an original screenplay for the foundation to judge. For aspiring screenwriters at schools like UCLA, Cal Berkeley, UC-Irvine, and UC-Riverside, it was your golden ticket. Previous winners included Francis Ford Coppola among an ocean of Oscar and Emmy Award winners. You won one of these things and the industry actually lifted its head out of the shit to smell you.

I was lying in bed staring at the ceiling in a despondent fog one morning when I got a call from one of my professors at UCR. "Congratulations!" he said when I answered.

"On what?"

He laughed. "Oh, Jesus Christ, you don't know yet? You're the talk of the department. Go check your email."

Well, that sounded exciting. I leaped toward the crappy folding table where my laptop sat.

"Dear Kevin Cramer – Your script, Zen Dog in the Clouds, *has been selected as one of the five Samuel Goldwyn finalists..."*

"Holy shit!" I said, leaping in the air. My inbox was already filled with emails from agencies either requesting my script or asking to meet with me in person. After all the glitches and repairs and delays, the flames underneath the rocket boosters of my career had ignited. The countdown had started. I was about to be launched into the stratosphere.

The next few weeks were a blurry whirlwind. Nearly every day I was driving into Westwood or Beverly Hills to meet with slick folks in expensive shoes who were interested in representing me. They'd take me to lunch at upscale cafés that served kale with everything, and we'd talk about the career I was about to have as if it was now ordained by a deity. I walked out of the awards ceremony with a $2,000 prize and business cards from people I couldn't have gotten into the same room with a month ago. My god, it was happening. It was really...

Six days later, Hollywood shut down completely.

The WGA (Writer's Guild of America) strike of 2007 mainly came down to the way television writers were paid. At the time, residuals from reruns typically accounted for somewhere between 25 percent and 40 percent of a writer's annual salary. But with better technologies allowing for faster internet speeds, the networks were beginning to put their content online after its debut and turning to cheaper-to-produce reality shows to fill out the summer season. It might not have been such a big deal if the writers were getting a comparable piece of the online advertising profits, but they weren't. So they walked off the job.

Though we weren't yet WGA members, my professors encouraged Rob and me to go out to the strike lines. Not only was it a great place to network, but we'd be operating under the new contract when we inevitably became eligible to join, so it made a lot of sense to offer support. Twice a week, we'd drive into Century City or Melrose where we'd spend twenty minutes fretting about where to park before ultimately approaching a crew of folks with crisply printed red-and-black signs proclaiming WRITERS GUILD OF AMERICA – ON STRIKE. We'd sign in, then spend a few hours marching around in front of the gates of Fox or Paramount or some other studio yelling slogans that would die out after seven or eight incantations. And because I mainly watch hockey, I apparently had conversations with a whole bunch of TV stars who Rob later had to tell me were famous. It was a bizarre time.

But what was fun for a while dragged on. Each day moved me further away from the energy around winning the Goldwyn Award. By the time the strike ended exactly one hundred days after it began, it had so razed the industry that many of the agents I'd met with in October didn't have jobs by March. When everything started to slowly crank back up again, I was somehow in a worse position than I'd been right after I graduated. All the effort, all the work, everything I'd put into chasing my dream had been demolished by something that was totally and completely out of my control. Only a miracle could save my career.

Back at Penn State, you were required to take one class outside of the counseling department in order to diversify your studies. Most of the other students took education or sociology or, ya know…something tangentially related to the field we were hoping to get jobs in. I took… screenwriting. My professor was an old drummer named Fig who was the type of guy who wore Hawaiian shirts under a long black trench coat whether it was ten degrees and snowing or ninety and sunny. As it turned out, we had a ton in common. He was from the town next to mine, and in a remarkable bit of synchronicity one told a story in class about being attacked in an alley one night by a bunch of mobsters who wanted a cut of the money his band had been paid for a gig.

"I'll never forget this one guy," Fig said with a sly chuckle. "He had a rope with fish hooks in it. He starts wailing on me, and I'm like, 'Hey, man, I'm just the drummer. I don't have any money!' Guy was out of his mind. Vinny Protavetta was his name."

I nearly fell out of my seat. "Vinny Protavetta?" I exclaimed. "That same asshole knocked out eight of my dad's teeth with a brick!"

And so assisted by the treachery of the Pittsburgh mob, Fig took a shine to me as his protégé. As it turned out, Fig worked in Hollywood through most of the eighties and had a couple good producer friends in Pasadena. He extolled and likely exaggerated my virtues, so they agreed to meet with me just after the strike ended.

The producers were an odd pair. Richard was a quiet, introspective guy who wore wrinkly shirts and had a giant pet hog while Jim was a tall, elegant man who always looked like he was on his way to an important banquet. They bought me a ham-and-egg croissant at a breakfast place in South Pasadena and told me about a script they'd acquired that they'd come to an impasse with and needed a fresh set of eyes on. But before they hired me, they wanted an example of my writing just to make sure Fig hadn't gone senile in the mountains of Pennsylvania and recommended a dimwit. I figured my Goldwyn script would do the trick, so when I got home, I sent it to them.

A week later, Jim called.

"Kevin, let me get to the point. We love *Zendog*. And we want to option it from you."

That was *not* what I expected. Truthfully, I wasn't totally certain what an option was. As I'd find out, it was a deal whereby they paid me to have exclusive control of the script for a year. If they didn't manage to move forward with it, the rights would be returned to me and I could either sell it back to them for another year or move it somewhere else. Which meant that in many ways my first big break in the industry didn't come about because of my various contacts or the Goldwyn Award—it more or less happened because my dad and my professor randomly got beat up by the same mob goon. Life is dumb.

While at a festival in Texas promoting their latest film, Richard and Jim happened to bump into William H. Macy, at the time known for such films as *Fargo*, *Mystery Men*, and *Wild Hogs*. Seizing the opportunity in front of them, they asked if he'd ever played a villain. As a man with a slightly droopy face, kind eyes, and a big smile, Macy was mostly pigeonholed as a doting doofus, the type of character who was more likely to spill a briefcase full of important papers than have knees buckle when he entered a room. So when they asked if he had any interest in playing the ruthless but philosophical drug kingpin in *Zendog*, he was intrigued.

I had no idea any of this was happening, so when Richard called a few weeks later to tell me Macy was now on board, I was astounded. "He wants to meet you," Richard said. "Do you have any time next week?"

"Richard, I'm an unemployed writer." I chuckled. "The only thing I have open next week is all of next week."

And so out of nowhere I found myself in the back of Jim's SUV heading into the Hollywood Hills. As we drove up there, my heart was beating like I suspected an ambush was imminent. I knew all I could possibly do at this meeting was fuck things up. Macy was going to see right through me—right through to the fact that I was just some grunt from Pittsburgh who didn't deserve to be in his house.

He was on the porch waiting for us when we exited the car. "Welcome," he said, shaking my hand. "Can't wait to get to work. We're going to create something great, just absolutely great." The man was just as nice as he seemed on television. He led us to a balcony filled with cool guitars where we sat down to discuss the script. Halfway through, his wife bounced up the stairs and popped her head in. I recognized her immediately as Emmy winner Felicity Huffman.

"Just wanted to drop by and say hi," Felicity said, placing a few bottles of spring water on the table. "I figured you all might be thirsty. Kevin, we just love your script. Such a great character. It's going to be Bill's Oscar."

Macy leaned forward. "Absolutely. This is the one," he said nonchalantly.

The world shifted. Everything was diagonal. A couple that each had a star on the Hollywood Walk of Fame had just casually proclaimed that my imagination was going to help land them the industry's most prestigious award. My mind began to race. I saw the red carpet beneath my feet. I saw actresses in expensive gowns, actors in tuxedos and sunglasses, cameras popping, fans screaming, and reporters asking questions. That was the future they were prophesizing. What seemed absolutely unimaginable just weeks ago seemed not only possible but probable. I sucked down that water like a horse as I watched all those dreams crystallize into reality. Unfortunately, it led to a situation where creativity wasn't the only thing desperate to flow.

During a lull in the conversation, I politely asked where the bathroom was and, after turning the corner, raced down the hallway like I was being timed. Once inside, I closed the door and hustled to the toilet, fighting to get my belt undone while my bladder screamed. As I unzipped, I looked around. It wasn't the type of bathroom I was used to. At my place, Rob shed a full Ewok every time he showered. Cleaning the mildew was not a pressing concern. It was a tad…unkempt. But here the far wall was a giant wooden bookshelf full of pristine hardcovers. Some kind of People's Choice Award was being used as a doorstop. It was half as big as the house I lived in. It was beautiful. Suddenly, I was struck with an overwhelming sense of dread.

I'm going to pee on William H. Macy's floor. This is how my career ends.

Consequently, I became a sniper who knew he only had one shot to take out an international terrorist.

Five degrees to the right. Down a tick. Deep breath. Slow your heartbeat. Steady your hand. You can do this. Trust yourself. Believe in your training. Target acquired.

Target eliminated. Mission accomplished.

When the meeting was over, it was like everyone saw through to my inner laborer because before I knew it, I was helping them move furniture around their backyard in preparation for a party that night. Oddly, it was the one thing that helped me relax. I wasn't totally certain how to act around rich and famous people, but I did know how to lift a couch. Under the strain of heavy furniture, I finally felt comfortable.

Through Macy, I'd end up occasionally having beers with big-time actors who I'd just seen on TV the day before. I was quickly being ushered into a world far beyond what I ever imagined was possible. But getting the pieces in place to make a movie takes a long time. And as it turned out, the economy was only months away from plunging into a ravine. Banks seemed to anticipate what was coming and were hesitant to loan to studios who'd just been shut down by a worker revolt for a hundred days. I didn't know any of this at the time and just naively assumed that with real Hollywood wheeler dealers and a couple recognizable stars on board, I'd be on the Oscar stage soon enough.

The challenge now was how to survive the interim.

CHAPTER 15

High Plains Drifter

As the writer's strike dragged on, I did the calculations. Even dipping into the retirement funds I'd earned from Stateline, even with the Goldwyn money, even eating meals that had the nutritional value of the box they came in, I had about two months. I was in a bad spot and thus willing to entertain ideas I would've otherwise discounted. Once when I was back on campus in Riverside, I ran into Chuck, who was now putting the finishing touches on *Adopt a Sailor*. He asked how things were going.

"Other than the fact that by March I'm pretty sure I won't be able to eat anymore, uh, pretty good, I guess."

He nodded. "Have you considered the Navy? You're still younger than I was when I joined. Best thing that ever happened to my life and my writing career. Just a thought."

Chuck went on to tell me about the position he had as a public affairs officer (PAO), which used his writing skills to combat foreign disinformation while highlighting the good the Navy was doing on a local and national scale. Being able to serve my country by telling stories was an exciting concept. So just after the new year, I found myself driving to the recruitment center on Slauson Avenue in southwest LA. They ushered me into a secure building where everything was disturbingly orderly. Next thing I knew I was in the office of a big man in a short-sleeve, khaki button-down. The finely polished nametag on his breast pocket said Chief Weems.

"So what brings you to the Navy, Kevin?" Chief Weems asked. "I'm interested to know why we're talking."

I told him about how I looked up to my cousin Eric who'd served in the Marines during both Gulf Wars. I told him about the deep connection I had with my grandfather who'd fought his way across Europe during World War II and was currently in the hospital dying of prostate cancer. (He'd pass away the following night.) I told him about Chuck and the writer's strike and how I was exploring all of my options. And then I told him about how I thought my education would make me a perfect candidate for a PAO position.

Before I met with Chief Weems, they'd had me fill out a bunch of paperwork and endure a few minutes of doctor's office–style poking and prodding. He read over my file and leaned back in his chair. "You have two master's degrees?"

"Yes, sir," I answered.

"It says here you ran cross-country in college?"

"Yes, sir."

"What would you say your average mile time is now?"

"Uh, if I'm running hard, six minutes. Maybe a little less."

"If we asked you to do a set of pushups, could you get to fifty without resting?"

These were much different questions than I anticipated. "Yesterday I crapped out at ninety-three. I do a lot of pushups. I don't have a lot going on right now."

He tapped on his clipboard. "I'm going to be straight with you, Kevin. I want you to fully understand how this works so you can make an informed decision. I know you're interested in public affairs, but that's not how the military works. We put you where your skills dictate. And we would not waste you behind a desk writing press releases."

"Uh…okay," I stuttered in response.

"With your education and fitness level, a better fit would be naval intelligence. A majority of our navigation officers are in their mid- to late forties and no longer in optimum shape by the time they acquire the necessary education—which, being frank, means they can be liabilities if needed to accompany our elite forces. You would not be."

I involuntarily leaned forward. "Elite forces?"

"The SEAL teams," he answered. "Now you wouldn't be expected to hit the same benchmarks. They're a special breed. But with the base you already have and the right training, you could keep up with them. You'd be an asset that's in short supply. So that's where you'd go. We'd love to have you, but I realize it's a big decision and probably not what you imagined when you walked in the door."

"That is, um…not what I imagined. No, sir."

Chief Weems didn't give me a big speech about my country needing me. He didn't suggest it was what my dying grandfather would've wanted. He was just straightforward, told me what they needed and where I fit in. And I respected the hell out of that. We scheduled a time two weeks later for me to go through an official fitness test and get the process started. But he was very clear that until I signed, I was free to opt out.

It was a lot to think about. I was currently trying to make it in an industry that throws up obstacles at every turn—an industry that's as difficult as it is self-absorbed. I had the opportunity to do something selfless, something for my country. And not only that, it seemed like I was needed. I could go from drifting aimlessly to being necessary, important even. And yes, the chances of getting blown up or shot would also increase significantly, but I did live in LA, so they wouldn't go up as much as you'd think. The reactions from my family were mixed.

"My god, you'd be perfect for that," said my sister.

"Kev, you've never followed an order in your life," said my dad.

But ultimately the deciding factor was the girl I'd been dating for a little over a year. Jessi was hesitantly supportive when she thought I might spend the next decade writing recruitment videos from behind a desk in San Diego. But when she envisioned me in Sudan or Afghani-stan or wherever some dangerous mission might take me, it suddenly forced us into a conversation about where our relationship was headed.

"I don't want to stand in your way if it's something you feel you need to do," she said. "I know things aren't working out right now and you need to find a direction. But I don't think I could constantly won-der where you were or whether you were safe."

The implication was if I chose that path, our time together would come to an amicable close. And as much as I wanted to find a purpose and finally at thirty years old quit toiling in the unknown, I also knew there was something special about this girl, and I didn't want to let her go. After a lot of soul searching and talking to my family in the days around my grandfather's funeral, I made a decision. I let Chief Weems know I wouldn't be coming in for the fitness tests. He told me he understood and to give him a call if I changed my mind any time before I was thirty-five.

The main consequence of my flirtation with the Navy was that Jessi and I now knew for certain we were going to try and build a life together. This was going to change a lot of things, mainly because before she'd left for California, Jessi got her first tattoo from a chain-smoking, Cadillac-loving rebel who owned a shop called The Underground in Laramie. His name was Jeff, and he was known throughout the moun-tain west as the guy to go to if you wanted a badass hot rod on your forearm. But when Jessi brought in a drawing of a minimalist angel, he was so impressed with her work that he offered her an apprenticeship on the spot—an apprenticeship she had to postpone for two years to attend UCR.

The whole time we were in school together, I knew Jessi was even-tually going back home to Wyoming to learn how to become a tat-too artist. If we were going to stay together, I had to follow her. So in August after three mystifyingly weird years, I said goodbye to Califor-nia and aimed my car toward the least populated state in the nation. I'd arrived in Pasadena with nearly ten thousand dollars in which to try and survive the inevitable hard times that awaited. When I closed my bank account, they gave me a check for $70.36.

Going from Los Angeles to Laramie was exactly the culture shock you'd expect it to be. In LA, it often took two hours just to get to the store. In Laramie, if you got stuck at a light for more than one cycle you assumed there was a funeral procession ahead. Until I moved there, I'd never seen a city that just *ended*. But Laramie full-out stopped south of town at the concrete plant. To the west was prairie and tumbleweeds the whole way to the snow-capped mountains in the distance—which unlike the mountains around Riverside, you could see clearly every damn day.

You wouldn't think there'd be a downside to clean air and no traffic. But the hard reality is that the better the air is somewhere, the less likely it is to be teeming with jobs. There was one high school in all of Albany County, and even if they had an opening for a counselor, it wasn't going to some East Coast outsider who showed up via California. Same for the University of Wyoming. You weren't getting a job in admissions or advising unless you were someone's cousin. Which really only left one option.

Founded in 1966, the Wyoming Technical Institute (known as WyoTech) was a for-profit institution that trained students in engine diagnostics along with collision repair and cool stuff like chassis fabrication and street rod design. Due to a slick marketing campaign and an engaging yet morally ambiguous team of recruiters, it attracted students from all over the country to pay quadruple what they would've spent at their local community college for basically the same education. I interviewed for a position in the career services department on a Tuesday afternoon just after I arrived in town. They offered me the job Wednesday morning—which, looking back, I probably should've seen as a red flag. But then again, my girlfriend was currently paying the rent, buying all the groceries, and covering the security deposit by working mornings as a barista before hustling to her unpaid tattoo apprenticeship. I couldn't have said yes fast enough.

My main focus within the department was to go around to the different classes and teach job search and interview skills, lessons that would presumably help the students land a position in their desired field upon graduation. A good 20 percent of the students recognized the potential benefits to their future from what I was teaching. The rest of them, however...

Trust me, you don't quite understand the term "hostile crowd" until you're trying to teach resume building to a bunch of dudes from small-town Nebraska who just want to be welding shit onto their rat rod. They are *not* pleased to see you. Especially because at the outset, the lessons seemed to be ripped from a fourth-grade unit on self-confidence meant to be taught by a person who wasn't averse to using puppets. It didn't exactly strike the right tone for the guys in class who'd endured firefights around Baghdad. After the first semester, I shredded everything I was given at the outset and decided to write my own lessons—which were mainly full of stories that ended with "don't be *that* guy."

One of my favorite teachable moments began with a phone call I received from a dude who was fifty shades of irritated about being unemployed since he graduated. "You guys never send me anything good!" he sneered. "Just entry-level jobs at dealerships. With my skills, I should be on TV building hot rods for basketball players."

"Okay," I said, taking his name and looking up his file. "You were an automotive graduate? And you're from Flensburg, Minnesota? Let's see what we have in your area."

"No dealerships!"

"Loud and clear," I responded, scanning through our jobs database. "Actually, we just got sent an opening for a fabricator at Little Falls Rod & Custom this morning. That looks like it's pretty close to you. If you're quick, you can jump on it before it goes out to the email blast."

Cue the dismissive grunt. "Ugh, I don't want that. It's two towns away!"

"*Don't be that guy!*" I'd bellow at the class. "His entire career plan is for one of the *other* two hundred people in Flensburg freakin'

Minnesota to open a world-class hot rod shop. And I'm pretty sure even if his brother started fabricating cars for Shaquille O'Neal right there in his mom's house, this doofus would reject it because, 'Ugh, I'd have to walk the whole way to the *garage!*'"

I'd get a few chuckles from the guys who'd fought their way out of Sadr City while the eighteen-year-olds from Goofrabbit, Oklahoma, stared at me blankly, still uncertain what the flaw was in the Flensburg kid's plan. And that was my job. At least it was supposed to be.

Other than the sappy, elementary feel of the original curriculum, the other reason the lessons needed to be altered so dramatically was because of an abrupt and unexpected change in the job market itself. On the morning of my very first day, I was talking to George, the department's clean-livin' assistant director. Out of eleven employees in the office, George was the only other guy, and though we were the same age, he was much, much older. His world did not include dancing or rap music or laser shows. That first morning we were discussing my role within the department when he got a phone call. Whoever was on the other line told him to check his email. And when he clicked on his email, his lungs deflated.

"Oh no," he said. You could tell he was trying desperately to stifle the first curse word of his life. "Oh...noooo."

The email contained a link to an article announcing that both Car-Max and Caterpillar were laying off thousands of mechanics across the country. Until that morning, those two companies were the largest employers of recent WyoTech graduates. Hundreds of other companies followed suit in the coming weeks as the oilfield, mining, and trucking industries began to take hits as well. The Great Recession had begun. We were suddenly staring at an economy that was dramatically retracting and now flooded with unemployed technicians.

I'd been on the job all of two hours.

The collapse of the economy was an earthquake for America's for-profit schools. For years, WyoTech's parent company Corinthian Colleges had been making money hand over fist in some pretty shady and borderline predatory ways. Everest Colleges, Corinthian's most known brand, offered degrees in diversified fields such as business, healthcare, and information technology at over one hundred locations in the US and Canada. They made money knowing that many of their students were in lower income groups and thus eligible for federal aid. To remain eligible for that aid, however, there was a stipulation that for-profit colleges needed to place at least 85 percent of their graduates in their desired field within twelve months of their graduation. Hitting that number was everything for Corinthian because it allowed the government to continue bankrolling the entire operation.

This next paragraph is super boring but stay with me. To calculate the placement rate, the career services department would keep track of all the graduates in four giant binders, one for each of the year's graduations. Two weeks after they received their diploma, we'd begin calling those graduates to see if they'd gotten a job in their field. If they said yes, we'd ask for their supervisor's contact info, and if that supervisor said, "Yup, Mike Platt works for Riverview Chevy as a level-one technician," we'd thank them, write the information down, and remove Mike's page from the binder. Then some independent company would later call Riverview Chevy to verify our findings. By the time you got to nine months out, there were typically only seventeen pages left in a binder that once held three hundred. At least that's how it was before the recession. Afterward, the binders remained...thick.

This freaked the hell out of the people at the top, whose good times were dependent on that sweet, sweet government money. With deadlines looming and projections not looking promising, the big wigs began looking for answers.

"We have to adapt," I told them. "I come from a guidance background. Right now, the students barely know us. We're just the people who bug them about whether they have a job after graduation. Each student should be assigned their own personal career services rep from the minute they arrive—someone who can tailor job listings for them based on a personal relationship built over time and a desire to help the student succeed."

I even wrote up a five-page proposal outlining my suggestions, which I gave to George to send up the chain. But what corporate decided instead was: "So what we're going to do is have each of you spend one day each week with the binders. For eight hours, you're going to lock yourself in your office and call these same eighty-four unplaced kids over and over again. Blow up their phones until they can't ignore us anymore. Call their emergency contacts. Harass, harass, harass!"

I despise bothering people. And now I was literally instructed to sit in my office all day and be a phone pest. I realize it wasn't intentional—the recession caught everyone off guard and management panicked, but it felt like I'd been caught in a bait-and-switch. Six months into the job and suddenly I was a glorified telemarketer.

Every day things got weirder. Corinthian began offering twenty-five-dollar bonuses for every new placement as if a small monetary incentive would somehow allow us to skirt the global economic forces in the way. The combination of the reward and the relentless daily pressure to hit placement goals led to some really fishy stuff at WyoTech's other campuses.

"You say you deliver pizza for Ted's Pepperoni Barn? Do you drive your own car? You do? Great! Have you ever fixed anything on your car? Oh, you changed the battery last week? Well, people wouldn't be getting their pizza if it wasn't for your automotive knowledge, would they? Sounds to me like you're working in your field!"

Another big problem was that WyoTech hired two part-time night callers that worked from six p.m. to ten p.m. after we'd all gone home. I'd spend all day talking with graduates, emailing them leads, getting them in contact with employers, and sometimes even scheduling interviews. And those students would happily email me to say thanks for helping them land the job—the morning after the night caller found out themselves, pulled the card from the binder, signed their name to it, and cashed in on a two-minute phone call. Some nights the part-time callers were making double or even triple what I was making working a full day. Suffice it to say, the day shift was *pissed*. But when we brought our concerns to management, we were told we were a "team" and we needed to be "team players" and it didn't matter who got the reward as long as the "team" was getting the company closer to the "goal line" and "other football metaphors." As is typical for such a situation, we all immediately got over our collective resentment that someone else was being compensated for our hard work and recommitted to excellence. Because that's how that works.

I, uh...didn't react well to the new direction. One because it was mind-numbingly stupid in every facet, and two because it was mind-numbingly stupid in every facet. I pretty much shut down. I barely spoke to anyone from the moment I walked in the door until the moment I left. If I did speak, I was unnecessarily combative. For a while there, I was *not* a good employee. I secretly hoped they'd say the hell with it and fire me. But they didn't. So I had to keep going in.

It didn't help that Laramie has two seasons. Those seasons are winter and July 27. There was a stretch in early February where the high for the entire week was -15. *Minus fifteen.* Every day I had to traverse ice ruts with the defroster blasting in order to get to a job I couldn't stand. I was supposed to be readying myself for six weeks in Montana watching William H. Macy secure his Oscar. I was supposed to have already gotten a six-figure payday. But due to the recession, banks were being especially stingy with their money. Trapped in a financial wasteland, Richard and Jim had already pushed production from the upcoming fall to the following spring—fifteen months away. The length of time I'd have to endure forty hours of misery per week kept getting extended. And I had a nagging feeling it would keep getting extended ever onward into eternity.

There was a hill on Route 287 just north of town. WyoTech was at the bottom of the slope. Every morning when I saw an eighteen-wheeler coming the opposite way, I'd think, *If I just steer to the left a little, I won't have to go to work today.* One or two times I actually touched the double yellow line before jerking back. Being stuck in a job you despise out of economic necessity wreaks havoc on your mind. Even when you're not at work, you're constantly fretting about having to go back. Your nightmares start featuring the conference room, and the image is so jarring you yearn for your subconscious to bring back the terror mazes and murder basements. It's a constant, cyclical loop of dread you can't escape.

Corinthian tried everything to get our placement numbers up. Their biggest Hail Mary came when they flew every single career services representative from Everest Colleges, Heald Colleges, and WyoTech to Chicago for a sales training seminar at the O'Hare Airport Marriott. To keep the office functioning, half of the office went one week and half the next. The crews were divided up by who the director wanted to drink martinis with, so the six women in the office in their twenties and thirties all went the first week. That left me, George, two older women, and our nineteen-year-old office assistant cramming into George's Buick for the two-hour ride down to Denver International the second week.

Sitting there at the departure gate, I realized that business trips are a special kind of hell. Though air travel itself sucks, when you're at an airport, you're usually heading somewhere at least nominally positive, often times for vacation or to see family and friends. But for the first time in my life, I was going to a place I didn't want to go with a bunch of people I didn't choose to be with to do something I had no desire to do. The travel department emailed us seven times about whether we'd prefer a window or an aisle seat. All five of us got crammed in the center. The emails were apparently so they'd understand exactly *why* we'd be disappointed.

After working eight hours in Laramie, driving to Denver, then flying all the way to Chicago the previous day, I had to get up early the next morning to head down to ballroom four where I was assigned to a table with a bunch of career service folks from different Everest campuses. As we nibbled on breakfast, two of them became mortal enemies over a free pen. Such were the type of people I was trapped with at a circular table in a flavorless conference room for hours on end.

After breakfast, a guy in an expensive suit strode confidently up to the front. "Ask the right questions to find the customer's pain," he bellowed. "Identify their struggle, then exploit it by letting them know our product can ease that pain. That's the key to any sale."

I zoned out, actively trying to ensure that none of his nonsense took up usable space in my brain. Although I must admit that lunch was pretty damn yummy.

On the second day, some corporate types from Corinthian showed us a PowerPoint on their innovative new system for keeping track of placements: a tally sheet with six columns. We were instructed to record our results for the day by putting the number of calls we made in column A, confirmed placements in column B, placements that still needed confirmation in column C, and some other junk in columns D through F. It was less complicated than drooling. But the presenters made a giant mistake at the end of the presentation.

"Any questions?" they asked.

Fifteen hands went up. "What if I call to confirm a student's job status and their supervisor is on maternity leave? What column does that go in? What if I call a student but their mom answers and says they're still asleep? What if they were on their way to their first day of work but lost their shoe in a ditch?"

If I was one of the presenters, I'd have shut it down after three questions. But they were absolutely unprepared for the Great Dumbstown Flood. After forty minutes of absurdity, I made sure George was looking the other way, stood up, walked out, and headed to the hotel bar. When I returned a half hour later, I walked directly into, "What if you wanted to write stuff down but some bitch next to you took your pen?"

"Bitch that wasn't your pen. It's been my pen the whole time!"

I spun around immediately, ending up on the curb next to a pile of slush outside the Marriott aimlessly staring off at traffic. It was a much better use of my time. Three hours later, I was mercifully on a plane headed back to Colorado. The one good thing about the entire experience was cracking up on the ride home with people that until then I didn't know particularly well as we recounted the hijacking we'd just survived.

George kept trying to toe the company line, insisting it wasn't that bad until finally as we approached Cheyenne, we got him to break. "Okay, the ninety minutes of questions about columns—that got a little tiresome," he said, stifling a laugh.

"George coming off the top rope with a thundering elbow!" I shouted.

"But the rest of it was very informative," he quickly insisted.

The car roared up I-80 powered by laughter and delirium. I don't have many good memories from WyoTech, but that was pretty awesome.

If you've ever worked a corporate job, it's no secret that if you walk into your office one day and, even though it's nobody's birthday, the whole space is filled with balloons and streamers, you're probably fucked. Management is obviously trying really hard to pass off something shitty as some sort of celebration, and they assume they'll be able to sneak it past you if there's bagels and confetti.

"Hey, why do these cupcakes spell out 'No more overtime pay'?"

The Wednesday after we all got back from training, each of us entered the office to see colorful decorations everywhere. One by one, we stopped at the door, took it all in, and muttered, "Goddammit." And for good reason. The bosses were running a surprise inspection of our phone calls to see if we were using the sales techniques we'd learned in Chicago. What fun!

Halfway through the morning, George knocked on my office door. "I've got to respond to an important email, but as soon as I'm done, you're up next." I nodded and gave him a thumbs-up. But I wasn't leaving this up to chance. My region to call was the mid-Atlantic, so while George was in his office, I dialed up Muffin Truck Chris back in Pittsburgh. As per usual, it turned out he was busy chopping meat and didn't answer the phone. Next up was my friend Darren, a handsome Italian film editor who Chris and I always dragged into our weird improv comedy skits back in high school.

"Hello?" Darren said.

"Yo, dude, it's Kevin. I need you to do me a huge favor. In ten or fifteen minutes, you're going to get another call from this number. When you pick up, I need you to answer, 'Darren's Auto Body.' And then just go with it. I'll lead you to the answers I need."

He didn't flinch. "Got it," was all he said.

Twelve minutes later, George came in and made himself comfortable, hitting the speakerphone button so he could hear the upcoming conversation. "Nervous?" he asked.

"Not really. I think I have it down." I pretended like I was looking at a spreadsheet on my computer but dialed Darren's number, which I had memorized. After two or three rings…

"Darren's Auto Body."

"Hi, I was wondering if I could speak to the owner or manager?" I said.

"This is Darren. What, uh…what can I help with?"

"My name is Kevin, and I'm calling from WyoTech in Laramie, Wyoming. Do you have a minute to chat about the benefits our graduates might be able to provide for your shop?"

"Uh, hold on," he said. "Larry! Have you seen my mallet? I gotta take a call, but if you find it, set it on the shelf in bay two!" He paused and closed a door. "Yeah, sorry about that. I'm gonna move into my office here."

I leaned back in my seat, trying not to let my sly grin give away the secret. "So your shop, do you do any custom fabrication or mainly just insurance work? I did a little research earlier. It seems like mostly insurance, is that right?"

"Yeah," Darren responded. "It's all local wrecks. Stuff like that."

"Lot of deer out your way?"

"Oh yeah," he said. "Get a lot of that. Had a guy hit a cow the other day."

For five minutes, we spoke of the damage inflicted on a make-believe car that ended up at a fake body shop through a pretend accident with a nonexistent cow—all of which I managed to tie back to the incredible opportunity he had to hire WyoTech students.

"Yeah, I got a guy I think is going to flake on me any day now," Darren said. "Boy, I'm really glad you called. I'll definitely be in touch when we have an opening. Send me over some info and we'll go from there."

When I hung up, George nodded confidently. "Well, someone learned a lot in Chicago," he said. "I don't think I need to see anymore. Keep up the good work."

I didn't even have to call my sister, who I also had on standby. Sadly, Kelly's Killer Kustomz was never bullshat into a brief existence. And Darren and I laugh about that every time we see each other.

In August, Jessi and I got married in front of friends and family on a beautiful day at a park beside the railroad tracks, then headed off to Sarasota for our honeymoon. But even laying on the beach in paradise, the following Monday was a devil creeping closer by the hour. I knew in a blink I'd be back wandering aimlessly around our career fair with the depressing knowledge that I'd used up all my vacation days. Summer turned back to winter again, and I still fought every day not to steer in front of a Peterbilt on my way down the hill. One way or another, I needed to get out for my own sanity.

Back in Pennsylvania, we'd just moved my grandmother into a nursing home and my parents were stressed out about the museum of Depression-era hoarding she'd left behind. I needed to head back home for a month to help them get rid of the boxes of decades-old tax documents and the sixteen never-opened coffee makers, among thousands of other things. George had recently been promoted to department director, so just after our March graduation, I walked into his office.

"Hey, I know this is a big ask, but I need the month of June to go back home and help my parents out with a bunch of stuff," I said.

He delivered his cold-blooded reply very warmly. "That is not an option."

I nodded. "Well then, this will be my last semester."

"Okay, then." He stood up to shake my hand. "I'll give you another handshake in June."

Knowing there was a light at the end of the tunnel was freeing. Every day I felt a little bit lighter knowing I was getting closer and closer to the end. I had about six weeks left when George went to a four-day conference at the corporate headquarters. When he returned, he called a staff meeting. We all pulled chairs into the center of the office, wondering what the big news was. George rolled his chair in front of the copier and handed out a bunch of papers.

"As we all know, this recession has been tough on the job market, which means it's been tough on our graduates," he said. "And let's face it, it's been tough on us as well. It's forced us to reexamine what we're doing. So at the conference, we came up with a bunch of ideas on how to move forward. But one plan stood out. We voted on it, and there was a consensus. So we're overhauling everything."

Wait for it...

George cleared his throat. "Right now, the students barely know us. We're just the people who bug them about whether they have a job after graduation. We're going to change that by assigning each student their own personal career services rep from the minute they arrive—someone who gets to know them. Someone who can tailor listings for them based on a personal relationship and desire to help the student succeed. We're doing this across all WyoTech campuses starting next semester."

Well, that sounds familiar.

I kept waiting for him to say something along the lines of, "Kevin actually came up with it," but he never did. Not even a hint. It was verbatim the proposal I'd typed up a year earlier. Which meant that immediately after I left, they were going to start doing exactly what I told them they should be doing all along, turning the job into a position I might've actually thrived in and, dear god, even enjoyed. As it turned out, my ideas reshaped all the career service departments at all the Wyo-Tech campuses across the country, and I didn't get a single thank-you from anyone. Not a Target gift card. Nothing. In fact, George insisted he didn't even remember my plan and that management had come up with it on their own during a brainstorming session.

Driving up the hill away from that place on my final day, the sky was bluer than it's ever been.

In April of 2015, Corinthian was fined $29.7 million in large part because the career services departments across their Everest, Heald, and WyoTech campuses were blatantly misrepresenting their placement rates, effectively defrauding the government and the students they served for two decades. The US Department of Education was tasked with dismantling the for-profit giant and selling off all eighty-five of the American schools under Corinthian's tent, including all five WyoTech branches. Undersecretary of Education Ted Mitchell summed it up by saying, "Corinthian violated students' and taxpayers' trust. Their substantial misrepresentations evidence a blatant disregard not just for professional standards, but for students' futures."

Did we fudge the numbers in Laramie while I was there? No. Nor was I ever pressured to do so. I can say that for certain. As frustrated as I was with George personally by the end of my time at WyoTech, he had a moral code that absolutely wouldn't have allowed such a thing to happen on his watch. But it was clearly happening elsewhere.

As for WyoTech, it was kept alive by the local community college long enough for a group of investors to raise the money to purchase it. From a distance, it seems to be thriving under new management. It would've been devastating for the local economy to lose it outright, and even though I disliked the place due to the corporate migraine it became, I know in the right hands it can be a great resource for hard-working, mechanically minded people looking to improve their education and overall job prospects.

And though WyoTech is still churning, it does bear the scars from the Corinthian debacle. For years after the settlement, the large building covered in cream yellow siding where I worked those twenty-one months sat abandoned at the bottom of the hill before finally getting torn down to build offices for the Laramie Public Works Department.

In the end, what I learned is that in the corporate world, ethics often stand as an obstacle to profit, and when forced to choose between the two, those making the decisions will always choose profit. I knew I'd rather not be a part of that type of broken machine ever again no matter what I had to do to avoid it.

CHAPTER 16

Gut Punch

When I returned to Wyoming after helping my parents take nine houses full of crap out of a single house, I was thrilled that I didn't have to get up and head to WyoTech anymore—for a day or so until I realized I had absolutely nothing to do. I began looking for a job, quickly realizing that there wasn't much available now that I'd eliminated one of the town's major employers. All I wanted was something, anything to occupy my time and help pay the bills. I applied to stock shelves, to drive auto parts around, to do facilities setup at the university...

Nothing.

It seems counterintuitive, but my education was a rock in my pocket as I tried to swim to the surface. Nobody wanted someone who they assumed would leave for a better job as soon as an opportunity presented itself, not realizing that the opportunities they assumed I'd leave for were purely hypothetical.

Luckily for me, my father-in-law is somewhere around the four-teenth most interesting man in America.[16*] Severely dyslexic, he was pegged as the least likely of his brothers and sisters to succeed and left Kansas City at eighteen to study geology at the University of Wyoming.

[16*] I swear I'm not sucking up here. Okay, maybe a little.

There he'd meet my mother-in-law and they'd spend their honeymoon in a tent while mapping the mostly inaccessible Absaroka Mountains around Yellowstone National Park. He'd get his PhD from UC-Santa Barbara, survive a grizzly bear attack in Alaska by hitting it with a pan, then settle in central Wyoming, where he began teaching geology at Casper College. There he started a lucrative business selling ancient mammal fossils, unearthed a Tyrannosaur, and led the team that exhumed the largest mammoth ever found in North America. If you ever see a guy named Kent with a giant beard and perpetually sunburned cheeks talking about ancient terror pigs on some Discovery Channel show, it's probably him.

Somewhere in the void north of Glen Rock, Wyoming, on the ranch of a family friend, Kent discovered a miles-long uranium roll front. It was the type of find that could keep new, sustainable nuclear plants running for years. The problem for his rancher friend was that due to the Homestead Act of 1916, landowners only held surface rights and didn't own the minerals beneath. This meant that if a mining company ever uncovered what my father-in-law knew, they could swoop in, claim the minerals, work the rancher's land, and cut his family clean out of the profits. In response, Kent started a company called Stegosaur Development whose job it was to do the tedious bureaucratic work of claiming the mineral rights. It was a deal that benefited everyone involved. The mining companies didn't have to front the initial costs or spend years going back and forth with the government in order to claim each little parcel of prairie. The ranchers let Stegosaur Development onto their land in exchange for a percentage of the revenue that the uranium would eventually bring in. And when all the test wells were drilled, and the mining company decided there was sufficient product underfoot, they'd have to buy that product from Stegosaur.

But it didn't end with the government signatures. In order to complete the process, you still had to physically assert the mineral rights by pounding in a claim stake every hundred yards over the entirety of the land in question—which for this project was an area larger than most East

Coast counties. Because it was such a massive undertaking, I helped out on weekends, bundling and labeling the wooden stakes that my brother-in-law had been cutting all week, and when I got the opportunity, I'd get up at 5:00 a.m., help them load the four wheelers onto the trailer behind Kent's F-250, and head out with them into the field.

The truck would bounce for twenty or thirty miles on dirt roads to a piece of land about as far from civilization as possible in the continental US. Along the way, pronghorn bounded across the road in front of us, prairie dogs popped from their holes, and sage grouse strutted around puffing their goofy little chests. Up on the ridgelines, you could see the Pumpkin Buttes and Bighorn Mountains to the north, and in every other direction you saw absolutely nothing. It was a place where the slamming of a truck door ripped through the silence like a gunshot.

While Kent and a bunch of his students zipped around on four wheelers, covering miles and pounding in hundreds of claims a day, I was only asked to secure twenty stakes at a time. It wasn't because they were going easy on the city boy. Nope, like the Navy would've—they sent me where my skills dictated. And in this case, it was into the places the ATVs couldn't reach. I'd get a mountaineering backpack, a small sledgehammer, a GPS device, a canteen of water, and wishes of good luck. The first time I accompanied them into the field, I looked to Kent before I trekked off into the abyss.

"So where are you guys going to be?" I asked.

"Oh, just on the other side of this ridge here. Not far. Couple miles at most."

"Ah," I answered, now realizing the full scope of my forthcoming abandonment. "Just curious—what happens if I break my ankle or get bit by a rattlesnake or something?"

"Well," Kent said, pausing. "I'd suggest not doing either of those things." He shut the tailgate. "We'll meet you back here at four o'clock. Have fun." And they drove off.

Alone on the prairie I'd walk in a straight line, climbing over barbed wire fences and veering around sagebrush until I hit whatever canyon had necessitated my special assignment. One time I skidded my way down into a dry creek bed surrounded on all sides by hundred-foot cliffs, amazed that I might be the first person to *ever* see that particular spot while also quickly becoming terrified it might become my burial plot. The bluffs around me were damn near vertical and not made of the sturdiest material—which made getting down a hell of a lot easier than climbing back up. After finding the coordinates and pounding in the stake, I tried five or six times to scale the walls only to get halfway up and find an overhang I couldn't get past. So I'd surf back down in a small landslide of the burnt orange rocks we were hoping to turn into green paper. When my boots hit the bottom of the draw after one of my failed attempts, I damn near landed on an old cow skeleton.

"Well, that's ominous," I said to myself. It was getting a bit dicey. I knew if I slipped and plummeted sixty feet, I'd be lying there for a long time trying to fend off buzzards until Kent discovered me. But it was either suck it up or stay trapped. On my seventh try, with my quads burning, I willed myself bowlegged up that cliff, grasping onto whatever I could, hoping the boulders I chose to grab didn't come out of the ground and send me tumbling. When I finally reached the top, I damn near emptied my canteen in one gulp.

And so it would go all afternoon, trekking up and down ravines that people with brains have been finding ways to stay the hell out of for centuries. Once after pounding in eighteen stakes, I got to number nineteen, which the coordinates said was smack dab in the middle of an absolute gorge. By that time, I was exhausted, and my canteen was dry. No one was around to check my work, so I reared back and javelined it into the hole. I wasn't too concerned. If anyone ever saw it lying at the bottom of the crevasse, logic dictated that a cow knocked it over. And the cows weren't saying otherwise.

It's still the job I get asked about the most on my resume. There's always a small flinch as the interviewer scans the page. "You were a uranium prospector?"

"Yes, I was."

Everything was setting up nicely for the project until March 11, 2011, when a 9.0 earthquake hit northern Japan, causing a massive tsunami that flooded the Fukushima Daiichi Nuclear Power Plant. The massive saltwater breach caused cooling systems within the structure to fail, leading directly to the meltdowns of reactors one, two, and three. Soon thereafter, radioactive isotopes began to flow into the Pacific Ocean. In the aftermath, Germany decided to phase out all of its nuclear plants. The price of uranium plummeted to the point where extracting it wouldn't be remotely worth the cost. Over a decade later, however, concerns over climate change and dramatic advancements in nuclear technology are putting fission-based energy back in the conversation again. So who knows? Twenty years from now, you might owe your lights staying on to the fact that I spent a bunch of weekends traversing Wyoming's finest gulches. Or not. Maybe by then we'll figure out how to get power out of bird shit or bad ideas or something else society has in abundance.

After a year of training, Jessi was finally getting paid to do tattoos and along with her 6:00 a.m. shift at Coal Creek Coffee was pretty much keeping us afloat on sheer will. In comparison, I felt like an absolute bum, and twenty hours every third weekend working for Stegosaur wasn't exactly challenging that belief. Enter my friend Devin, a squat little punk rocker who went to college with Jessi and was somehow a regular at bars he'd never set foot in. We were having beers one Friday night at a place called The Library, which was directly across Grand Avenue from the University of Wyoming. It was a modern bar by Laramie standards. Half sports bar and half pool hall, it was connected to a popular restaurant of the same name as well as a small six-pack shop. It was mostly a hangout for grad students and chill locals and thus didn't typically invite the wild west mayhem that often rose up at the cowboy bars in town.

As Devin and I were regaling each other with yarns of our underemployed lives, a small bald guy in a brown polo pulled up a seat next to Devin and sat down. His name was Brian, and he owned the bar. Devin knew every bar owner from there to Pueblo, so the interaction was in no way unexpected.

Brian patted Devin on the back. "What are you doing back in town?"

"Here for the game," Devin said, sipping his beer. "What's new here?"

"Ugh," Brian answered. "We had a brawl last night. Six, eight guys swinging pool sticks, throwing haymakers. One of the bartenders got his nose busted trying to break it up."

Devin's eyes lit up. "A brawl? On a Thursday night? In *here*? The only time I've ever seen shit go down in this place is when Colorado State comes up for the Border War."

"I know, right?" Brian said. "Never thought I'd have to hire bouncers but I'm thinking about it. I'm just worried I'll get meatheads who show up all amped to fight and make it worse."

Devin didn't hesitate. He pointed at me. "I got your guy right here." He went on to tell Brian I had a master's degree in counseling and was trained in de-escalation all while exaggerating my rust belt toughness. By the end of the night, I'd filled out an application, neglecting to mention that during my bachelor party the previous August, I'd slammed a dude's face off a table when he wouldn't politely agree to stop throwing chicken wing bones at my cousin—which ironically meant The Library hired a guy who'd already been in a fight at the bar they were paying him to prevent fights in. Anyway, two weeks after Devin recommended me, I picked up my uniforms—a couple black T-shirts that said, DON'T LIE TO MOM, TELL HER YOU'RE AT THE LIBRARY—and started work as a doorman.

The Library had two entrances, one facing Grand Avenue and one at the back corner closest to the parking lot. The two entry points necessitated two new hires. And since they already had a lanky guy, they decided to pair me with my physical opposite. Calvin was a soft-spoken but intimidating kid from Arizona with a shaved head and tattoo sleeves. And while I was six-foot-two and 175 pounds, Calvin was my height and 350. Like I said, I was a doorman. Calvin was a *bouncer*.

It was a much different vibe than the last time I'd checked IDs as a twenty-year-old at the Greensburg Sheraton. Every Friday night, there was live music. This sounds amazing until you realize that no band in American history has ever seen an eight-foot-high drop ceiling and a capacity limit of 135 and thought, *Ya know, maybe we're not trying to reach the last row at Red Rocks*. But even though I still can't get rid of the ringing in my right ear, the bar buzzed with a college town energy that made it fun to go to work. It was pretty much the inverse of the uptight corporate sphincter clench I'd quit earlier that summer. My shifts were full of late-night sports, micro-conversations with strangers, and the occasional flirtatious drunk girl spilling Shock Top on my jeans.

Because the bar had never placed anyone at the door before, my first few nights were full of surprised patrons wondering why I was tapping them on the shoulder as they entered. In general, most of them were pretty cool about it, but a small faction were unnecessarily prickly. When I'd ask for their ID, they would blow me off, always saying the same thing, "Oh, I'm a regular."[17]*

I had the same response waiting every time. "Sounds like you need more fiber. I still need to see your ID."

At this point, 90 percent of them would act like pulling their driver's license out of their purse or pocket was akin to a full-body cavity search. "Oh my god, I've been coming here for a certain length of time that I believe designates me as superior to these serfs and not subject to such tyranny. I'm going to talk to Brian and he's..."

And they'd rail for ninety seconds about the five-second process of getting their birth year confirmed while I ignored them, smiled, and told them to have a good time.

Eventually I'd get to know all the regulars and just wave them on through—everybody except one guy. He was this little fake hard ass

---

[17] * You really need to say this out loud in order to get the joke.

who wore a leather jacket and peacocked around all night. The first time I tried to card him he scoffed and said, "Yeah, no," then batted my arm away and strutted into the bar. Obviously, I wasn't letting that slide. I followed him to his seat.

"Yo buddy, I need your ID," I said.

The bartender saw what had happened and nodded to me. "He's cool. He's friends with one of the cooks. He's in here all the time."

And that little fucker smirked at me from his bar stool and said, "See? Now piss off."

I actively try to be considerate to everyone I meet. But if you act like a scumbag anyway, I will make a hard turn in the other direction. So every time I saw this dude enter the bottle shop on his way into the bar, I'd slide over to block the door.

"ID," I'd say nonchalantly.

"What the fuck, man? Let me through."

"I will. After you show me your ID. That's how this works."

At this point, he either had to fight me or show me his license, and I was fine with either. "Jesus fucking Christ! Are you fucking kidding?" And he'd soil his undies and stomp around. When he'd finally relent and slam his license in my hand, I'd take an unnecessarily long time comparing his face with the photo. Like waaaaaay too long. Every. Damn. Time.

After our third or fourth interaction, he absolutely flipped. "What the fuck, dude? Are you stupid? You should know who I am by now!"

As I looked at his license, I grinned. "I do know who you are. I just don't like you and know this drives you insane. And I'm going to do this every fucking time you walk in." I handed his license back to him. "Have a good night."

He complained to Brian about it, but Brian didn't like the guy, either, and found it almost as funny as I did. Honestly, it became a game. A couple times I carded him again after he ran outside for a smoke. I even pointed him out to Calvin on the off chance the asshat tried to come in through the front. All the guy needed to do was be cool one time and I'd have stopped. But nope. I was still carding this dude in May.

Working the door at a popular bar becomes challenging in unexpected ways. Checking IDs on Halloween, for instance. I'd get handed a license, look at a photo of a clean-shaven engineer named Matt, then up at Chewbacca, then down at the photo, then back up at Chewbacca...

"Yeah, I'm just gonna take your word for it, man."

Behind him would be Catwoman and Optimus Prime and slutty Elmo, and I just gave up checking anything but their birthday. The Library also hosted the after party for the university's popular drag queen bingo night. When the show let out, the carnival arrived on our doorstep. As the line formed, I'd look a fabulous six-foot-five woman in a sequined dress up and down, glance at the name on the license, and say, "Have fun tonight...Bob."

"Oh, honey, tonight it's Shania."

"My apologies. Enjoy your night, ma'am."

I secretly hoped there'd be a brawl between the drag queens and some cowboys because that'd be a fight I wouldn't mind sacrificing a few teeth to say I broke up. But I found out that drag queens are the most flamboyantly entertaining group of humans you can find in the universe, so if any of the good ol' boys objected, Shania and friends would've just show-tuned them into submission. So truth be told, it was one of the easier nights of the semester.

Laramie is a college town, so fake IDs were pretty common. Brian told me not to be a hard ass unless the ruse was impossible to miss. He only wanted plausible deniability in case the cops decided to come in and crack down, so I'm sure I let one or two a night slide by that wouldn't have gotten through the door at, let's say, a swanky club in LA. But of the few fakes I confiscated, one stands out as the absolute best. A quiet nineteen-year-old girl entered the bar with a friend one Thursday night and casually handed me a New Mexico ID. I looked at it and immediately knew something was off. I just wasn't sure what.

"Hold on," I said, walking her license into the bottle shop. I went up to the guy behind the register, a chill, long-haired ski bum named Mark. "Hey, Mark, I know there's something wrong with this, but I can't put my finger on it."

We both stared at it for a minute as the girl stood next to us nervously. "I can just leave," she said, tapping her foot on the ground. "How about I just leave?"

"I got it," Mark said, smacking the license. "That's a New Mexico ID with a Grand Canyon background. And the Grand Canyon is in…"

"Arizona." I laughed. "Oh, that's hilarious." And while the girl uneasily chewed on her finger beside us, we both nearly cried at the ridiculousness of what we'd been presented. "Wait a second," I screeched. "The Liberty Bell isn't in New Jersey! This looks suspect."

Mark doubled over. "Hold on, South Dakota doesn't have palm trees!"

Meanwhile the girl is standing there meekly, praying that her entire life isn't about to unravel. "So, can I have my ID back or…"

"Oh, hell no," Mark snapped. "We're keeping this one. Little advice: go to someone who knows geography next time. I hope you didn't pay too much."

She hung her head and walked out the door to me shouting, "When did they move the Statue of Liberty to Delaware?"

The best thing about the job was that they'd hired me and Calvin because of a huge brawl, and in the entire ten months I worked there, there were only two minor skirmishes that we quelled damn near immediately. And that was it. The typical customer was someone just looking to get a little happy, have some laughs with friends, and stumble back to their apartment.

But even though major scraps never materialized, we were definitely prepared to deal with them. Calvin and I were told it was a virtual certainty we'd be putting folks in headlocks on the day of the annual Wyoming vs. Colorado State game known as "The Border War." Winner takes home an old boot as a trophy, so you know it's going to be

intense. The Library was right down the street from the football stadium, so before we opened that morning, Brian prepped the two of us
like we were about to enter the octagon.

"Two years ago, there were four fights. And we didn't have another
one until right before we hired you guys. Just be prepared. People are
going to get stupid. Anyone comes in wearing green, try and keep an
eye on them so they don't get jumped."

We opened the bar at nine that morning. Immediately, it was a zoo.
There was a line halfway down the block before the game that somehow became longer at halftime. Calvin and I were tasked with double
duty selling cans of Miller Lite to people in line. As soon as we stocked
one cooler, it got kicked and we'd have to haul another one up. At certain points, my pockets were full of hundreds of dollars of crumpled
fives and tens that I didn't have time to shuffle back to the registers.
But thankfully the mood was light and jovial despite the overwhelming
crowd. I think it helped that Wyoming won 44–0, so whenever Cowboy
fans yelled, "Hey, you suck," at the Rams fans, the Coloradans were
like, "Yeah, that's accurate." The lopsided score meant that a lot of folks
just sulked back to Fort Collins before the game ended and didn't flood
the bar with postgame tension. About all I really dealt with the whole
day was folks leaning on me for support as they swayed from side to
side waiting to get in the door.

And though I never had to break up a big fight, I did get punched
once. I was checking the IDs of a couple of joker frat boys when I
noticed the guy in front of me bring his fist back to his hip. I didn't
have time to block the cheap shot he was about to throw, so I just
clenched my abs.

THUD!

It hurt a lot more than I let on, but I didn't move. I barely grunted. I
guess his plan was for all the women at the bar to see it and jump in bed
with him? Maybe for the frat house to commission a statue? Whatever
the motivation, his demeanor changed abruptly when I just stood there
and answered his strike with a homicidal glare.

His lips quivered. "Ya gotta be prepared," he stuttered. "I was just… testing you."

I handed him back his ID. "You can turn around and walk out on your own or I can throw you out on your fucking head. Your choice."

Luckily, they weren't the type of frat bros that were out seeking chaos. They were looking for beer and whatever girls might be drunk enough to find them amusing. But after this dude hit me, his buddies couldn't wait to be the first to apologize. "Steve, what the fuck was that? Are you kidding? Why would you punch the bouncer? We're sorry. He's an idiot."

Steve pleaded his case. "I was kidding. I was just goofing around!"

I watched them until they exited, then turned around to face the neon Rolling Rock sign behind me. I bit down on the back of my hand and let out a groan that was briefly heard over the jukebox. And though I never got to break up any real fights, I did have to survive four hours of karaoke every Thursday, which was a lot like being elbowed in the face over and over.

The Library provided me a critical sense that I was, however briefly, part of a community. I got to know the bartenders and the wait staff as we lamented being stuck in the same voyeuristic trip—forced to watch *other* people have a good time. All of us were crucial to the vibe yet somehow oddly divorced from it. But after WyoTech, it was exactly the type of breezy, low-pressure job I needed. And though I wasn't exactly raking in cash, I no longer felt like a complete bum, either. At thirty-three, I didn't have what anyone would call a career, but at least I was contributing *something* financially. Being able to earn money in a place that smelled like wing sauce and abounded with laughter was a bonus.

After three years, Jessi's apprenticeship ended. She had an offer to stay at The Underground, but while she adored that shop, there was a clear ceiling for her in Laramie. If she wanted to become truly success-ful at this new endeavor, she'd have to go somewhere with, ya know, people—one resource Wyoming lacked. For a while, Denver was the front-runner. We had a bunch of friends down there, and it would've been a super-cool place to land. But then we peered into the future and wondered what would happen if we had kids someday. Who would watch them when we had to work? We needed to be near family. And everyone in Jessi's family lived in Wyoming, a place she desperately wanted to escape. Which left one familiar option.

CHAPTER 17

Storm Clouds

C onveniently, when Jessi and I arrived in Pennsylvania, there was an unoccupied and now decluttered house waiting for us in Greensburg. The plan was for us to live there rent free while Jessi looked for a job at a tattoo shop and I did the necessary fixes that my grandparents had neglected over the previous two decades. From there, I'd try to find a school counseling position, and we'd eventually move to a place that made sense for both of our commutes.

To our pleasant surprise, Jessi found a job almost immediately at a busy street shop called Salvation Tattoo on Pittsburgh's Southside—a two-mile stretch of bars and restaurants popular with the city's college crowd. She started making money almost immediately doing the type of little flash tattoos that kids get on their eighteenth birthday. So once I'd completed the repairs at my grandparents' house, we decided to cut Jessi's commute in half by moving into a three-story townhouse in Murrysville. It seemed a bit excessive, but after the cramped apartments we'd endured in Laramie, we felt like we deserved something with a little space. We signed a year-long lease and happily moved what little we had into a big, empty place we assumed we'd soon fill with a lot more stuff.

And then the bottom fell out.

Two weeks after we'd moved into the townhouse, I was driving to the gym and saw Jessi's car pass by at a time when she should've been at work. It was one of those moments when you feel like you swallowed a rock. I immediately turned around. When I walked in the door, Jessi told me that her boss's friend had moved to town from Baltimore and randomly showed up looking for a job. The dickhole who ran Salvation told him, "Sure. You can have Jessi's," and cut her loose with no warning. This was disastrous in a few ways, but mainly because the calculations we'd done on whether we could afford the townhouse were based on what Jessi was pulling in per week. Once Salvation let her go, we actually ended up in worse shape than we'd have been in had she been unemployed all summer.

Adding to the stress, the recession was choking the amount of money coming into the state. In response, the legislature began hacking away at the cash they allocated to assist Pennsylvania's five hundred school districts. It was a great plan because stiffing our children is obviously preferable to anything that might possibly shrink corporate profits or make the wealthy less comfortable. As for the school districts themselves, asking them to *postpone* the five-million-dollar upgrade to the football stadium was just as preposterous. What was reasonable, however, was designating positions like music teachers, librarians, and school counselors as "non-essential personnel." Basically, this meant that when a counselor retired, many districts simply dissolved the position and divided their students among the remaining counselors. Thus, there were no openings to pursue.

Every day, Jessi and I felt like we were falling with no hope of landing. Running out of money and in dire need of work, Jessi managed to grab a job at a coffee shop that had just opened between the laundromat and a tanning salon down the hill. And without many options, I slumped my shoulders, held my nose, and walked into a place I thought I'd left far behind.

"Welcome to Emerald. What can we help you with today?"

I took a deep breath. "I just need an application."

Four days after I applied, I walked into the garage and started filling up soap buckets at the Emerald location on the ground floor of the Jonnet Building, a ten-story brown monolith that rose up from the parking lot of strip mall in Monroeville on a stretch of depressing Americana just west of the Turnpike. The garage was constructed on the site of a former bank drive-thru. It had two bays flanked by sets of glass garage doors, which meant we could pull cars through without having to back them out. All in all, it was fairly warm in the winter and airy and light in the summer, which was about all you could ask for as a car prep.

I was organizing the supplies when a six-foot-four Jamaican man in his early sixties jammed his way out of an old station wagon covered in Steelers bumper stickers and entered the garage. He paid me no mind as he walked in, put his lunch in the mini fridge, and began meticulously fiddling with the radio until he found the Top 40 station. I had no idea I was about to meet my favorite coworker of all time.

He turned around, saw me putting soap in the bucket, and feigned a heart attack. "Did they send someone to help old Kingsley?" he said, hand on his chest, eyes wide with surprise. "I don't believe it! Go away, mon, you are a dream."

"I, uh…always assumed I was real," I replied. "Although I'm less certain now that you've called it into question. I didn't assume my day would start with an existential crisis."

As he made his way over, I couldn't tell if he was about to hug or dissect me. "The last guy quit in the middle of the day! Six weeks Kingsley has no one to help. I'm an old man! Do you think I should be doing this job, one man, all these cars?"

"Wow, that really suck—"

"No waaaaay, mon!" he said, clutching his back. "Everything hurt." He stared right into my eyes. "What is your name?"

"Cramer."

"Cramer, are you going to be the reason Kingsley's back scream at night?"

"No. I need the money too bad."

He squinted with skepticism. "You make it one month, we can be friends. You don't, I will haunt you, mon. I will haunt you."

And that became my life, day in and day out, me and Kingsley hanging out in the garage. I learned early on that it was going to be much, much different than the other four locations I'd worked where unnervingly trashed cars were a bit of an anomaly. But due to our proximity to the Turnpike, we got a ton of folks going on vacation—which meant that a large portion of our rentals were treated with the care dogs afford chew toys.

One minivan came back from the Outer Banks filled front to back with an inch-deep layer of Cool Ranch Doritos. At minimum, it was the contents of fifteen full-size bags. I don't care how long you had the vehicle, there's no way to make that big of a mess without Cookie Monstering them into your forehead over and over the whole way to the ocean and back. Unfortunately, that particular van wasn't abnormal. Every day at least three or four cars came in with enough food on the floor to restock a Grab N Go. I swear to god, the people of Monroeville could get crumbs out of a grape.

But the most alarming difference between Monroeville and the other branches is best relayed with a story about a trip to a small impound lot in Swissvale right around the corner from my grandmother's church. Upon arriving at the lot, I waited outside as our assistant manager, Anthony, paid to get one of the branch's Dodge Chargers out of automotive jail. He had to rush back to the office, so he left me with the keys and told me to hurry back. As he drove off, the lot attendant came over to open the gate.

"Which car you got there?" he asked.

"The black Dodge Charger," I said, pointing at the muscle car against the fence.

"Ooh, that one," the attendant said, accompanying me toward the car. Nothing about his demeanor gave me the slightest hint about what was to come. As I opened the driver's door to hop in, he simultaneously opened the passenger door and pointed to the interior panel, which was spattered with what looked like streaks of week-old coffee. "So we're thinking it must've been the driver who shot him due to where all the blood ended up."

I peered across the seats in the first stages of realizing I was staring at a crime scene. "Hold on, buddy, you're saying there was a *shooting* in this car?"

"Did you guys not know that?"

I kicked at the gravel. "If the office knew, they failed to relay it to me."

There was an awkward silence. "Well, if you'll pop the trunk you can see..."

"Whoa, dude, please tell me the dead guy isn't in there."

"Oh no. No. That stuff goes to the coroner *way* before it comes here," he replied as if that type of surprise was somehow impossible.

Thrilled I wasn't about to see a corpse, I popped the trunk. Dried coffee everywhere. Enough dried coffee to satisfy a vampire for weeks. I just shook my head. I could either refuse to drive this car and be stranded in Swissvale or just put the damn thing on the Parkway and drive the speed limit back.

The guy nodded. "We wiped down the steering wheel for you."

"That was considerate. Thank you," I said, sliding in and shutting the door.

Narcotics and murder were always hovering on the periphery of my daily duties. During my time at Monroeville, I saw three or four cars I'd cleaned earlier in the day inside rings of police tape on the eleven o'clock news. A good quarter of our business came from drug dealers changing up their vehicles every week in order to throw off the cops. The first time I found a bag of cocaine in the glove compartment, I showed it to Kingsley and asked, "So what the hell do we do with *this*?"

His eyes lit up. "It go straight in the trash, mon. You never see it!"

"We're not supposed to like...let someone know or..."

"You let someone know, the cops show up. Then you got to testify, mon. You want to testify at a drug runner trial?"

"No, I do not."

"It go in the trash, mon," he said sternly. "You never see nothing."

The drugs, however, did provide their share of lighter moments. One of the various office workers during my stint in Monroeville was a sorority blonde named Amy who'd just graduated from Edinboro or Slippery Rock or one of Pennsylvania's other state schools. She was sent up Route 28 to retrieve a car that had been impounded after a police chase. It was a Tuesday afternoon and relatively slow, so when she came peeling around the corner and braked abruptly in front of the garage door, I knew something was wrong. I hit the green button, opening the door so she could drive into the bay.

Inside the car, Amy was shaking—but not in a frightened way. It was more like how you'd shiver if you got bird poop in your mouth. Too embarrassed to make eye contact, she reached over and pressed the power window button.

"Cramer, get the Shop-Vac!" she squealed. "I'm covered in crack!"

I glanced down at her lap. She wasn't lying. I don't know what the going rate is for that stuff, but there had to have been hundreds, perhaps thousands of dollars in little crystals clinging to her sweater and dress pants. "Whoa," I replied. "You are indeed covered in crack."

"Can you please vac me off?"

I didn't know her well enough to reach a nozzle into the area where most of the drugs were. "How about I hand the hose through the door and you do it yourself?"

She nodded. I fed the hose through the window, flipped on the power, and to anyone who ambled by I'm certain it looked as if she was using the Shop-Vac to help herself, uh…relax. When she was done and stepped out of the car, there was some residue in places she couldn't see, which I helped with very tastefully and totally in accordance with the guidelines in the sexual harassment manual about how to proceed when a coworker of the opposite sex begs you to vacuum drugs off their ass. Though many lines were lost, no lines were crossed.

When Amy could breathe again, she told me how she'd opened the center console and noticed a bunch of CDs. Sick of listening to the radio, she thumbed through them at a stoplight and picked one to pop into the player—except that instead of containing the urban truths of the Wu-Tang Clan, the case held copious amounts of unbound crack rock bathed in coke, which upon opening exploded all over her. Such is how a blond girl from the suburbs briefly became the world's worst drug mule. And how the street value of our Shop-Vac skyrocketed.

It should be evident by now that the Monroeville office was an absolute zoo. The job itself sucked, but I spent the day listening to Kingsley sing off-key Beyonce songs and belly laugh like Santa Claus, so at points it was almost tolerable. Nothing can really describe the insanity of the office, though, like the day before Thanksgiving in 2011. We had sixty reservations. And that was before a tanker truck decided to leak driveway sealant all over a five-mile stretch of the westbound Turnpike, destroying over four hundred cars that drove through it, leading many people to wonder...

"Why isn't my car moving anymore? And why is there a Mastodon stuck in the road?"

So we're running everywhere all day because people headed from New Jersey to Illinois for Thanksgiving are trapped in Monroeville with a fossilized vehicle. For my manager, a thirty-year-old new mom named Jamie, it was a nightmare of epic proportions. Halfway through the afternoon, it led her stressed out, post-pregnancy mind toward the worst decision I believe I've ever witnessed. As we scrambled around for cars, Jamie told me that she immediately needed a silver Ford Flex that had just returned. So I hustled out to get it, jumping in the driver's seat only to be overwhelmed by the smell of gasoline. I stumbled out into the parking lot hacking pathetic little coughs as I circled the car, opening all the doors to dissipate the fumes. Upon examination, the back seat and floor mats were soaked in regular unleaded as if someone had been interrupted before they could set the car ablaze. I took a few moments to quell the headache I'd gotten from my unintentional huff, then traipsed back into the office.

"Hey, Jamie, we can't use the Flex," I told her. "The back seats are soaked in gasoline."

"Cramer, I need that car. Right now. Go."

"I almost blacked out when…"

"Go!"

My concerns repulsed, I returned to the car, rolling all of the windows down before pulling into the garage. Maybe it wasn't as bad as I was making it out to…

Before I even put it in park, Kingsley reeled back. "Cramer, this car smell like gasoline!"

"I know. Back seat is soaked in it. Jamie said she said she wanted it anyway."

Kingsley put his hands on his hips. "I'm not breathing that. You go up and tell her we're not cleaning this wretched thing. This go to the detail shop."

When Jamie saw me again, her hands involuntarily clenched into fists. "What now?"

"You really have to come down and—"

"Aaaaah!" she shrieked, stomping across the office and down the stairs. As she stuck her head in the car to give it a sniff, it was obvious that the smell nearly made her wretch, but at that point her mind could only travel in one direction. "Ugh, just spray twice as much citrus scent around as you usually do. And hurry up. I don't have time for this." And she scurried back up to the office.

Defeated, Kingsley and I began to do as we were told. I vacuumed the front while he misted an entire bottle of citrus in there—enough to turn the inside of the car into a foggy morning on the Cape. All it did was make the interior smell like jet fuel and grapefruit, a lemony horror that was worse by a factor of ten.

Kingsley finally threw up his hands. "We can't rent this car. The woman crazy."

I nodded, kicked away the Shop-Vac, and marched up the steps to give Jamie the bad news. "Look, I don't care if you fire me. We're not renting that car."

Her response may have been the dumbest thing another person has ever said to me. "Cramer, the woman we're giving it to smokes out every car we ever rent her. They'll be ashes and cigarette butts everywhere the minute she takes off, so who cares what it smells like?"

I must've blinked forty times. "Your plan is to give the gasoline-soaked car to an avid smoker? This is what you're telling me?"

"I'm tired of debating this. Just go pull it around!"

"You want me to throw some dry brush back there, too? Maybe an oxygen tank just to add to the liability?"

Behind her eyes, I actually saw a moment of clarity in the middle of her profit-driven madness as if she briefly pictured a Ford Flex bursting into flame on the Parkway. It was short-lived. To have one more car out on rent, she'd risk it. "Cramer, give me the keys."

There was only one way to save Jamie from herself. "Hey, Anthony!" I yelled across the office. "Congrats! After the lawsuit, you'll be the new manager!"

It seemed to finally dawn on her that the consequences of this decision could negatively affect her career. "Fine! We'll find the woman another car. Jesus."

I nodded and headed for the door. "Don't forget to thank me when you're around for your daughter's first birthday."

In much the same way as Stateline and WyoTech, my time at the Monroeville Emerald was slowly killing me inside. But unlike those two jobs, this one damn near actually killed me. The second time I nearly died at work[18*] was the day of the 2012 baseball trade deadline. I only

---

[18] * Remember Swearing Mike and the crashing crates of doom?

remember this because for the first time since I was fifteen years old, the Pirates didn't suck out loud. That was really all that was on my mind all day. The Monday rush that typically spills into Tuesday morning was over, so Kingsley and I were getting caught up, washing cars at a reasonable pace instead of at hyper speed. At about three thirty, our intern, Kaylee, a business major at LaRoche College, came down into the garage and asked if I could pick up a customer at a condo complex off of Northern Pike.

"Sure. Just let me help King finish this car," I said. She nodded and headed back upstairs. Now normally if I was asked to pick up a customer, whoever did the asking would give me keys to the car they wanted me to take. I figured Kaylee had gone upstairs to grab them and would be right back down. But a few moments later, I saw her backing out a red minivan as if she was headed somewhere. So I set my wash brush against the wall and went out to flag her down.

As I stepped into the parking lot, I noticed that the air felt heavy. A few minutes prior, it was bright and sunny, but now the sky was more of a dirty gray. I walked about ten yards from the garage to get to Kaylee's van. Seeing me, she rolled her window down.

"Hey," I said. "You never told me what car to take. Does it matter?"

She gave herself a soft palm smack to the forehead. "I left the keys on the shelf. I just forgot to tell you. I think it's a silver Honda Civic. I'm sorry."

I laughed. "No worries. Just wanted to make sure what the plan was."

She held up a small leather satchel. "I'm headed to the bank, but I should be here by the time you get back."

"Cool," I replied, waving and turning around. She rolled up the window just as a couple big raindrops began to sparsely hit the pavement. I began to walk back toward the garage. It was about as mundane a moment as possible—a slice of time that typically gets swallowed by the sameness of it all and filtered right out of your brain.

But then something compelled me to look up.

In a dark cloud above the building, there was a tiny flash, the type you'd see if you ran across the carpet in socks and then touched a doorknob. Upon seeing it pop into existence, I swore this tiny spark and I were connected, as if there was a corridor opening up between us and I could just float into the sky and grab it. Then suddenly and menacingly that adorable little zap branched out. The cloud around it lit up like the windows in a haunted house. The spark zipped to the right, seemed to bounce off a mirror and then...

WHACK!

The bolt shot down from the sky at terrifying speed. There was a blue flash in front of my eyes and what felt and sounded like a bullwhip being cracked on my left shoulder. I had to have leaped three feet in the air. When my shoes hit the ground, I sprinted for the safety of the garage in a time that could've landed me an Olympic medal.

"Jesus," I said, trying to catch my breath. Still a bit tingly from the jump scare, I grabbed the Honda keys that Kaylee had left me and walked out the other side of the garage into the intensifying raindrops.

On the way to pick this dude up, I learned the Pirates had made a trade with the Marlins for an underwhelming first-baseman, then was treated to a recap of the customer's fender bender. The storm itself was easing to a drizzle as I dropped the guy off in front of the building. All in all, it was about ten minutes after the bolt.

And this is where it gets freaky. As soon as I entered the garage, Kingsley stopped washing the car in front of him, dropped his brush, and stared at me like I was a voodoo demon.

"Cramer, are you a ghost?" he yelled.

I flipped the Civic keys into a small wicker basket on the shelf. "What?"

"You got hit by lightning, mon!" he shouted. "I saw it with my own two eyes!"

I laughed it off. He was clearly joking. "King, if I got hit by lightning, I wouldn't be talking to you right now."

"The lightning hit you!" he insisted. "And you jump in the air, run in here, get the keys, and drive off like nothing is wrong. Are you the devil?"

"Yes, King. The devil washes cars in Monroeville. It's a great cover."

King had back problems and spent most of his day slightly hunched, but he'd always jolt straight up if something caused him surprise or alarm—which was exactly what he did. "You think Kingsley is joking you? I'm not joking you, mon! You got hit by fucking lightning. And just run away!"

At this point, I wasn't convinced. Obviously, King had misinterpreted what he saw. Also, he was a bit of a prankster and I was pretty sure that any minute he was going so say, "Ha ha, Cramer, old King is just messing with you."

That's the story I told myself until Kaylee returned from the bank. She parked the van and slowly began walking toward the garage holding the petty cash satchel. Her reaction was much more subdued than King's, but she also gazed upon me as if I was an apparition.

"Cramer, are you...okay?" she asked. "You...got hit by lightning."

From behind her I hear, "What did King tell you, mon!"

I knew Kaylee had been at the bank and didn't have time to coordinate with King on some elaborate story. Also she'd been sitting in the van in the parking lot, which meant that I had two witnesses from two totally different angles who both insisted that I got hit by a bolt of lightning (a bolt that knocked out power in the entire ten-story building, mind you). What actually happened, I have no idea. I'm pretty sure I didn't get hit because from everything I've ever heard, you *know for sure* when you've been hit by lightning.

The most plausible explanation is that I was about to step over a three-inch-by-three-inch metal grate that was part of the old shelter for the bank drive-thru and the bolt hit *that*, grounded itself, traveled into the building, and blew out all the power. That's really all I have. And if that's the case, I might be one of the only people in the world to ever be grazed by lightning. Also, it means another half step and I was dead.

The suddenness of the whole thing shook me to the last atom. After everything I'd done, everything I'd worked for, only a sheer miracle saved me from dying as a car washer—perishing in a bolt of dullness, my last act trying to locate keys to a Honda Civic.

So not only did life feel totally hopeless, I was shown in no uncertain terms that it could also be taken in a literal flash. I mean it'd be like reading a chapter in a book, waiting for a dramatic conclusion or some lesson to be learned, but instead the author just ended it without any of the

CHAPTER 18

Outlets

W hen your job is washing cars in the winter, the only thing you care about is keeping your feet dry. The moment your boots get wet enough that the moisture seeps through to your socks, a nap in a butterfly garden couldn't turn the day back north again. And it is impossible to wash thirty-two cars in a day without getting your feet wet. Damp gloves are no picnic, either. When forced to recall the eleven months of utter despair I spent at the Emerald branch in Pittsburgh's Oakland section, that's the first memory that pops to mind: an icy, shivering hell starting in my toes and rising up inch by inch to consume my entire body. The second thing I can see clearly is the giant flock of crows that swarmed over the busway bridge every evening at sundown, seemingly waiting for me to keel over so they could peck at my frozen bones.

When the lease on our townhouse in Murrysville ran out, Jessi and I ditched it like a murder weapon. By this time, Jessi was augmenting her coffee shop money by tattooing at a skeezy shop a few miles up the river from downtown, which meant driving close to an hour each way to do small tattoos for whatever tweekers happened to walk in. The pay wasn't justifying the travel, so we decided it was time to move into the city. Because of it, Emerald transferred me to the nearest branch, a busy, crowded mess of a location a half mile from the University of Pittsburgh.

The Oakland branch looked like it was once a corner market. Surrounding it was a fenced-in parking lot that was about twenty spaces too small for the number of cars it needed to contain on a typical Friday afternoon. Next to the lot loomed the six-story brick wall of a self-storage place that cut off half the sky and made the whole site feel like a prison yard. The manager at Oakland was named Megan, and unlike Jamie in Monroeville, she didn't have a baby to use as an excuse for her inept, remorseless decisions. She was just a terrible person. Before you discount my assessment of her character as being overly harsh, I present what happened when I arrived at work on a particularly Arctic morning.

Megan was wandering the lot checking in cars that had dropped overnight. Before saying hello, she pointed up to the garage. "Cramer, I need the car in there immediately for an important client," she said, adjusting the black-framed glasses that only partially hid the evil in her eyes. "And keep the garage door shut. I want the car to be warm when they get it."

I nodded and trudged up toward the garage, entering through the side door. After two steps inside, my lungs felt like they'd been set ablaze. My eyes began to sting. To my utter horror, I found myself in the middle of a toxic death cloud. *Oh my god, the car is fucking running.* Using the skills I'd picked up at the chemical plant all those years ago, I pulled my shirt up over my nose to create a shield impervious to toxins and leaped outside to catch a decent breath.

As I stood there trying to psyche myself up to run back in and hit the garage door button, I heard Megan yell at me. "I told you I need that car right away! Quit messing around!"

I was so angry I could barely function. "You left the car running with the garage door shut knowing I was about to walk in there? Are you *kidding* me? Do you know what I just breathed in?"

"Don't take that tone with me. I'm your boss," she said with zero empathy or even a lick of understanding of what she did wrong. "I will write you up."

It was obvious that she either didn't know or didn't care that she'd set me up to inhale poison, and I'm not sure which scared me more. After she repeated the folly twice more, I actually had to beg the regional manager to tell her why leaving cars running in confined spaces was a bad idea. That's the kind of twit I was dealing with.

As a thirty-five-year-old with two master's degrees, I was making $8.25 an hour. I had over fifty thousand dollars in student loans and was paying for healthcare out of pocket. Luckily, there was a ray of light on the horizon in the form of the recently passed Affordable Care Act. One provision of the ACA stated that any employee who worked over thirty hours for a company with over fifty employees would now be eligible for healthcare through said employer. Emerald had always been careful to give their car preps no more than 39.5 hours a week, so they weren't forced to give us the benefits of full-time employees. But now that the threshold had been lowered to thirty, the frigid drudgery might almost be worth it. Eight bucks an hour would be more like eighteen if we didn't have to pay for health insurance. Hell, we might be able to start putting a little bit of money into a retirement account. We could begin saving to buy a house. This was really going to change things for the bett—

Megan called me into her office one Monday morning. "Cramer, we're going to have to cut your hours from thirty-nine to twenty-nine starting next week. No more Thursdays or Wednesday afternoons. Okay, that's all. I need the white Buick Regal like yesterday, so make sure you hurry."

Emerald was an operation that made $15.4 billion in 2012 on the backs of people like me busting their ass for almost nothing. To reiterate: fifteen point four *billion* dollars. And they couldn't sacrifice any of that ridiculous windfall to give healthcare to the people doing actual work while management was going on business lunches and golf outings. And not only that, I now got $82.50 less per paycheck. Let me be clear, I still think capitalism is the very best economic structure our society has come up with and it's not close. But the fact that the system rewards greed above all else, thus elevating the morally bereft assholes among us who do the least for their fellow humans into places of prestige and power, is eventually going to be the iceberg that sinks the ship. Somehow, some way, sympathy for the less fortunate has to be part of the equation or we're all doomed.

As for Emerald, I desperately tried to get out.

Once when I was eating lunch at the sandwich shop next to Emerald in Monroeville, a group of guys in dress shirts and jeans came in. In the group was a cocky-looking athletic dude I swore I recognized. Later, on his way to the bathroom, he passed my table and stopped. "Why do I know you?" he asked.

"Hold on," I said. "I'm doing the same thing you are, looping through all my memor..." And it hit me. "Your name is Adam. I was your RA in college."

His eyes jumped open. "Cramer!" he said. "What's up, man?"

I laughed. "You're not from here. What are you doing in *Monroeville*?"

Adam shrugged. "Ugh. Long story. After Flagler, I drifted around, ended up going to LA and getting a master's degree in screenwriting, got fucked by the writer's strike, and somehow ended up here. How about you?"

This jackass stole my life's story. "Dude, you're never going to believe this, but..."

The unexpected meeting at the sandwich shop led to an introduction to the other guys Adam was having lunch with. At the time, Western Pennsylvania was in the middle of a natural gas boom due to numerous untapped Marcellus Shale deposits. Adam was being compensated handsomely by a company out of Louisiana to meticulously go through two centuries of farm and land deeds so as to know who to approach to set up drilling and extraction. They were paying $250 per day. And they needed people.

Two weeks later, I was talking to the mid-Atlantic regional manager of a company I'll call Louisiana Development. After describing my time working on the uranium project in Wyoming, we shook hands, and he told me as soon as he got word from the big bosses in New Orleans, I'd be coming aboard. I spent the next half of the day shadowing Adam as he showed me the exhilarating process of tracing property transfers back to the 1800s. I didn't care how boring it was. For $250 a day, I'd watch milk expire. Jessi could quit getting up at 4:00 a.m. to go into the coffee shop. She could stop putting in sixty-five hours a week and coming home weepy and exhausted. And no matter what the weather was, my feet would be warm.

Every day I went into Emerald wondering if it was my final day of being an invisible, poorly compensated afterthought. I waited. And I washed cars. I played poker at Adam's house on Friday nights with the guys I was about to work with. For two months, I anticipated the final go-ahead. Until it became clear I was waiting on the same dream I'd been waiting on for most of my adult life—a dream that was mostly just fog. Due to the whims of the energy market, two months after I shook the regional manager's hand, Louisiana Development went on a hiring freeze. My job was permanently on hold. Adam watched all of his coworkers gradually peel off for other projects. The poker game got smaller. We both realized that not only wasn't I coming aboard the train, it was slowing down to let Adam off.

People who've never struggled wonder why it's so hard to break the cycle. It's because you need a lot more than just work ethic, skill, and desire. When you're near the bottom, every time you think you're on your way up, the ladder sheds a rung. And I started the journey, like, 41 percent of the way up. I had a support system. I can't imagine how difficult it is for the folks trying to get out of the hole from below me. I often wonder if they *ever* get to glimpse the surface.

By this point, *Zendog* had gone through four different directors. While I kept getting paid a thousand bucks a year for the rights, each turn of the page was accompanied by fierce optimism that would eventually flame out into yet another heartbreaking stay in career purgatory. Whenever my feet were freezing, I'd warm myself by glancing around at the Oscars crowd in my mind and beginning my speech with, "Eighteen months ago, I was cleaning rental cars." But it was starting to become obvious that no grand opportunity was going to fly me away to the promised land. There was no other side of the hill. Just struggle without gain. If you did all the right things, had talent, and busted your ass for years, weren't you supposed to be rewarded *at some point*? Everyone had always told me, "Just don't give up, and someday it will all come together." And it hadn't. As a consequence, I started to become bitter, angry, and defeated.

And I still had to get up and wash cars for people who viewed me as a drone. Even when I saved them from certain doom.

Once when I was in the garage, I watched Megan circle a brand-new BMW X3 with a guy who was renting it for a business trip to Philadelphia. The X3 was a sleek, compact SUV that looked cool and drove like you were gliding on ribbons. But it also had one massive design flaw. For some reason, the engineers decided to fiddle around with the most basic and necessary premise imaginable: the process of putting the vehicle in park. On most every automatic transmission in circulation since 1948, the driver slides the shifter until it lines up with the P residing in the very final spot. As far as I know, not a soul in the world thought, *I wish there was another way.* But the Germans decided, "We'll go ahead and fuck with it anyhow." On the X3, the final position at the top of the shifter channel was *neutral.* You then had to tap a button on top of the shifter to actually put it in park—adding an extra step after most people assumed the sequence had ended.

Anyway, this guy backed the X3 toward the garage, which was up a slight hill from the office. Before he exited, however, he noticed something on his bill that he wanted to clarify, so he stopped the car and stepped out, focused intently on his receipt. As he crunched the numbers in his head, the open driver's door of the X3 began to slowly creep away from him. Having almost wrecked one or two of these stupid things myself, I knew exactly what was happening.

"Sir!" I yelled from the garage. "Sir! Your car is—"

It was time to become the action hero I'd always hoped to be. I dropped the pressure washer and sprinted past the guy, trying to catch the car as it rolled away, gaining speed as it headed toward the front door of the office. In seven or eight big strides, I caught up to it, grabbed the steering wheel, swung my legs inside, and jammed on the brake just before it clipped the back of a Sonata and crashed into the waiting area.[19*]

With my foot on the brake, I tapped the button on top of the shifter as the guy came ambling toward me, looking absolutely tormented. "My god, did I forget to put it in park?"

"You have to, uh," I said, breathing deeply, "tap this silver doohickey until the light comes on. Otherwise it's in neutral."

The guy abruptly switched from being angry at himself to mystified with BMW. "I've been doing it one way my whole life. What's the point of... Why would you *change* that?" he said, tugging nervously on his shirt.

It was at this point that Megan slammed open the front door. "Cramer, what the hell are you doing?"

"Other than saving your business and quite possibly your life?"

She pointed to the garage. "Why is that Avenger still soapy? The customer is waiting!"

I pointed at the X3. "This thing was in neutral and rolling toward the office. I literally ran it down and stopped it like Bruce Willis. You're welcome."

Megan remained wholly unimpressed. "Okay, but now you should be finishing up the Avenger so..." And she waved me away with a flick

---

[19*] Which was filled with toddlers, puppies, and nuns.

of the wrist. My god, she was the real-life embodiment of one of Cinderella's wicked stepsisters. With no recourse, I headed back toward the garage.

"Thanks, buddy!" the X3 guy said. "You really saved my ass. Hope you get a bonus or something."

"I won't!" I replied without turning around.

Day after day, that's how things went. For a while we had a decent assistant manager who provided an adequate check on Megan's ditzy callousness. But in January she got a job with fleet services, and they transferred in a piece of human bubblegum named Rachelle to take her place. And when Rachelle was in the garage by herself, the order of IQ from highest to lowest went as follows: trashcan ants, dead hornet, drain muck, washer fluid barrel, Rachelle, stack of tires. And I'm only putting her ahead of the tires because I feel like being nice.

As long as I'd worked there, Emerald's main business policy was, "Hurry, hurry, hurry. Don't stop to think. Hurry, hurry, hurry." But I'd at least had a few managers who realized that profit margin and customer satisfaction aren't solely predicated on speed. Rachelle did not. She'd roll into the garage with a car she needed "immediately," and while I was crawling over the seats cleaning up crumbs, I'd watch her run around the car in her pants suit like she was on some sort of Japanese game show while indiscriminately thrusting the brush toward the side panels. Imagine a two-year-old with a coloring book and you'll understand how Rachelle cleaned a car. Then she'd run around closing the doors, nearly always slamming one on my ankle so she could spray water wildly around the garage. When she was done, everything in the place was drenched yet at least two windows were still soapy.

There was a single outlet in the entire garage. It was on the wall beside the shelving unit. This outlet was critical because we used it to plug in the Shop-Vac. Until Rachelle showed up, it had a flip-down plastic cover to prevent the socket from getting wet and shorting out. But two weeks after she arrived, Rachelle managed to snap the little pin that kept it in place. So now the garage's one outlet was exposed—and if it got water in it, we couldn't use the Shop-Vac until it dried out. Which meant we'd have to bring the cars down by the office and run an extension cord out from the break room to clean the interiors. It also meant that on cold days, you were further away from the heater, and on stormy days, you were vacuuming in the rain.

Even so, it really shouldn't have been a big deal. One morning I walked into the office and politely asked if everyone could refrain from squirting water toward the outlet. "When you're cleaning the roof of a car, if you could please walk around to the driver's side and spray back toward the opposite wall, that'd be awesome," I said. "If you don't, the outlet will short out and we won't have a vac for three or four hours. So let's not do that."

Later that day, I got back from picking up a car at Midas and noticed in the rearview that Rachelle was in the garage squirting off a car, doing exactly what I asked her not to. Before I could get up there, she pulled out and took off. When I got up to the garage, the outlet was soaked. I flipped the switch on the Shop-Vac, and when there should've been a roar, it just clicked. Which meant I had to haul the thing down to the office and find the extension cord—just as it started to rain.

This would happen twice a week. Each time I'd remind her. Each time she'd ignore me. Then came the time she pulled a car in and immediately began squirting water in the wrong direction. I hadn't even gotten to turn the Shop-Vac on before it died.

"Rachelle!" I yelled, flipping the switch on and off only to hear the dead click over and over. "I've asked you ten times to quit spraying water toward the outlet. What is it you don't understand about this?"

She was taken aback that I had the audacity to question her. "I'm in a hurry, and I don't have time to walk all the way around the car to start squirting it off."

"It's all the same!" I yelled. "It doesn't matter where you start. You still have to spray off the whole car, so it doesn't take any more or less time."

In the tone of someone sending back a perfectly good meal, she responded, "Well, this is the way I do it."

I was about to pull a fender off. "When you short out the power, we can't vacuum and wash simultaneously. Your customer will get their car six or seven minutes later than they otherwise would've because of your attempt to save four seconds that you *aren't actually saving!*"

"Well, I don't agree," she answered. "And why aren't you vacuuming? I told you I'm in a hurry!"

AAAAAAAAAAAAAHHHHHHHHHHHHHH!

Afterward, I begged Megan to tell Rachelle to stop squirting water at the outlet. Megan's response was, "Well, she says that's the way she does it because it saves time."

AAAAAAAAAAAAAHHHHHHHHHHHHHH!

I finally lost my mind in mid-July. I was in the garage cleaning out a Ford Fusion when a crabby old woman scared the shit out of me by tapping me on the elbow. "You need to stop working on this car and get mine done!" she yelled.

I was not a fan of customers wandering into the garage. "Yeah, you're not allowed to be in here," I snapped at her.

Undeterred, she pointed to a maroon Buick 200 that was parked on the side of the garage where we put the trashed cars that needed extra time to clean. "You should be working on that one!" she shouted. "That's the one the girls in the office said they're giving to me."

I clasped my hand over my mouth to make sure that regrettable statements didn't fly out, then glanced at the car she was pointing at. The last customer had essentially wiped out the tobacco industry's class action losses inside that car. It was coated in ash and smelled like a chimney.

I walked over and peered in the window of the smoked-out car. "Are you sure they said you were getting *this* one?"

"Yes!"

Despite the fact that this lady had marched into the garage to boss me around, I still tried to be as pleasant as possible. "Just so you know, the last customer smoked a hundred cigarettes in that car. It's like Pompeii in there. It would take a minimum of a half hour before I'd be comfortable giving it to you."

Hearing this, the woman turned and marched down to the office with flames trailing behind her. I shrugged and returned to cleaning. Not my problem. But apparently this lady went berserk because ten minutes later Megan and Rachelle were walking her around a Cadillac. While they were doing so, I grabbed another set of keys from the peg-board behind the desk and walked out the front door. Outside Megan and Rachelle were waiting to pounce.

"We need to have a talk," Megan said.

I sighed. "About what?"

"How many times have you been warned to *never* to tell a customer about the condition of a car?"

"I don't know," I replied. "Once? Six months ago?"

"So you admit you were warned," Rachelle interrupted.

"Look," I said, "the lady barged into the garage to yell at me because the smoked-out car wasn't ready. And nobody told me to start on it. I said it would take a while. I was just being honest."

Rachelle was incredulous. "There are plans going on in the office that you don't know about. It's not your job to give customers information."

It was all so ridiculous. "So when they ask me questions, you want me to pretend I don't speak English?" I asked. "I do a pretty good Russian. *I no speak. Just vash car.*"

"It's not funny!" Rachelle shouted. "She's going to give us a bad customer service review because of you."

I laughed. "If you get a bad review, it's because you were being shady and jerking her around. Don't blame me for something you guys screwed up."

Megan rolled her eyes. "Rachelle, take him into the office to do the paperwork. I can't deal with him right now."

Rachelle's eye was twitching. "Follow me," she said, throwing open the door and leading me back through the office. She sat down at the manager's desk and rifled through a filing cabinet, pulling out a folder. Then she slid a paper toward me that was essentially a run-on sentence detailing my insubordination.

"What the hell is this?" I asked.

"It's a formal reprimand for your file. You need to sign it at the bottom."

I laughed. "You're writing me up for being honest with a customer?"

"You disobeyed orders," Rachelle said.

"Orders? You're not a five-star general, Rachelle. You're the assistant manager of a rental car place. Orders. You realize how condescending that is?"

"Well, I don't think it's condescending at all. Because you work for us. And we pay you to do what you're told."

Something in her dismissive tone made me snap. I couldn't take it anymore. I'd rather starve than be beholden to these vapid nitwits another moment. I stood up. And without looking back, I walked out the door. I wish I'd have said something intelligent on the way out, but even if I'd yelled, "May you be scorned by history like the other incompetent fools whose shoulders you fell from," she wouldn't have understood. It all happened so quickly that I forgot to ram their most expensive car into the brick wall of the self-storage place on my way out, which was how I'd always planned my exit in my head. But I plum forgot. I just needed to get the hell out of there.

I drove home with the windows down and the radio up. Those corporate airheads hadn't gotten the best of me. I was done washing cars forever. I was happy. I was vindicated. I was...unemployed.

I may have forgotten to mention that Jessi was seven months pregnant.

CHAPTER 19

Everything Everywhere All at Once

O ur brains love to put new things in familiar compartments. It's why we ask lazy questions of strangers we meet on an airplane. One of our first inquiries is typically, "What do you do for a living?" It's a simple way to find out a lot about someone in very short order. While there's typically no malice behind it, our drive to know comes from a subconscious need to put this new person in a particular tier. Whether we realize it or not, we're trying to establish who has the social power in the encounter.

When you're a stay-at-home dad, nobody knows where to put you. Most people assume they're supposed to celebrate the reversal of gender norms, but even the most liberal folks you meet don't respond with the same body language as they would if you told them you were, let's say, a prison guard.

"Prison guard? What's the most insane thing you've ever seen? Tell me more."

When you're a stay-at-home dad, you get the same response every time.

"Oh that's great. That's so great. That's just... Wow, it's just so great!"

I've never been a stay-at-home mom, so I can't speak to that particular experience, but let's be honest here, it's still more widely accepted by society. I know moms have their own problems like the rest of the world expecting them to be annoyingly perfect, but when you're a stay-at-home dad, it's hard to enjoy the time you're spending with your kid because of the nagging feeling that you should be out earning money instead of pushing a stroller on a Tuesday afternoon. As much as you tell yourself your contributions are impactful, if you were raised as a blue-collar kid in the rust belt hearing stories of your grandfather busting his ass in a factory for forty years, you end up spending most of your mental energy trying to convince yourself you aren't a useless loser.

My son Henry was born two months after I quit Emerald, and with no money coming in, it put a ton of pressure on Jessi to get back to work well before she felt ready. I was applying to jobs all over the place but kept running into the same problem: I needed to find something that paid enough for us to afford daycare. If I picked up a part-time job at Home Depot or FedEx, we'd actually be losing money. Somehow getting a job was the least economically viable option. So for a full year I spent my days dealing with a fussy infant who desperately wanted Mama and not the other person in the house who didn't produce milk on command. As Jessi hustled to make ends meet, I was involuntarily spending my days becoming increasingly isolated at home. When I took Henry to the park, all the other parents were women in their late twenties who I had nothing in common with—women whose husbands were out laying pipe or driving trucks. I was so far from where I always thought I'd be at thirty-six.

We made so little in the first two years of Henry's life that our family didn't even qualify for the Children's Health Insurance Program, a Medicaid-based plan that assists with medical expenses for kids under eighteen. In case it's unclear what that means, what I'm telling you is that we didn't make enough to hit the *bottom threshold* for our infant son to qualify for medical assistance through a program designed to help out poor kids. Every decision I'd ever made in life was suspect.

Every time I chased a dream instead of stability, every time my Scots-Irish obstinance wouldn't allow me to submit to empty-headed authority—every time I rebelled, quit, or revolted—had led me to an existence where I was closing in on forty depressed, stressed, and broke. If I'd had just a little less pride, I could've been depressed, stressed, and financially comfortable, a slightly preferable existence otherwise known as living the American Dream.

For our child, our bank account, and my own sanity, something needed to change. What I needed was a way to earn money from home. I needed to be a writer again.

Enter Jessi's friend Kara, who a few years earlier had quit a corporate job to start a small home repair business. In order to gain customers, she'd joined a local networking cult group that helped her locate folks who might need their sunroom renovated or kitchen backsplash redone. Basically, it was a bunch of small business owners who all got together over coffee each week and stood up to deliver a one-minute pitch detailing the type of clients they were looking for. There was a chiropractor, a lawyer, an accountant, a financial planner, a real estate agent, an HVAC guy—twenty-four people who were all on the lookout for potential revenue for each other. Though the meetings were exactly as dull as the description implies, it was a savvy idea and really helped Kara grow her business. She suggested it to Jessi as a possible avenue toward getting more tattoo clients. But Jessi saw a different opportunity. She asked if they had a writer in the group. They did not.

Turned out they didn't have a writer in the group because they had absolutely no need for a writer. I'd come to this sinking realization about three months after signing up when I was barely making enough from the group's referrals to cover my monthly dues. As far as my writing career went, it was another catastrophic failure. And that really should've been the end of the story. But somehow it wasn't. Of all things, it turned into a new beginning.

About six months into my time with the networking group, a tightly wound rich woman named Lonni joined us. She owned a business called White Rabbit Linens that rented elegant table coverings for weddings, banquets, and large charity events. Early on, Lonni asked me if I'd proofread her new brochure, which established a good working relationship. Then one morning instead of asking for wedding or Bar Mitzvah referrals, she asked the group if anyone knew someone who could hack down a bunch of overgrown brush that had taken over the back of her warehouse.

After the meeting, I approached her. "Hey, Lonni, if you don't find anyone else, I could do that for you this Sunday."

"But you're a writer," Lonni replied.

"I also have a kid who's growing out of his onesies," I replied.

So that Sunday I headed to White Rabbit with my loppers and hacked away at the tangled jungle of vines and thorn bushes that had crept their way down from the hillside. It took nine hours, but when I was done, Lonni could park a car back there again, and I had a cool $108. For a day, at least, it was like my old paper route. No supervision, no one behind me critiquing my lopping skills, nobody monitoring my breaks. I just showed up, did the work, and left. I came home sweaty and covered in little scratches, but all in all, it was the most pleasant day of work I'd had in years.

I'd done a good enough job clearing all the brush that Lonni asked if I'd be interested in fixing the retaining wall. So I did. And then she inquired if I could scrape and paint the exterior of the warehouse and showroom. So I did that, too. When the exterior was done, I painted the interior. And then I tore down the rotting housing for the giant sign out front and put up a new one. Suddenly, I was there almost every morning. Out of nowhere, when strangers asked me what I did for a living, I was telling them, "I'm the maintenance guy at a linen warehouse."

"How'd you come about doing that?"

"I don't really know."

My proficiency in moving cinder blocks, painting, and nailing stuff together had fooled Lonni into thinking I was handy, completely obscuring the fact that I really had no idea what I was doing. Most times I'd fuck up whatever I was asked to do three or four times before ultimately finding a solution that worked. What would've taken someone with basic handyman skills a half hour to complete, I'd sometimes spend two days on, often completing it only after I'd given up and watched a YouTube tutorial. But then I'd proudly show Lonni the completed work and she'd be super thankful. And I'd be given yet another task.

Once Lonni's son got sick right as she needed to do a big linen pickup downtown. Since I was there painting anyway, she asked if I could make the run for her. When it all went smoothly, she seemed to realize that having someone else do most of the heavy lifting freed her up to entertain clients, fluff napkins, and talk about fabrics—which was more in line with her personality than lugging bulky forty-pound bags of dirty tablecloths in and out of service elevators. So I started heading to fancy hotels, museums, and college campuses where I'd find all the dirty linens that had been cast into the corner, stuff them into a bunch of highlighter yellow bags until they were about to burst, throw two or three at a time on my back, and walk them out to my two-door Chevy Cavalier. Unable to see out the rearview mirror after cramming my car to the brink of explosion, I'd carefully return to the shop, separate the linens by colors, throw out all the sugar packets and half-eaten vegetables that had been trapped inside, and haul the piles to the industrial washers in the back.

Before long, Lonni even had me driving up to her house on multiple acres of beautiful land in Beaver County to cut the grass. Her husband showed me how to use their huge, super-fun NASCAR lawnmower that you steered with two big levers instead of a wheel. With all the hills, trees, and other obstacles, it'd take around five hours to do the whole thing. The only problem was that I couldn't do it on my schedule. As soon as Lonni's husband felt the grass was a millimeter too high, he'd be on my ass about it—calling and texting, asking when

I was going to get there. Over time, the acreage I was asked to cut kept getting larger, adding an extra ninety minutes to the job for the same flat fee of a hundred bucks. Add in the forty-five-minute drive each way and it chewed up the better part of a day. In order to get some of my time back, I started prioritizing speed over precision. This occasionally meant that items left in the yard became inadvertent confetti. Also, the fence by the pool and their Airstream trailer ended up with a moderate case of mower rash.

After three years of getting along quite pleasantly, out of nowhere I got a nasty text from Lonni's husband featuring a bunch of pictures documenting all of the stuff I'd supposedly[20]* nicked up. He told me not to show up to cut the grass anymore and that because of my negligence he wasn't paying me the last three hundred bucks he owed me, either. The implication was also that I no longer worked at White Rabbit. I was completely blindsided. I'd hustled my ass off for these people, missing more than a few family events because "the grass couldn't wait until Monday." I felt betrayed. All he had to do was talk to me and we could've worked something out. But instead he just lashed out and cut me off.

What Lonnie's husband forgot was that I still had a key to White Rabbit and knew where Lonnie kept the money. I was on my way home from a friend's house one night when I decided to pull into the lot. With nobody around, I got out of my car, inserted the key in the side door, and walked right in. I stood there in the dark on the floor where I used to sort linens debating whether I had a right to take the three hundred dollars they owed me out of the filing cabinet or not. They'd stolen three days of my time. I wouldn't be robbing them so much as evening things up.

What I learned from the ordeal is that I'd have been a hell of a burglar if I just got rid of my conscience. Lonni had been great to me. It wasn't her fault she was married to a shithead. I never made it up to

---

[20] * Although if we're being honest here, I should probably change "supposedly" to "most likely."

the office. I did, however, go around to all the doors and unlock them knowing it would most likely result in some low-level paranoia when she showed up the next day. That was all the revenge I got. I threw my key in the bushes and drove off. And that was the end of my time at White Rabbit.

In the summer of 1995, just after the Muffin Truck insanity, the smart aleck center fielder on my baseball team asked me if I wanted a couple days of work. His name was Josh, and his girlfriend's dad had bought out a couple of fledgling companies over in Johnstown and needed some muscle to help rid the buildings of all the crap inside. I agreed and soon found myself headed over the mountains in a U-Haul with Josh and a leather-tough old guy named Rod.

The businesses we were clearing out were old family-run companies that somehow found themselves financially underwater. Me, Josh, and Rod moved office chairs, computer monitors, filing cabinets, and machinery into the back of a twenty-four-foot truck for transport to a warehouse back in Irwin. Other than Rod, there was one other guy with us that day: the acquisitions manager at Stephanie's father's company. His name was Lester, and he wore slacks and bright red polo shirts. And as Josh and I turned the corner with a behemoth desk we were bringing down from the third floor, I heard Lester in an adjacent room say something like, "That's not your call anymore."

Lester's snide comment was followed by a totally different voice screaming, "This is bullshit! That wasn't in the buyout! You mother-fuckers! I'll see you in court!"

"If you had the money to go to court, we wouldn't be here," Lester responded coldly.

A second later, this paunchy, middle-aged guy with a gray mus-tache came storming into the hallway with double birds raised in Les-ter's direction. The dude was *pissed.* And he really, really wanted to storm down the stairs and slam the front door. Unfortunately for him, there were two high school kids in his way meticulously trying to get a two-hundred-pound wooden desk down to the lobby. So he had to... wait. Like a guy whose bus was late. He was forced to just sort of furiously...hang out. The dude was allowed one angry step every thirty seconds as Josh and I unsuccessfully tried to force chuckles back down our throats.

"Laugh it up, jackasses," the guy grumbled.

I nodded to him from the landing. "You want us to lift it up so you can crawl under?"

"What I want is for you to shut up and keep going," he snapped.

"Whoa, buddy, calm down," Josh replied in the smarmiest, most dismissive tone possible. "Santa's listening."

I swear the guy briefly raised his hands toward Josh's neck.

After the guy barked at us, it was sort of inevitable that our subsequent rate of exertion would've caused snails and turtles to be like, "Okay, guys, let's pick up the pace a bit." When he finally got to the door a few minutes later, he slammed it like six times.

"Hey, buddy, you mind holding the door for us?" Josh said in the middle of his tantrum.

He did not hold the door for us.

Anyway, after we'd cleared the building, we checked with Lester to make sure we were good to drive back to the warehouse—to which Lester entered the break room and looked at us like we'd just asked to joyride in his Lexus.

"It doesn't look to me like everything is loaded yet, so what do you think?" he said.

Josh and I glanced at each other. "I'm pretty sure we got everything. Building is empty."

Lester pointed to the break room counter. Sitting there were about fifteen individual Heinz ketchup packets, the kind you'd get in a drive-thru bag from a fast-food place. "If everything is gone, what's all that?"

"You want us to take the *ketchup packets*?"

Lester was adamant. "Everything in this place is ours now. Everything."

"Hold on," I said. "Just to be clear, you don't want us to throw them away. You want us to physically take them back to Irwin with us?"

"We own everything," Lester replied.

So as instructed, we gathered up these freaking ketchup packets, threw them in the back of the truck, and returned to Irwin where I assume their procurement led directly to record-setting profits. Because of the sheer ridiculousness of it, when we'd cleared the adjacent building the following day, Josh and I were relentless.

"Hey, Lester, this spiderweb in the corner—we taking that? Lester, where do you want this old pretzel? Yo, Lester, all these mouse turds, what box do you want them in?"

One morning at the networking group, I told that story to Bryan, the owner of a small but reliable moving company called Iron Town Movers. Bryan was a brawny nerd who somehow got rear ended while sitting at a stoplight once every other month. As a result, he moved through the world tensed up as if waiting to be sucker-punched.

"They made you bring the ketchup?" Bryan laughed, cringing as a jolt of agony shot down his neck. "Hey, weird question, but since you've done it before, would you ever want to fill in with us if one of our guys drops out last second?"

And suddenly I had my second part-time job.

The first thing I discovered about being a mover was that nothing we were told by the office was ever accurate. One time we were told the client had twenty-five boxes. They had 118 boxes. This is mathematically the same as the client having ninety-four boxes and the office telling us, "They have one box." And the clients weren't much better. You'd go to pick up what all context clues told you was a pretty light plastic container only to feel your L5 vertebrae explode. Seeing you clutching your back, they'd say, "Oh, yeah, I know that tub is labeled 'SWEAT-ERS,' but it's actually our vintage cannonball collection. So be careful."

You also had to constantly ask questions of people you didn't know on what for them was often a very stressful day. Once, it quickly became obvious that we were helping a girl move out of her longtime boyfriend's apartment. As we're hauling stuff in and out the front door, it was impossible to avoid snippets of their conversation.

"Heather, we can make this work. I know we can. What do you need me to be?"

"Charles, we've been together four-and-a-half years. That's long enough to know that you don't have it in you to be what I need you to be."

"I've made some mistakes. I'll be the first to admit it. But I can change if you just give me a chance. Look in my eyes and tell me you don't still love me."

"So the guitar stand," I'd interrupt. "Is that staying? Going? What's the deal?"

It also became readily apparent that there was always a reason people hired movers instead of giving it a go themselves. On every move I'd think to myself, *If I grab the office chair, maybe it'll force Eddie and John to get the treadmill.* Meanwhile, John is thinking, *If I grab the television, maybe it'll force Eddie and Cramer to get the treadmill.* And Eddie is thinking, *If I just run away into the woods...* There was always an unspoken tango as we tried to force the other guys into taking the heaviest crap. But it just postponed the inevitable. At some point, I'd find myself trying to find a grip on the underside of a NordicTrack.

But without a doubt the worst item I encountered working for Iron Town was a 908-pound Winchester gun safe. Giant Norwegian guys named Magnus who tie ropes to their waist and pull airplanes would've been like, "No, thanks." At the load-in house, it took all four guys on the crew that day just to get the beast onto the appliance dolly. Simply getting it out of the garage and up the ramp into the truck was exhausting enough to justify a weeklong nap.

But we all knew that getting it into the truck was only half the battle. Along with a load of furniture, we drove it across the city to a big house overlooking the Ohio River. And when we got there and set eyes on the delivery house, we knew one of us was most likely going to the hospital. It was a big, ornate old home, most likely built in the 1800s for some long-forgotten steel baron. In the front, thirty or so steps led up to a large wraparound porch and double front doors. In the back, a small driveway brought you to a paved parking area with a sidewalk that curved down through the garden toward the back porch. Unlike the load-in house, there was no prefab two-car garage to roll the safe into.

The client smiled and pointed at a pair of open storm doors that revealed twelve concrete steps leading to the basement. "The gun safe needs to go down there," he said casually as if he hadn't just sentenced one of us to death.

It was me, a big dude with glasses named Patrick, an old skateboarder named Robbie, and a Kenyan college student named Mousa who I believe was in the US studying to be a doctor. We all peeked over the edge of the stairs like mourners peering into a grave.

"All right," said the client. "I'll leave you guys to it."

The truck wouldn't fit between the trees and the shed, so we had to park it on a side street. Imagine four guys trying to push a dead Triceratops up a hill and you'll get a better picture of what getting this thing over to the house was like. If the dolly wheels could manage human expressions, their faces would've resembled a kid whose older brother was sitting on his head. Finally, though, after multiple fits and starts, we pushed the thing the forty yards from the street to the edge of the storm doors only to encounter the biggest obstacle yet: a half-inch-high strip of metal just before the stairs. It might as well have been the Great Wall of China. Baffled, we did what all enterprising young men do when faced with a monumental challenge.

We stood there for a half hour exhaling loudly and saying, "Well, fuck."

When none of us managed to remember how to build an ancient pulley system capable of lowering half a ton, we came up with the best solution we could. We covered the steps with moving blankets, built a tiny cardboard ramp over the lip, and strapped four ratchet straps around the safe and the dolly, the ends of which we wrapped around our hands like boxer's tape. The plan was to push it over the lip, steady it at the top of the stairs, then slowly lower the whole dolly on its back by pulling our combined might against gravity.

"Should we call an ambulance ahead of time?" Patrick laughed with just the right amount of concern mixed in.

"We got this," Robbie said. "Let's get it done. On three."

Realizing there was no more postponing it, we wrapped the straps over our knuckles, tilted the dolly back to get more leverage, and got in position.

"Okay," Robbie said. "One…two…three…"

We pushed as hard as we could. And much to our delight, our cardboard ramp worked. The whole apparatus went up and over the great lip of Brighton Heights. But our relief didn't last. As Newton's Seventh Law states, "A nine-hundred-pound gun safe in motion isn't just going to stop because you're not ready for it to go down the stairs yet."

We all made the same horrified face when we realized the tires had cleared the ridge of the first stair. The four of us desperately tugged on our ratchet straps, only say in unison, "Nope, it's going." It was like the moment you realize you're hydroplaning and no matter what you do, you're just along for the ride. The metal lip put a trench in my knee as I tensed every muscle in my core trying to slow the thing down. As it careened down the blankets toward the door, Musah and Robbie got dragged on their stomachs down the first few stairs. Somehow, I managed to unwrap my ratchet strap fast enough to keep from being jerked down into the canyon along with them.

Was the safe under our control? Absolutely not. Was it completely out of our control? Also no, which for us was a giant win. It slid down in a clump of blankets and landed perfectly on the concrete landing in front of the basement door.

Prone on the stairs with his chin resting on the sixth step and his shoes up beside me at the top, Robbie stated the obvious. "Well, that didn't go according to plan."

"Whatever," Patrick said. "It's down there and we're alive to talk about it."

There were whoops and high fives when we gathered it up, wheeled it into the basement, and placed it against the wall. It felt like we'd beaten a dragon.

I worked a few moves a month for Iron Town over the course of two years until a combination of new state regulations and financial mismanagement forced the company to shut down. I'd love to say I never moved another treadmill again, but my time at Iron Town made me the go-to friend to ask for help when any of my buddies' wives find a good internet deal on exercise equipment. So far, every damn one of them has had to go upstairs.

During the summers, I also worked as a referee for the Midwest Division of the American Ultimate Disc League, a professional ultimate frisbee league founded in 2012 that currently has twenty-four teams based in the US and Canada and a television deal with Fox Sports. Sprinting around in front of hundreds of fans with the smell of burgers and dogs wafting over from the concession area was a hell of a way to earn some extra cash. I even got on Sportscenter once when a dude from the Indianapolis AlleyCats flew through the air to make a ridiculous layout defense right in front of me, and it ended up #2 on Top Ten Plays of the Day. It was a great job that I absolutely loved until I stupidly jumped an eight-foot-high fence to confront a fan who'd been shouting obscenities at me all game.

After the final whistle, the hard ass yelled through the chain links, "You're lucky you're on the other side of the fence or I'd be kicking your ass!"

He melted into a puddle of goo when I landed in front of him. "Well, I'm on this side of the fence now. Your move."

And that was the end of that job.

White Rabbit, Iron Town, and the AUDL—when I started those jobs, my boy was pretty much an adorable lump who laid on a blanket all day and was amazed by his toes. By the time they all disappeared, he was reading and playing ice hockey.

Three jobs had come and gone. But during Henry's toddler days, I was actually working five. The two I haven't mentioned yet were remarkable seeing how I stayed at both longer than I'd stayed anywhere else to that point in my life. And as of now, one of them is where this long road full of potholes and detours ultimately led.

CHAPTER 20

Dumpsters
and Whiteboards

The most uninteresting story you can possibly tell is about getting an email, so instead I'm going to describe one morning when I was pinned down by helicopter fire somewhere in Central America. A thirty-year-old woman with hipster glasses came crawling toward me through the mud and the sweat and the flames. Explosions rocked the jungle around us.

"Look out!" she screamed, pulling a pistol from beneath her over-size sweater and firing past my ear. Shocked, I turned to see an anaconda fall dead at my feet.

"You really saved my ass," I said to her. "Now it's time to return the favor."

With every ounce of strength that remained in my body, I grabbed the lifeless reptile and hurled it through the sky until WHACK—it wrapped itself around the helicopter's rotor.

"Nooooo!" screamed all of the Philadelphia Flyers as their chopper began to spiral out of control toward a lake full of flesh-eating bacteria.

I turned to the woman and gave her a well-deserved fist bump. "Looks like we saved the world."

She smiled and answered, "Hi, my name is Victoria, and I'm a client of Lonni's. I have a bedroom that needs to be painted, and she said I should ask you for a quote."

I had no idea what the going rate was for painters, so I told Victoria that if she bought the materials, I'd do the job for fifteen bucks an hour, which was three more than Lonni was paying me and seemed like a bonanza. So one day I went over to Victoria's house in Swissvale and painted her bedroom purple and white. She loved it and recommended me to her sister. A week later, I was headed out to Greensburg to paint her kitchen olive green. Then their friend in the South Hills needed the whole interior of her house done in a weird creamsicle orange. Suddenly, I was driving to random places all over the city once or twice a week, taping windows, laying out tarps, and rolling walls while listening to sports talk radio all day.

I was on my sixth or seventh job before I realized, "Do I have a small, commercial *painting business* now? What the hell is going on?"

This was on top of the linen deliveries, moves, grass cutting, and refereeing. As I tried to do anything I could to support my wife and the growing little boy who wanted to eat and have shoes and stuff, I was running from one job to another, often putting in fourteen-hour days. When I wasn't working, I was chasing around a maniac two-year-old whose favorite pastime was jumping off of shit he wasn't supposed to jump off of. I was exhausted. And it was about to get crazier.

In the networking group, there was a fast-talking, easily bored mortgage guy named Tony whose volume at a whisper was still an eight out of ten. He was New York Italian and so slick you walked away from every interaction assuming he'd convinced you to sign up for an insurance policy you didn't need. Tony was attempting to slide out of the mortgage business and into flipping houses, so one morning we met at Panera Bread to go over a flyer he asked me to edit for his new venture. I assumed the meeting wasn't going to land me much more than fifty bucks and a free breakfast sandwich. I was very wrong.

"Kev," he said excitedly. "The Pittsburgh market is red hot right now. You can make a killing with investment properties. A *killing!*" His well-intentioned advice was obviously meant for an imaginary version of me that had money to throw around, but it was what he said next that surprisingly changed the direction of my career. "Just bought a place in my subdivision. Want to get it on the market in the next month. What I really need is someone to paint the interior if you know anyone. Sooner the better."

I took a sip of my free orange juice. "I mean, I just painted two places last week."

He leaned forward. "I thought you were a writer."

"Yeah, well, the universe seems to think otherwise."

The house he bought was a split-level ranch in a residential neighborhood just off I-79 in Butler County. The previous owner had apparently passed away and left it to her kids, who all lived in Ohio. While it was sitting vacant, a pipe burst in the basement and turned it into a frozen Everglades, which allowed Tony to snatch it up for well below market value. By the time I arrived on scene, the basement had already been pumped, the game room carpet removed, and new drywall put up. I got to work rolling primer and color on the game room walls and ceiling. Two long Sundays and it no longer looked like the inside of a boxcar.

As it turned out, Tony wasn't just a mortgage guy. He was pretty knowledgeable about home repair and was coming in at night to remodel the kitchen and bathroom. Remarkably with our efforts combined on the day he'd designated for getting the house to the market...

...it was still an uninhabitable mess of scattered tools and sawdust. Tony had massively underestimated both the amount of work necessary to get the house back in shape and his own availability to do it. But since he was so far behind, when the painting was finished, he said to me, "If I show you real quick how I want this subfloor done, do you think you could level it?"

Tony was under the same fallacy that had befallen Lonni. Based on my work ethic, he was assuming I had a larger array of skills than I actually possessed. This was actual carpentry—a definite step up from using a paint brush and roller. And yet I didn't have many painting jobs on the horizon and wanted to keep working so…

"Uh, sure. Just show me what you're looking for."

His tutorial was to point at the living room floor and say, "Okay, see all these sections that aren't even? I need them to be flush. There's a bunch of scrap wood in the garage. Saw is plugged in. Tape measure is around here somewhere. I gotta run to the office. I'll see you in a few hours. Maybe tomorrow. Call me if you need anything."

And I found myself alone in this house tasked with a building project the likes of which I'd never attempted before. I hadn't done any carpentry since *Adopt a Sailor*, and most of what I accomplished there only seemed impressive to actors and producers who'd never used a hand tool in their life. I was now in the world of actual contractors who presumably knew what they were doing. My work would need to be inspected at some point. Eeeegggggh.

I must've stood there staring at the floor for twenty minutes until I told myself, "Just start. Just do *something*." I noticed two of the old boards were warped and cracked, so I pried them up with my crowbar. Then I spent a half hour trying to match the thickness of the plywood with the scrap in the garage. When I found a comparable piece, I measured the gap in the floor, marked the scrap, and after longer than I care to admit figuring out that you had to hit two buttons concurrently to make the saw start whirring, I carefully sliced through the board. When I was done, I had a rectangle that fit the corresponding hole. I headed to the living room and nailed it in. I put the level on it. The bubble stayed in the center.

Holy shit.

Look, I realize that for actual carpenters this is the equivalent of catching a soft popup, but leveling a subfloor was a huge deal to a baseball and frisbee player with degrees in education and screenwriting. I'd fucking *built* something. When a family someday walked across that floor without thinking, *Well, this is lumpy,* it was because of me. I could almost see my grandfather standing next to me with a flathead screwdriver and a Folgers can full of wingnuts, nodding his approval.

As I was finishing up, the radio DJ started babbling about the Oscar nominations that had been announced that morning. Even if *Zendog* had been delayed for seven years before ultimately getting greenlit, this would've finally been the year I hit the red carpet. And instead of celebrating, I was putting in a subfloor on a house that had tried to drown itself. At that moment, the candle on my Hollywood dreams finally went out. The DJ quit talking, and the first few chords of a Nirvana song ripped through the house. There was nothing I could do about the course of events. I'd exhausted my anger about what life had and hadn't allowed me to achieve. This was where I was. For the first time in my life, I realized how useless bitterness is as an emotion. I shrugged and got back to hammering.

In the coming days, I found myself ripping down and replacing drywall in the garage, installing light fixtures, and cutting up the old garage door so we could fit it in the dumpster—all of the simple stuff Tony didn't have time to do. Three months after Tony had earmarked it to hit the market, the house sold. He used the money to buy another house up on Mount Washington, which I painted as well. But I also cleared the basement, fixed the deck, caulked the archways, and restored the old Victorian banister. Five months later, that house sold as well. Suddenly there were three more places over in Bellevue. Eight months had gone by and I was somehow working almost exclusively for Tony. Then one day the script at the top of my paycheck was different. Instead of Tony's name, it said "Lombardo Properties, Inc."

When he handed me the paystub, I almost toppled over. "Hold on. Are we a legitimate construction company now?"

"In name only, brother, but it's a start," Tony said, giving me a fist bump.

And that's when things got weird. As we snatched up more projects than Tony and I could handle on our own, Tony was forced to spin the wheel of laborers. And what you find is that the wheel doesn't often land on "hard working and relatively intelligent." Nope, most times it lands on "flaky and unreliable" or "often drunk" or "on probation for shit you don't want to know about." Once Tony texted me to say there was a guy coming to help me rip out an old kitchen. He was a kid named Ryan who helped me get the stove and the fridge down the hall and into the front yard for the scrapper. Somewhere in the middle of the sink removal and cabinet smashing, he relayed how glad he was to be out of prison and how he was never getting behind the wheel totally plowed again. At the end of the day, I said, "See you tomorrow," and he replied, "Yeah, man. See you tomorrow."

The next morning, I got a call from Tony as I arrived at the house. "Hey," he said. "You're on your own again today. Ryan got another DUI last night."

And so Tony gave the wheel another spin.

As Tony gathered properties, I was going around doing the demolition, working with guys on Monday who I'd already forgotten existed by Thursday. A lot of the dudes that you hoped stuck around didn't. Many you wished never showed up stuck around. One of those guys was a Tennessee hick in his late fifties named Daryl. In my life, I've never run across anyone who so dramatically overestimated their intelligence and ability. I believe Dunning and Kreuger once had a brief encounter with him and were suddenly struck with an idea for a paper. My first project with Daryl was removing all the old shingles from the roof of a three-story house. Like everything else in Tony's queue, we were doing it at the worst possible time. We once waited two years to move a couple 450-pound iron deck beams from behind one of our properties because presumably Tony found the task much too easy and wanted to delay until there were fourteen inches of fresh snow on the ground before we slogged them up the hill. As for the roof, April or October would've been a nice, pleasant time to be up there. Not so much in August when the heat turns your vision squiggly and gives you a solid understanding of what it's like to be a hamburger cooking on a grill. And while an average roof pitch is somewhere between five and nine, this one was a twelve. If you're not certain what that means, here's the closest diagram I can provide with my keyboard.

$$/\backslash$$

So not only could you feel the heat searing through your boots, gloves, and knee pads, you had to wear a hoodie and jeans so you didn't scald yourself as you desperately clung to the roof like an action hero who'd just jumped onto a train. I wore a harness that was roped into an iron ring bolt at the apex of the house because if you slipped, it was the last thing keeping you from casketville.

Daryl, on the other hand, refused to wear his harness because it interfered with him taking off his shirt, which he did every day five minutes into our stint on the roof. When Tony told him he had to wear his harness or get taken off the job, he lost his mind and spent the next day boycotting. "I gotta sweat to death up here because Tony and all you guys are jealous of my muscles and my tan? Hell no. I ain't working with people who don't respect my freedoms."

"Yeah, Daryl," I said, doing actual work while he sat by the gutter and pouted. "You figured it out. Your beer gut is killing my body confidence."

"I knew it! I knew it ain't a safety issue. That's your problem, not mine! I ain't doing no work. I'm too hot, and this roof is too steep. I'm gonna fall off and die! And then Tony will see what happens when you fuck with *me*!"

I'd have to climb down the ladder and sit in the shade for a minute so I didn't snap and toss Daryl off the roof. *"My fault. I thought he was an old shingle. Admittedly they were all just lying there next to the tools, so it was an easy mistake to make."*

You'd figure his constant bitching would be the worst thing I had to deal with, but I actually preferred his hysterics to the meandering word glop he thought were stories—all of which were about the trials and tribulations of his attempts to buy cigarettes for a thirty-four-year-old meth addict he called his "old lady."

"Kev, I gotta find thirteen dollars by the end of the day," he'd tell me. "Old lady needs her smokes or we ain't getting freaky tonight. The cigarettes she likes are thirteen dollars at the GetGo by my house, but if I pay the extra two dollars and take the bus to the West End, they're only eleven, so it's a deal. She is one sexy mama. Yep, if I can find thirteen bucks, we're getting *freaky* tonight when I get off the bus."

I fumbled my hammer when I finally realized how bad his math was. "Daryl, you realize you're paying thirteen bucks either way, right?"

"No, her cigarettes are only *eleven* bucks in the West End. I just need two for the extra bus fare so it *adds up* to thirteen. But the cigarettes are only eleven. I'm saving two dollars."

Look, I'm not the brightest nut on the tree, but sometimes I feel like an astrophysicist compared to the rest of the population.

But by far the stupidest Daryl moment came after he convinced Tony that he was an expert arborist. We were at a huge house in Bellevue that Tony bought off a guy who hadn't thrown anything away since 1951. With no power in the house, the basement was a horror film. It had no windows, so I had to strap a headlamp to my forehead and plunge like a coal miner into a dank suburban cave that was cluttered with old paint cans, rusty tools, matchboxes, chemical bottles, broken windows, and random bicycle parts. Defying all odds, there was nothing of any value in the entire place. Even his extensive vinyl collection was just church hymns sung by plump women in horn-rimmed glasses. I was pretty certain even the vintage record store wouldn't pony up for a dusty copy of "Dorothy Mumford – Live at the Winklestown Methodist Church," so I just frisbeed them all into the yard.

The rubbish from the house filled six-and-a-half construction dumpsters before I even started the demolition. But as dumb as that was, nothing could prepare me for Daryl's tree-cutting shenanigans. This giant old house had an oak tree in the side yard that had to have been fifty-five feet tall—one of the biggest in the entire neighborhood. And Daryl told Tony that if he had a crew of three guys, he could get it down with a single chainsaw.

Blinded by savings, Tony believed him.

I arrived one morning to see a stoner named Cory sitting on the front stairs as Daryl examined the enormous tree. There was no way the three of us were getting this thing down. We had a better shot at winning a Nobel Prize. But Daryl was convinced we could do it if we just got in some practice with a smaller, skinnier birch tree in the back that also needed to come down. Cigarette in his mouth and no shirt on, he tied a rope around the trunk, fired up his chainsaw, and yelled to me and Cory that when it started to fall, we should tug as hard as we could away from the house. I was skeptical, but like everything else, Daryl insisted he'd been doing it for thirty years. The first thing I learned from Daryl that day is that longevity itself does not ensure mastery.

Daryl was cutting through the trunk in a hail of wood chips when we heard a loud crack. "Here it comes!" he yelled. So Cory and I tugged as hard as we could in an attempt to steer it toward the nice flat lot adjacent to...

The second thing I learned from Daryl that day was that two humans with a rope have the same effect on a tree's eventual landing spot as a moth does on the trajectory of a bus. As this tree toppled toward the back of the house, all I could think about was the weeks of work I'd put into a place that was about to be condemned.

The old birch crashed to earth in a loud popping of branches and wailing of raccoons. Unbelievably, it crushed the bottom of a down-spout we were going to replace anyway but otherwise missed the house—by six inches at most. Standing there with his chainsaw and a doofy look, Daryl screamed at us. "What the fuck, guys! I told you to pull!"

"The tree weighs a thousand pounds, Daryl," I yelled back. "It went thirty degrees west of where you said it would!"

"Shittttttt," Cory said, his eyes bleated and red. "I need a smoke."

I really should've walked away after that debacle, but Daryl insisted on starting the fifty-footer, and I really needed to put in a few more hours before I went home. The lowest limb on this tree was about eight feet off the ground. Learning nothing from the previous fiasco, Daryl leaned a ladder against the tree, climbed it, and tied a rope to the branch, instructing Cory to tug when he heard it snap.

While most companies have signs around that remind workers they have a "Safety First" mentality, Daryl's overall mindset was "Safety Eleventh," so he's leaning off the ladder with a running chainsaw in his left hand and hugging the tree trunk with his right. Like a moron, I was holding the ladder for him, mainly because I didn't want to see a severed arm that afternoon. And just as the thought, *This is not going to end well*, ran through my mind, the branch snapped. Instead of falling straight to the ground like Daryl envisioned, the enormous limb swung back toward us like a pendulum. I leaped out of the way, and the whole thing crashed into the ladder with a BANG they heard three blocks away. Daryl slammed into the tree and dropped the chainsaw. Seeing the ladder tipping, I jumped back over and caught it, saving Daryl a nasty fall, but he still sliced his hand open on the splintered nub where the branch had once connected to the trunk.

"Cory, Jesus Christ, you're supposed to pull!" Daryl screamed with blood running down his arm. "Kev, you gotta hold the damn ladder! Jesus, what kind of stupid guys is Tony giving me to work with?"

"That's it," I shouted. "We're done. Daryl, you don't know what the fuck you're doing." And I called Tony and told him we needed to hire a tree service or one of us was going to get killed. It was a sentiment that Daryl vehemently opposed, continuing to claim he could get the tree down if he just had competent help.

Based on my previous experiences, what happened next was absolutely shocking. *Tony listened to me without hesitation.* He let me make the call to stop a project cold based on my assessment of the situation. He didn't drive out to the house to check it out, and he didn't weigh his options; he just trusted what I saw. A boss who had my back? I'd forgotten they existed. I was going to work my ass off for this guy until the company folded or my body broke down.

A few months later, Daryl fell off a ladder into a bunch of bushes and fucked up his back. I wasn't there, which is beneficial because not having memory of the event lets me picture him dropping in slow motion like Hans Gruber plummeting off Nakatomi Tower at the end of *Die Hard*. After his accident, he went on disability, and we never saw him again. Tony heard a rumor he's in jail somewhere in rural Tennessee.

Cory shot and killed a heroin dealer outside a bar on Mount Washington and is doing twenty-five years.

Every day was different. I dug trenches for gas mains. I knocked down walls. I tore out frozen carpet and soaked insulation. I got to see how far I could throw a toilet way more often than you'd think. One day I'd be up on a ladder tearing off awnings and gutters, and the next I'd head into a clammy basement to do masonry repair. My friends would ask what kind of skills were necessary to do the work I was doing. "You can't have an aversion to spiders or cracking your head on pipes," I'd answer. My hands were always nicked up and bleeding. Each day I came home with a sore back and covered in grime. And yet unlike previous jobs where I dreaded the sunrise, I blissfully got up every day to do it again.

And that's when out of nowhere I finally got the opportunity I'd always hoped for.

The minute I walked up in front of my first class as a teaching assistant at UC-Riverside, I knew what I wanted to do with my life. Passing on my knowledge and passion for creating stories while essentially doing improv comedy for ninety minutes was everything I ever wanted out of life, even if I brought home stacks of papers to grade that overwhelmed my apartment.

Because of the Goldwyn Award and some sparkling TA ratings, the theatre department was planning to bring me aboard as an adjunct faculty member after I graduated—right up until state budget concerns prompted a system-wide hiring freeze for all University of California campuses. After moving to Laramie, however, I kept my teaching dream alive, applying anywhere and everywhere I heard of an opening. SUNY-Oswego, Lehigh, Emerson, Emory, Eastern Michigan, Ferris State—I was sending resumes and cover letters all over the country. But my hopeful enthusiasm soon turned into the depressing understanding that without a big-time film to punch up my credits, I just couldn't compete with folks who'd been in the industry for years. And so I ended up washing cars in Pittsburgh. Which in a weird twist was how I finally got my break.

Like every other Monday, the Emerald in Oakland was slammed. I was in the garage squirting off a car when one of the rental agents walked out of the office and flipped me a set of keys. "Customer needs a ride. Blue Elantra."

I took the keys, walked down, and opened the driver's door. The customer was already inside. "Where to?" I asked him.

"I'm headed up near Magee Hospital. I'll give you directions once we get over there."

I nodded and pulled out of the lot. We chatted about the Pirates and traffic and all the typical small talk that occurred when a rider disliked silence.

"Okay, up here you're going to turn on Craft Avenue," he said, pointing. "It's just before the light."

"You mean the theatre? Three Rivers University?" I asked.

"Yes," he said, surprised I knew of it. "You drop someone off here before?"

"Uh no. A couple years ago, we had rehearsals there for a play I wrote."

The guy looked at me like I'd just told him if I pressed a button on the dash, the car turned into a submarine. It was not what he expected from the dude in the grease-stained shirt. "You write plays?"

"Yeah, I have a master's in screenwriting, actually," I said nonchalantly as I pulled into the parking area to let him out. "From UC-Riverside out near LA."

He started ruffling through his wallet. "Do you teach?"

"I did. Out in California. Now I wash cars."

As he got out, he handed me his business card. "You should send your resume to Three Rivers. Email me. We're always looking for adjuncts."

Apparently, the guy was one of the lighting professors in the theatre department. That night I emailed him my resume. He in turn forwarded it to the department chair. I got a prompt reply saying they weren't looking for anyone at the moment, but they'd keep me in mind.

Three years later, I was in the middle of a set of pushups when my phone rang.

"Hello," I panted.

"Yes, I'm trying to reach Kevin Cramer. This is Joseph Bartleman, Chair of the Theatre Department at Three Rivers University."

"Oh," I said, bewildered. "How are you?"

"Well, as it turns out we need to add an extra section of Intro to Screenwriting this semester and are looking for someone to teach it. I was calling to gauge your interest."

I hadn't pursued a teaching job in years. And now one had found me through a shitty job washing cars that I'd walked out on two years before. "Well, I am interested." I laughed.

Long story short, after a brief interview process, I was back in a classroom again. And other than the paltry adjunct pay, it was everything I ever wanted out of a job. I was showing great movies, then breaking them down and examining themes, character development, and pacing. The students not only seemed to be having a good time but were tangibly improving their writing skills as the semester went along. Through all of my bizarre stories and dumb metaphors, they were actually *learning*. Every week I walked out of the building so charged up I couldn't touch doorknobs.

The following year, Three Rivers asked me to come back, and not only that, come back to teach an upper-level class. They apparently liked what I was doing because by my third year, I was teaching three classes per semester including two sections of Advanced Screenwriting—a 400-level class that typically wasn't given to adjuncts.

The rest of the faculty didn't quite know what to do with me. And for good reason. They were cool intellectuals who sipped Cabernets and spoke of Italian cinema of the 1950s as if describing the touch of a former lover. They'd be at a faculty meeting discussing the flaws of neo-realism when their heads would rotate to catch me scurrying into the room in my grubby construction clothes straight from spending the morning in a cloud of drywall dust. Add in my tattoo sleeves and raggedy beard and I did *not* look the part—though I was normally good at separating those two worlds. On the jobsite, I let my thick Pittsburgh accent come "aht" around all the contractors, then slowed my speech and worked to annunciate clearly to sound more professor-like when on campus.

Like I said, I was *normally* good at it. At faculty meetings, I often didn't say much as the full-time academics talked of administrative issues that didn't affect me. But suddenly at one gathering, the head of the department looked in my direction. "I've had five students tell me that Story Analysis was the most impactful class they had this semester," he said. "That used to be the one they hated the most. Kevin, is it okay if I forward your syllabus to the whole department so everyone can see what adjustments you've made?"

I beamed at the compliment and nodded. "Yeah, whatever yinz need."

Fuck.

You could tell they were baffled that this dude in a dusty baseball cap who talked like their mill trash cousin was sitting in a faculty meeting with them, let alone thriving in the job. But to their credit they were good people and rolled with it. Then again they were used to rolling with things because college is full of, ya know, college students. Much like teaching middle school, it helped if you were a little...off. I once got really excited about a line of dialogue that a student had written and leaped out of my chair to run around the room. As I was celebrating, I heard a thud and turned to see another student bonking his head on his desk. Beside him, the girl who'd written the dialogue was slyly pointing at him and sticking out her tongue.

As I returned to my seat, I noticed their peculiar interaction. "Hey, what is this?" I said to them curiously. "What is happening here?"

Both of them froze like they'd been caught sneaking a lollipop. "Nothing," the girl said. "We were just, uh…nothing." Soon thereafter, the entire class began to giggle.

I sat back down. "Okay, now I know something's up. And I'm not giving any more script notes until I find out what you jokers are up to."

After thirty seconds of silence, a girl on the other side of the class meekly raised her hand and held up her notebook. "We, uh, have a contest going. Every time you leap out of your seat and run around like a border collie, whoever inspired you do it gets a point. Curtis was way ahead last week, but Heather just caught up," she said. "Winner gets a milkshake."

I stopped. I stared at them coldly. I was a professor, goddammit— someone to be respected, not used as a vehicle for a silly game. I pointed to the girl with the notebook, who was obviously the ringleader. "That," I replied, "is *awesome!*" And I got up and sprinted around the class-room five times just to mess with their scoring system.

By the spring of 2020, I'd been teaching at Three Rivers for six years. My students were winning awards. They were having their films screened at festivals. I beamed with pride that I was having a meaning-ful impact on their lives and careers. I was *good* at this. After twenty-five years of wandering and wondering, I'd finally found a job that was a perfect fit. And as it happened, the chair of the screenwriting depart-ment was retiring at the end of the semester, which meant that for the first time since I was hired, there was an opening for a full-time profes-sor. I hoped they'd consider me. Having taught at least one section of every class offered, I was the obvious choice. But you never knew who else with better credentials might apply. Also, let's face it, I wouldn't have been doing much to make the faculty more diverse, a concern that you might imagine was ultra-important to the students in an artsy department that leaned so far to the left it nearly toppled over. Consequently, I, uh, wasn't expecting much.

Which is why I was shocked and moved one afternoon when a bunch of my students flagged me down as I walked toward my Advanced Screenwriting class.

"Kevin, did you hear Steve is retiring?"

"Yeah," I replied. "Going to be weird here without him."

One of my best students, a big gay kid named Charlie, smiled. "Actually, Olivia and I have a plan. At the end of the semester, we're all going into Marjorie's office and telling her they need to hire you to replace him. Aliyah, Mark, Curtis, Heather, Dmitri, Cheyanne, Nathan…like everyone you've taught is coming with us. We're going to make a big scene."

I almost dropped my backpack. "What? Really?"

"Absolutely," Charlie replied. "It's dumb that you're not full time already."

I'm not a guy who cries easily. I was once sanding the paint off a metal railing when the grinder kicked back, cut through my glove, and put a canyon across my fingers. I just grunted and went back to work. But this was different. Here were my students giving me confirmation that I'd had a clear, quantifiable positive influence on their lives.

"Wow, thanks, guys. That means a lot. Truly. Thank you," I said, trying to scurry away before they noticed the water pooling at the edge of my eye. "I gotta get to class."

If all went well, I was about to land my dream job. I was going to be a full-time professor in the fall. I didn't walk as much as float into class that afternoon. Like previous sessions, we acted out and discussed pages from the first drafts of my students' full-length screenplays. We read a drama about a female sheriff in the old west, a zany action flick about two guys who found a baby Mothman, and a road trip comedy about four seniors who'd escaped a nursing home. I leaped from my seat and ran around a bunch. It was Wednesday, March 11, 2020.

That week, all faculty had been getting updates from the chancellor in relation to a mysterious new flu that was ravaging China and Europe and had recently started popping up on the East and West Coasts. The emails read as such:

Sunday: *We're aware that some schools in New England and California have recently gone fully remote. In the unlikely event that Three Rivers has to follow suit, we will reach out with instructions. But don't worry. We're in Pittsburgh and we're pretty certain it won't be that bad here.*

Monday: *Just another update. Everything's looking good to complete the semester in person unless this virus can somehow survive on an airplane. Wash your hands for at least twenty seconds and we should all be fine.*

Tuesday morning: *Okay, so yesterday we said that moving to online classes was pretty unlikely. And let's be clear here, we're not saying it's now likely, but it's also far from unlikely. We don't really know, so look for another email later today.*

Tuesday afternoon: *Here's a bunch of instructions on how to move your classes online. Again, just a precaution. We're not cancelling classes. Probably. Unless we have to. Which is looking more likely.*

Wednesday: *Set yourself on fire to avoid the plague!*

Advanced Screenwriting was a three-hour block once per week, so I always gave everyone a fifteen-minute break halfway through class to recharge. Like normal, the minute I said, "Be back at three forty-five," students began to reach into their purses and backpacks to get the social media hit they'd been craving since class began. Suddenly, the light, jovial mood we'd established over the past ninety minutes began to change. The students who remained in the room began to show each other their phones, staring at their screens with a mix of excitement and confusion.

"Pitt just cancelled classes for the rest of the semester," one girl said. "This posted like four minutes ago. Oh my god."

There was a ding from another girl's phone. "Carnegie-Mellon did, too." DING. "And Duquesne. This literally just happened."

It slowly began to dawn on us that this was probably our last class together—at least the final class that was anything resembling normal. If the other schools in the city were cancelling classes, Three Rivers wasn't far behind. We read and discussed two more scripts and then had a very awkward goodbye.

"All right, I guess maybe I'll see you guys next week? Or...have a nice life?"

And they all filtered out. I threw on my hoodie, picked up my backpack, turned out the lights, and walked down the street to the parking garage. And that was the last time I was in a classroom. The kids who were going to tell the department chair to hire me didn't even get a proper graduation. Their college run just...ended. Flaccidly. It goes without saying that they never got to vouch for me. Due to the pandemic, enrollment was way down in the fall of 2020. I was offered one class, in person with masks and social distancing. But by that time, I had another concern. Jessi was pregnant again and due in September, right as I was supposed to go back to teach. There were no vaccines yet. And for $927 (minus $140 to park for the semester) with no supplemental health insurance, I wasn't going to risk bringing COVID home to my baby. I'm not tech savvy or patient enough to run an online class, so when they couldn't offer me an outdoor space, I turned them down.

The following year, nobody inquired whether I was available.

Once again, my big break...wasn't.

Sorry if I fooled you into thinking all the twists and turns had led to a clean, happy ending. As I often told my students, "Sorry, kids, Hollywood ain't real life."

CHAPTER 21

Falling and Landing

"**R**emain absolutely still. There's a good chance you have serious internal bleeding," said an incredibly gruff and tactless medical technician as he pushed my stretcher through the hallway. As I laid there constricted by a neck brace watching the florescent lights on the ceiling roll by, I swore he was saying batshit-crazy stuff based on no hard evidence like, "Your lungs could've disappeared, your aorta might be dirty, your pancreas might no longer believe in the moon landing, *and that's just the beginning!*" I couldn't wait until we finally got to the MRI room so I didn't have to listen to this doomsday prophet anymore.

When we got there, I was instructed to lay very still while the guy went to track down some other medical personnel to help lift me onto the MRI machine's rock-hard bed. For a moment it was quiet. Other than random beeping and far-off conversations, it was just me alone with my thoughts in a sterile hospital room. Lying there motionless, I distinctly remember thinking, "Damn. I should still be at work."

Tony's most ambitious project was a decrepit dive bar that had been shuttered for the better part of four years when he bought it. It was a big place that massively exceeded our capabilities. Before we'd really figured out a good system for flipping houses, we were tackling a large commercial space with all of the accompanying regulations. And we were doing it with just me, Tony, and a constantly rotating cast of stooges. It didn't seem remotely worth it.

Except for one thing.

If you've ever seen the iconic shot of Pittsburgh looking down on the confluence of the Allegheny and Monongahela Rivers, it was most likely taken from the platform of the Duquesne Incline, a giant pulley that hauls tourists four hundred feet up the face of a cliff in cute little red boxes to the stunning realization that the city is no longer America's black lung. It's one of the most majestic urban views in the country as you stand at the very height of the skyline looking down three different river valleys at all the trains, trucks, and tugboats traveling over and under something like twenty-five different bridges. On nice days, the platform is packed as people from all over the world snap pictures. And the bar Tony bought was directly across Grandview Avenue from the incline, the second-floor windows looking out over the exact same breathtaking panorama. If we did this right, it was going to be a gold mine.

As for the bar itself, two tiny windows perfect for neon Bud Light signs were cut into the brick façade facing the street. Inside was a sea of brown. A huge old wooden bar, the type you'd see at an American Legion Hall, dominated the front space while the restaurant area tried to fool you into thinking you were in a hunting lodge with floor-to-ceiling wood paneling. The kitchen was cluttered with heavy and now useless appliances including a massive iron stove and pizza oven. Upstairs was a jumbled mess of booths, tables, and at least four chairs for every person allowed by the occupancy limit. It needed some work, but Tony was optimistic. As he walked me through the place pointing out all the walls he'd spray painted with an "X" signifying what needed to be knocked down, he looked at me with a straight face and said, "I'm thinking we're open by New Year's Eve." He meant the ball dropping into 2016. Just a fun fact to keep in mind.

The bar was a massive project. I took out three interior walls, four bathrooms, four stairwells, and two storage closets. I knocked down the brick façade and put up temp walls and giant plywood barriers. We cut through the floor and used a pulley system to hoist giant I-Beams in to support the ceiling. I jackhammered a hole in the cement kitchen floor for the stairs that would eventually lead down to the new prep kitchen. After they redid the sewer lines in the basement, there was a massive pile of dirt that I had to shovel into orange Home Depot buckets, which I'd then shuffle out to our van and drive two miles to one of our other properties to dump over the hill. As the weeks and months went by, Tony's optimistic timeline turned into a punchline. By New Year's, the place was an outright disaster full of open studs, crumbling bricks, and exposed nails.

"Man, this place was hopping last night," I'd joke. "Girls everywhere. Bartenders told me they ran out of all the top-shelf stuff. All of it."

"Ha ha," Tony would grumble. "Get back to work."

One cold January morning, I was ripping out the ceiling in the bar area with a kid named Jordan when from across the room I hear him yell, "Oh fuck!" He scrambled down off the ladder like he'd uncovered a rattlesnake. A second later, all the drywall fell to the ground to reveal the biggest goddamn beehive in the city. If it hadn't been twelve degrees in there, I'm pretty certain all ten thousand of them would've immediately gone berserk, causing us all to run into the street dancing like cartoon characters. But we lucked out and they were so cold and sluggish they barely noticed. I was suddenly real glad I hadn't started with the ceiling back in September.

The colony extended across two-and-a-half ceiling joists. Honey literally began dripping from the ceiling to the floor in long, goopy strands. It looked like a terror cave in the underworld of some distant planet where the away team was about to find out exactly what happened to the first set of astronauts who never returned to the ship.

I'd been filling our van with debris and was about to make a run to the dump when we uncovered the hive. Figuring there wasn't much I could do in the moment, I left the bees behind and drove across town to chuck a bunch of wood, glass, and bricks into a giant pile of similar construction waste. What I found when I returned to the bar was as vexing as it was dismaying. At the time, we had a dude named Clyde working for us. He was an educated burnout whose dad was a well-known local politician. He came from money and knew it. In fact, I'm pretty sure he was only working with us as a condition of his probation after he got busted selling weed.

When I walked in, Clyde was on a ladder pumping Raid into the hive. Below him on the floor were literally thousands of dead bees. Jordan was leaning against the bar supervising.

"Dude, what the hell are you doing?" I shouted. "Don't kill the bees!"

Clyde's eyes were glazed. "Oh shit, they're already dead, though. Why?"

"The food chain!" I yelled somewhat incoherently. "All the pollination! Without bees we all die! How do you not know this?"

Jordan looked up from his phone. "What do you mean without bees we die?" he asked. "That's dumb. Bees are little assholes."

"Hornets are assholes. Wasps are assholes," I screeched. "Bees are our fucking friends, you dumbasses!"

Jordan scoffed. "Bees aren't my friends. You're a weird dude."

Clyde looked at the can. "Shit, I forgot about the pollinating. And they do little dances to communicate. I like bees."

"Then why did you massacre them?" I yelled.

"Shit, I don't know," he said, climbing down the ladder. And just when I thought he couldn't do anything more confounding, he walked out to his car, returned with two mason jars, climbed the ladder, and started collecting the honey. "Free honey if anyone wants it," Clyde said, happily licking his finger. "This is super good. Fresh. Like organic, man. Right from the hive. No preservatives or any of that unhealthy shit."

I turned away from pulling nails at the other end of the bar. "Other than the straight-up poison you just coated it with."

"If I tried to get the honey before I killed the bees, they could've stung me, man. You gotta think," he replied.

"Jesus Christ," I said. "I'm not sweeping up the fuckin' bees."

I absolutely ended up sweeping up the fuckin' bees. I felt so guilty about not being there to save them that I now donate every year to a giant pollinator preserve in Maryland.

Working in a high-traffic area on a building people are eminently curious about leads to a lot of unwanted interruptions. After we removed the old front door, we covered the entrance with a giant sheet of plywood. But it was a huge pain in the ass to screw back in and sliding it across the entrance while you were working made the site dark and depressing. On nice days, it was amazing to just let it open so you could see the sunlight and feel the breeze. Unfortunately, it also led to a bunch of hoopleheads deciding it was cool to just wander in.

One morning, some dude appeared out of nowhere. "Well, what's going on in here?"

I turned around. "This is a construction site. You can't be in here."

"What's this gonna be?" he asked, knocking on the wall to test its structural integrity.

"A bar," I answered.

"A bar!" the dude exclaimed. "We got enough bars up here. What we need is a corner market! I gotta walk the whole way down to Virginia Avenue to get my Skoal!"

"I'll pass that along to the boss," I answered. "You really can't be in here."

He stood there asking questions until I quit answering entirely. No sooner had he wandered out than an old woman popped her head in. "What's this gonna be?"

"A bar. Like I told the guy who just left, you really can't be in here."

"A bar?" she sneered. "Last thing we need is another bar. We need a deli!"

"Yeah, it's really not my call. I'm the demolition guy."

"You didn't even consult with anyone who lives around here to ask what we all want!"

"Ma'am, I'm about to set off some explosives so…" Thankfully, that sent her scurrying. As soon as she left, though, a young woman pushing a stroller shouted in from the sidewalk. "What's this going to be?"

I was tired of dealing with the crankiness of the neighbors. "What do you want it to be?"

"It'd be nice if it was a daycare."

"Well, you're in luck," I said. "That's exactly what the plans are."

Work on the bar stretched all the way across 2016. Waiting on building permits and city inspections was an unnecessarily grueling process. We were constantly discovering problems in demolition that necessitated a change to the architect's plans. It would take months to get them approved because no matter what city you live in, the permit office has no incentive whatsoever to take their hands out of their pants and do any work. It didn't help that the bar had been on that corner for nearly a hundred years and thus grandfathered through a century of new regulations, all of which we now had to make sure were up to code. Twenty-seventeen dragged into 2018. And then 2019. For over two years the building sat ugly and vacant with plywood covering front as we waited for the rusty gears of bureaucracy to grind out the necessary authorizations. Any work we did on the place happened in fits and starts until early in 2020, we finally got the green light to go full steam ahead.

It was just before everything in Pennsylvania screeched to a sudden halt. It was just before the outside world became a memory. It was just before Jessi and I began watching a financial sinkhole begin to open in the distance.

The approaching void was jarring because after years of climbing, we'd seemingly reached the surface. Far from the days of doing Pirates logos for forty bucks a pop, Jessi had meticulously refined her work and built a reputation for doing stunning linework florals. In the span of eighteen months, she went from a nearly empty schedule to being booked weeks in advance. Then an internationally renowned artist asked her to come work for her in her private studio, which sent Jessi's requests into the stratosphere. Clients were driving hundreds of miles just to get her art on their skin. Suddenly, shockingly for the first time I could remember, money wasn't something to fear. I damn near quit thinking about it altogether. Within four years, we went from being on state assistance to buying a house in the city. To repeat, we bought a *house*. When money has been your number-one worry a majority of your adult life, you assume it will be a gray cloud above your head until you die. But suddenly it wasn't. I didn't even realize the weight had lifted until one day it was just...gone.

Yet in the end this wonderful new existence had nothing to do with me. Jessi was the one whose hard work had paid off. I was just riding her coattails. My paycheck every two weeks was what she brought home in a day. For me, all the stability felt fake. I hadn't earned shit. The realization that I couldn't survive on my own—that without her I could barely scrape by at best was the new cloud above me. But when the world shut down, so too did her revenue stream.

Tattooing is like wrestling or sex—you can't do it effectively from six feet away. The tiny financial cushion we'd built was going to dwindle quickly if the pandemic stretched on for more than a couple months. And nobody at the time had any idea how long it would go on. Just as the sun had come out, it was starting to get dark again. Until Tony and I found a workaround.

Because the shutdown was based upon limiting your exposure to other people, each day Tony chose a property for me to work on by myself. He'd drop off supplies before I got there, text me what needed to be done, and I'd go do it. I'm pretty sure that technically what we were doing was about as legal as moonshining, but I justified it in the notion that I saw less people at work than I did at my house. While the world stayed indoors, I was buying us time, putting in fifty to sixty hours a week. I knew it was just scooping water out of a sinking boat, but the boat definitely wasn't going down as fast. Everything else about the spring of 2020 sucked elephant nuts, but the feeling that I was contributing in a meaningful way let me sleep a little better at night.

On Wednesday, February 6, 1901, my great-great-grandfather went to work as a stone mason at the Cambria Steel Works in Johnstown, PA. It was just over a decade since the facility had been ravaged by a wall of water and debris that had smashed its way down the Little Conemaugh River Valley after the collapse of the South Fork Dam. John Kirtley had survived one of the deadliest disasters in American history, yet it was a regular day of work that put the final date on his gravestone. Nobody in the family is exactly sure what happened except that he didn't come out of blast furnace #1 alive. Obviously, we never met. I was born seventy-six years after he died. But I've thought about him a lot since Thursday, June 18, 2020. About how he seemingly went into work that morning with no idea he'd never see his kids (my great-grandmother and her twin sister) again. About how it all must've ended so abruptly.

It was about two weeks after Allegheny County moved into the "green" zone, a threshold by which COVID spread was at low enough levels that parts of life were allowed to ramp back up again. For Lombardo Properties, it meant that we no longer had to isolate from each other. We could finally get together and accomplish tasks that required multiple people. So we focused on the bar, hauling in lumber to complete the build-outs the city had finally approved. On Wednesday the 17th, I'd moved all the old appliances out of the kitchen. We took down the grease-caked oven hood that had been bolted into the back wall since 1974. We removed the sinks. We cut the old gas lines. For the first time since I first set eyes on the place, the kitchen was empty. It allowed Wayne, a quiet, vehemently pro–Second Amendment carpenter from rural Georgia, to get on a ladder and cut out a section of the ceiling for the outflow channel that would eventually be connected to the new, larger oven hood.

I spent the morning trudging up and down the stairs carrying mangled plastic braces from the drop ceiling I'd ripped down earlier that week. The drop ceiling had hidden a massive cache of electrical conduit, all of which was now exposed. There was no power in the building, so my next job was to take all the conduit down, remove all the outlet panels, and get all the metal and wires downstairs in preparation for a trip to the dump the next day. It was as glamorous as it sounds.

It was just before one o'clock. I was thinking about taking lunch but first wanted to get a decent inventory on just how much conduit I needed to pull. As I walked around the second floor looking up at the ceiling, tracing these long silver snakes from one electrical box to another, it was impossible to guess that I was mere seconds from the third time I'd almost die at work.

Earlier that morning, Wayne had been framing out the wall that would someday separate the manager's office from the oven hood's exhaust port. Whenever one of the screws dropped off his drill, it would fall through the hole he'd cut the day before and ping to the tile-covered concrete floor twelve feet below. I could hear him grumbling about it all morning as I walked up and down the stairs. But after a while, the pinging stopped. What I didn't realize was that at some point, he decided to eliminate the falling screw problem by taking the large square of floor he'd previously cut out and placing it back in the hole.

He forgot to remove it again when he finished up and headed downstairs.

My eyes were following a tangle of wires up toward the roof when I stepped toward the back wall to see if they went over or under the ceiling joist.

Okay, this one looks like it goes up and ov—
SNAP!

If you've never suddenly and inexplicably had the ground disappear from beneath you, let me assure you it's just as shocking as you assume it would be. There's no momentary feeling of bliss, no illusion of floating—no slow motion. It all happens before your brain has any idea how to react. My hands involuntarily shot into the air. I think all the blood rushed out of my head because all I remember is total darkness as if I was plunging down a mineshaft. And then I hit. My heels met the ground first, buckling my knees, causing my lower back to smack the tile with an impact that sent a galaxy of light rushing up my spine. Momentum sent my head whipping backward. First my shoulders, then my hands, then the back of my skull rocked off the concrete floor. I was certain I was dead.

Somewhere in the cold, black distance of the external world, I heard Wayne's voice. He was twenty feet away, but it sounded like he was shouting at me from across a river.

"Holy shit, man, what was that? Are you okay?"

"No," I managed to grunt as I flopped over to my stomach.

Knowing I'd been on the second floor, he sprinted up the steps to find me. I could hear him frantically running around up there as I tried not to fade to black. Then on the way back down, the clomping of his feet stopped abruptly when through the open wall he caught a glimpse of me lying on the kitchen floor next to the piece of wood he'd forgotten to remove. "Oh shit." And he ran outside to grab Tony.

My brain was completely dark. All I could feel in my body was a numb tingling as if grains of sand were being pumped through my bloodstream.

Okay, you're still conscious. At least for now. But you fucked up your back really bad. That's probably it for walking. This is going to be a long, arduous rehab process, but at least you're still here. Life will be different, but you can do it. You'll adapt.

What surprised me the most was how calm and accepting I was.

Above me, I heard Tony's voice. "Kev, do we need to call an ambulance?"

The question brought me back to reality. "Give me a few minutes," I grunted.

For ten minutes, I laid there with my eyes closed, my forehead pressed to the hard tile floor. Eventually I realized that I had to test my body to see if any of it worked. I absolutely expected the worst. But when my brain told my hand to move my fingers, they began to wiggle. A wave of pure gratitude washed over me. I could move my hands. I could shrug my shoulders. I'm not sure I've ever been so thankful to do something so simple.

As Tony repeated, "Take all the time you need," I felt myself reentering the world. Color and images returned to my thoughts. Sounds were beginning to make sense again. My back was throbbing like I'd been felled by a sledgehammer. But that was good. I could feel pain. Suddenly, I realized my ribs were sore and my left wrist and right thumb were on fire. I'd never been so glad that so much of me hurt.

Hold on a minute.

It was the moment of truth. I needed to see if my legs worked. If they didn't, my life was going to be very different going forward. But there on the floor, I accepted whatever the result would be. I was alive. I was going to see my boy again. I'd be able to hold my daughter three months later when she came into the world. My brain sent a message to my knees to bend and bring my heels up to touch my butt.

And they did.

The feeling of elation and appreciation was like nothing I've ever felt before. Even in the moment, I knew that falling twelve feet to concrete is often a death sentence. (And technically my head fell eighteen.) Yet somehow for me it wasn't. I laid there a good fifteen minutes until my head finally let me lift it from the floor. I made my way to one knee. Once I mastered that, I stood up. I looked at Tony and Wayne, who were staring at me like I'd just exited a tomb.

"Should we call the ambulance?" Tony asked again.

I looked around the empty kitchen, taking in all the debris that had fallen through the hole with me. I blinked, not believing what I was about to say. "Actually, I think I'm good. I'm gonna go eat lunch."

I hobbled off without assistance, snagged my protein bar, my water bottle, and my apple, and sat there on the stairs trying to process what just happened. But I couldn't. There's no processing something like that. I was still around, and that was as far down that path as I was willing to go. As I was eating, I reached into my pocket and pulled out my grandfather's old screwdriver, which I'd been using to take the face plates off the electrical boxes. Coincidence? Probably. But I like to think he was looking out for me. Even if he wasn't—even if his soul wasn't actually hanging around—that's what I'm going to believe because it's more comforting than realizing that life at its core is completely and totally random.

I called Jessi and told her I'd be home early and that we were going to have our semi-annual ER date that afternoon. When I finished lunch, Tony drove me home in my car with Wayne following behind in the work van.

It was about two hours after they'd shot me up with iodine and ran me through all the machines when the doctor who'd been treating me barged into the room with a big grin and undid my neck brace. "Well, first thing's first. You don't need this thing." He chuckled.

I was stunned. "What, really?"

"You fell twelve feet to a concrete floor, and other than the bruises and scrapes, you're fine," he said, looking at my chart. "What kind of superhero are you?"

It was as stunning as being grazed by lightning or avoiding a tumbling crate of window and door tracks. I could've walked home if I wanted to. For an hour as I waited on dismissal paperwork, I was a minor celebrity among the ER staff.

"Oh my god, you're the guy who dropped twelve feet to a concrete floor?" one of the nurses said. "Shouldn't you at least be limping? Have you been secretly running around at night saving the city from villains?"

"Shhhhhh," I said, finger to my lips.

The day after I fell, tattoo shops in Allegheny County were finally allowed to reopen again. After three months and a day, we got Jessi's income back. Later in the year, it would disappear again for another three months after my daughter Miranda was born. But this time we knew we could make it. I put in fifty to sixty hours again while Jessi stayed home with a newborn. We made it to Thanksgiving, after which I took over dad duty again.

As for the bar, it finally began to look like something. They poured the concrete for the patio. The HVAC, plumbing, and electrical guys started rolling in and out. The drywall went up. Nice garage doors replaced the shitty old plywood on the front. We built the upstairs and downstairs bars. All of the tables, chairs, and booths got delivered. The beer taps went in. I spent days in a hail of sparks grinding through a hundred sheets of corrugated steel, which we then installed on the front of the building to create a new aesthetic. Once that was done, I spent a week in a bucket truck pressure washing the chipping yellow paint off the back half of the building and painting over it with battleship gray.

As I was thirty feet in the air slopping color onto the bricks, a random guy shouted at me from the street below, "You should be doing a mural on the side of that building!"

I turned and shouted back, "I am! You don't like it? I'm one of the foremost single-color muralists in the country. Nobody understands monochrome art!"

He had no idea what I was talking about, but he left without bitching that we were turning the building into a bar, so I was fine with it.

I was touching up the paint around the garage doors in mid-January of 2022 when the inspector finished up and said to Tony, "Everything looks good. We'll send over the paperwork."

"So that's it?" Tony asked. "We passed?"

"You passed," the inspector replied. And he gathered up his shit and walked out.

Tony and I stared at each other like we'd just been exonerated after a lengthy trial. I swore I heard a symphony. "Holy shit," I said.

"Holy shit," he replied. I'm sure he heard the symphony even louder than I did. "Brother, we have a bar."

I had my first beer at the brand-new Steel Mill Saloon on the night it opened, just before St. Patrick's Day 2022—six-and-a-half years since I first put a hammer into the wall. I walked over to the giant window on the second floor and stood there looking over the city. In the reflection, I could see people laughing, joking, drinking, watching basketball, and eating barbecue jackfruit tacos. It was surreal.

I was having a beer at a bar that I'd *built*.

As hard as I tried for so long, maybe I was never meant to escape the blue-collar life I was born into. Maybe some of us are just destined to be what we are. I have no idea how long I'm going to work construction. I can easily envision Tony selling the bar someday for millions of dollars, dissolving Lombardo Properties, and moving to Vegas. And I'll have to move on again. I'll work part time at a grocery store or hook on with my buddy's landscaping company or something else I can't possibly envision yet. I'll go wherever the road takes me.

And wherever that is will be okay.

Afterword

A good friend of mine is a brilliant character actor named Randy who has most likely appeared in at least one of your favorite television shows at some point in the last forty years. He never became the household name he most likely hoped to be when he was young, but his career is filled with credits that begin with 1978's *Dawn of the Dead* right up through more recent television appearances in *Parks & Recreation* and *American Rust*. He's essentially the king of "also appearing." You'd think I met him through the theater, but I didn't. I met him at the gym.

One day as we were packing up to leave after our workouts, I asked him how things were going. "Good," he said. "I was just filming in New York City last week."

"Oh, how was that?"

He stuffed his shoes in his gym bag and looked off pensively at all of the gym owner's weightlifting trophies. "It was fine. Great, in fact. Very fun."

It was obvious he was holding something back. "You need to deliver the lie with more enthusiasm, man." I laughed. "The audience needs to *believe* it."

He sighed. "Oh no, I just, um…" He paused, debating if he should continue. "I stayed with some good friends. Dynamic people. Just so creative. They have an apartment in Manhattan overlooking the park. I don't even want to know what it costs. She's an artist and he's one of my mentors—one of the most successful people I've ever met. Produced, written, and directed more hit Broadway shows than I can count. Three amazing kids who are all thriving in their own right…"

He trailed off, so I jumped in. "Sounds amazing," I said.

"It is," he replied with a heaviness I didn't expect. "And he's miserable."

His assertion stunned me. There had to be extenuating circumstances. "Is he sick or something?" I asked.

"No. He's just upset because he wants to put on a specific show at a specific theatre and management doesn't think his preferred script would resonate in the current climate, so they asked for a different one. And he was irate because he thought he should be able to dictate his own terms. He kept saying he'd 'earned the right.' The whole week I don't think I saw him smile. He couldn't let it go. It was sad."

The story was like a horse kick to the chest. Randy was describing a man who was living my dream: a life filled with writing success and accolades that not only lifted me from financial straits but put me at the literal top of the world. His friend had everything I'd always yearned for yet was seemingly living a cynical, joyless existence.

I walked out of the gym flush with the knowledge that happiness is a *choice*.

Through my twenties and thirties, I was of the belief that happiness was a destination. I'd eventually be happy when I got a solid job with benefits. I'd be happy when *Zendog* got made. I'd be happy when I got an agent. Happy when I got a professorship. That's where the happiness was—out there somewhere in a future where I'd met certain metrics of success. But the story of Randy's mentor made me understand that if checking predetermined boxes was the criteria for happiness, I'd always be chasing it. I'd never arrive.

I decided right there to untether from the brick I'd been hauling around. I let go of the measuring sticks I'd been using. I decided to concentrate on all the things I had instead of all the things I didn't.

Yes, maybe I wasn't where I desired to be. Hell, I wasn't anywhere near where I should've been. But Randy's story highlighted the fact that "should've" is the most bullshit contraction in the English language.

Should've implies there's a different past or future based on nothing but our own flawed expectations of how events would unfold. Should've has nothing to do with reality. No matter who you are, there is only one path that your life thus far has actually taken. And you can accept it and move forward or wallow in what isn't.

That's it. Those are your choices. It doesn't mean quit working hard or stop dreaming. It just means that if you truly put in the effort and those dreams don't materialize, you haven't done anything wrong. Most people you know are dealing with the same head full of frustration and angst that you are. Nobody has it made. And if you're comparing yourself to others, you're most likely competing with an illusion they themselves don't even believe. So just accept what you have. And let go of what you don't.

Now I'm fully aware I was able to gain this insight after Jessi and I started to settle into something resembling financial comfort. Trust me, I've been there and know that down in the hole, enlightenment isn't really an option. All I'm saying is that if you find yourself on the surface, there's no reason to hide from the sun.

Just after the bar opened, Pittsburgh had a rare late March snowstorm that put down five to eight inches of powder around town. After they cleared the roads, I was on my way to the bar to do some paint touch-ups when Tony called.

"Hey," he said. "I gotta send you up to the shop today. We got a problem."

"Well, that doesn't sound good."

"It isn't. You're gonna need a shovel. I'm on my way with some bleach."

The Lombardo Properties "shop" is actually an old real estate office in the North Hills that Tony bought to flip before realizing that if he just kept it, we could finally have a place to store our van and our tools and all our extra supplies. Above the shop is an apartment that Tony gets rent from each month. Below the shop is a garage and a laundry room.

Overnight, the tenant in the apartment had flushed something that didn't agree with the plumbing. Combine it with the unexpected freezing temperatures and I opened the door to find the drain cover slightly askew and two weeks of goopy wet toilet paper all over the floor. The whole place smelled like... I mean, I don't have to say it. You know what it smelled like.

I shook my head and trudged into the garage to grab a shovel and a bucket. It was the type of moment that I'd have ranted and raved about earlier in life. *I've worked so hard. I should be past all this!* But I can honestly admit that in the middle of it, I was struck with an emotion I absolutely didn't expect. It wasn't rage or irritation or even mild annoyance. Nope, halfway through, the squishy plopping of the toilet paper into the bucket involuntarily made me chuckle. And once I started, I couldn't stop. For a good fifteen minutes as I was scooping up this slop, I was laughing like I was at The Comedy Store and the headliner was busting out top-shelf material. The only thing going through my mind was, *My entire journey has led to this moment in time. This is where I'm supposed to be right now.*

PLOP!

It was all so fucking silly.

When I was finished, I threw the contents in a double contractor bag and set it out for the garbage. Still waiting on Tony to arrive with bleach to disinfect the washroom floor, I walked outside into the snow and leaned against our broken old cargo van. The sun was out and the snow was pretty. I knew that when I eventually got back home, I'd tickle my daughter just to hear her laughter echo through the house, then take my boy to hockey practice and beam with pride watching him zip around the ice. I was alive and healthy in this moment.

I took a breath of the crisp, snappy air.

Yup, I sure had a lot to be happy about—for a shit shoveler.

I hope some of the stories triggered a good memory or two. Thanks for letting me share my journey.

9 781955 026741